SEX IN PSYCHO–ANALYSIS

(Contributions to Psycho-Analysis)

Sandor Ferenczi

and

THE DEVELOPMENT OF PSYCHO–ANALYSIS

Sandor Ferenczi
and Otto Rank

Two Books Bound as One

DOVER PUBLICATIONS, INC., NEW YORK

This new Dover edition first published in 1956 is
an unabridged and unaltered republication of the
first edition of the work published under the titles
Sex in Psycho-Analysis and *Contributions to Psycho-
Analysis*. It also includes an unabridged and unaltered republication of the first edition of *The
Development of Psycho-Analysis*, by Sandor Ferenczi
and Otto Rank.

Library of Congress Catalog Card Number: 58-13674

Manufactured in the United States of America
Dover Publications, Inc.
180 Varick Street
New York, N. Y. 10014

SEX IN PSYCHO-ANALYSIS

(Contributions to Psycho-Analysis)

Sandor Ferenczi

Authorized Translation by Ernest Jones

DOVER PUBLICATIONS, INC., NEW YORK

TRANSLATOR'S PREFACE

Dr. Ferenczi is known as one of the leading exponents of psycho-analysis, and, apart, of course, from Professor Freud, has perhaps made more original contributions than anyone else to that subject. Before taking up the study of psycho-analysis he had for many years been engaged on neurological, psychiatrical and medico-legal work, and had made a number of contributions particularly on neurological and psychotherapeutic subjects. His extensive personal experience with the methods of hypnotism and suggestion gave him a specially favourable opportunity to compare and contrast the results thus obtained with those he was able later to obtain by the use of the psycho-analytic method. The greater part of his work has been published only in Hungarian; from that which has appeared in German I have selected for translation, with Dr. Ferenczi's approval, some fifteen papers, which are here reproduced in the order of their original appearance. Of these only two, forming Chapters I and III, were written from the point of view of popular exposition; the others are all of a more technical and advanced nature, being addressed to an audience already familiar with psycho-analytical principles. While this fact increases their value for serious students of the subject, there being little enough of such literature in English, it exposes many of the conclusions to ready misconception unless it be constantly borne in mind that a considerable knowledge of previous work is assumed throughout by the author. To those readers approaching the subject for the first time the following books are recommended as a preliminary study: Hitschmann, "Freud's Theory of the Neuroses," Brill, "Psychanalysis," and the translator's "Papers on Psycho-Analysis." In the translation I have tried to render the author's thought and language as closely and accurately as possible, judging this to be the chief desideratum in dealing with a scientific work, even at the cost of retaining some foreignness of style.

I am indebted to Miss Barbara Low for reading through both the manuscript and the proofs.

Portland Court.

London. W.

CONTENTS

The Development of Psycho-Analysis follows page 288

CHAPTER I

THE ANALYTIC INTERPRETATION AND TREATMENT OF PSYCHOSEXUAL IMPOTENCE*

ONE of the few objective arguments brought against the method of treatment ' of the psychoneuroses inaugurated by Freud is the criticism that it effects only a symptomatic cure. It is said to cause the pathological manifestations of hysteria to disappear, but not the hysterical disposition itself. In regard to this Freud quite rightly directs our attention to the fact that the same critics shew much more indulgence towards other anti-hysterical procedures, which cannot even effect a *final* cure of one symptom. We may also bring forward against the argument just mentioned the fact that the analysis, penetrating into the depths of mental life, (a process which Freud tellingly compares with the excavating work of the archaeologist), not only effects a cure of the symptoms, but also results in such fundamental change in the patient's character that we

*Published in the Psychiatrisch-Neurologische Wochenschrift, 1908, Jahrg. X.

no longer have any right to call him a sick man.[1]
We are the less justified in doing so, in that after the
analysis is finished he is well armed also against new
psychical conflicts and shocks, pretty much as well as
the non-analysed "healthy persons," who—as we now
know with certainty—carry about with them throughout life a multitude of repressed ideational complexes
that are at all times ready to increase and exaggerate
with their affect-value the pathogenic action of
psychical traumata.

Besides this, the burden of proof completely disappears in the cases where our medical task is comprised in the curing of a single symptom. Among
these tasks the treatment of psychical impotence has
constantly been regarded as one of the most difficult.
So many of my patients came with this complaint, and
so great have I found the mental misery due to this
symptom, that I have been untiring in the application
of the most diverse medicinal[2] and suggestive[3] methods
of treatment. Now and then I have had success with
both of these, but neither of them proved to be reliable.
I count myself all the more fortunate to be able now
to report much more successful results, for which I
have to thank Freud's psycho-analytic method of
treatment.[4]

[1] Jung and Muthmann in their works come to the same conclusion.
[2] Ferenczi. Arzneimittelschatz des Neurologen. Gyógyászat, 1906.
[3] Ferenczi. Ueber den Heilwert der Hypnose. Gyógyászat, 1904.
[4] Freud's works may be referred to in this connection, as well as the following ones by two Vienna physicians: M. Steiner, "Die funktionelle Impotenz
des Mannes," Wiener med. Presse, 1907, Nr 42, (also Die psychischen
Störungen der männlichen Potenz, 1913, by the same author: Translator's
Note), and W. Stekel, Nervöse Angstzustände, 1908.

I will first relate, without any theoretical discussion, the cases I have observed, and interpolate my own remarks.

I was consulted by a workman, aged thirty-two, whose apprehensive and almost abject appearance allowed the "sexual neurasthenic" to be recognised even at a distance. My first thought was that he was being tormented by conscience-pangs due to masturbation, but his complaint proved to be a much more serious one. In spite of his age, and in spite of innumerable attempts, he had never been able, so he told me, properly to perform cohabitation; an inadequate erection and *ejaculatio praecox* had always made the *immissio* impossible. He had sought help from various physicians; one of them (a notorious newspaper-advertiser) spoke to him roughly, saying "You have masturbated, that is why you are impotent," and on this the patient, who in fact had indulged in self-gratification from his fifteenth to his eighteenth year, as the result of this consultation went home convinced that the sexual incapacity was the well-deserved and irrevocable consequence of the "sins of his youth." Nevertheless he made further efforts to be cured, and went through among others a long hydriatic and electrical treatment, without success. The patient would already have bowed to the inevitable, but that he had recently become attached to a very suitable girl; the wish to marry her was the motive of his present attempt to be cured.

The case is a very everyday one, nor did the anamnesic exploration and the examination of the patient bring out anything special in addition. It became evident that besides the impotence he suffered

from a neurotic symptom-complex: various paraesthesias, auditory hyperaesthesia, pronounced hypochondria, disturbed sleep with unpleasant dreams; altogether,
therefore, an anxiety-neurosis in Freud's sense, for
which an adequate explanation was to be found in the
lack of sexual gratification and the frequent frustrated
excitations.   The patient, although the coitus-mechan-
ism completely failed at just the critical moment,
indulged in phantasies, both when awake and when
half-asleep, the content of which was entirely comprised
of sexual situations, and during these experienced the
most intense erections.   This circumstance aroused
in me the suspicion that besides the nervous results
of the abstinence he might also be suffering from a
psychoneurosis, and that the cause of the impotence
itself would have to be sought in the inhibiting, inter-
dicting power of an unconscious psychical complex,
which became operative just at the moment of the
wished-for sexual union.   This pathological condition
has, under the term "psychical impotence," long been
known to us, and we have known that with it the inhibiting action of morbid anxiety and fear makes im-
passible the otherwise intact sexual reflex-arcs.   It
was formerly believed, however, that such cases were
fully explained by the "cowardice" of the patient or
by the conscious memory of a want of success sexually,
and our medical activity was confined to calming or
encouraging the patient, with successful results in a
certain number of cases.   With a knowledge of Freud's
psychology I could not remain content with such
superficial explanations; I had to suppose that not
conscious fear, but unconscious mental processes,
having an absolutely definite content and taking their

origin in infantile memory-traces, probably some childish sexual wish that in the course of the individual cultural development had become not only unobtainable, but even unthinkable, would have to be made responsible for the symptom. I received merely negative answers to the questions put to him along these lines. Nothing special had happened to him in a sexual connection; his parents and the family had always been very decent and reserved in this respect, and as a child he had not bothered himself in the least about "these matters;" he knew himself to be entirely free of homosexual impulses; the thought of the functioning of "erogenous zones" (anal- and oral-erotism) filled him with repugnance; the doings of exhibitionists, voyeurs, sadists and masochists were almost quite unknown to him. At the most he had, rather unwillingly, to admit a somewhat excessive fondness for the female foot and its covering, without being able to give any information as to the source of this fetishistic partiality. I allowed the patient, of course, to relate exactly how he had gained his knowledge of sexual matters, what his phantasies consisted of during the period of self-gratification, and how the first attempts at cohabitation, unsuccessful from the start, had passed off. Still even this detailed anamnesis did not elicit anything that I would have been able to accept as an adequate explanation of the psychosexual inhibition. We know, however, since Freud's work that such an account of the illness does not reproduce the real story of the individual's development, even with complete honesty and a keen memory on the part of the person questioned; so cleverly can consciousness "overlook" and "forget" thoughts and memories that have become disagreeable that they can be withdrawn from the repression or made conscious only by laborious analytic work. I did not hesitate, therefore, to apply the analytic method.

In the analysis it soon turned out that the suspicion as to the presence of a psychoneurosis was justified. With closer attention the neurotic nature of the paraesthesias mentioned above was recognisable ("pains" and "crackling" in the tendons, "agitation" in the abdominal and crural muscles, etc.), but besides these there appeared a number of undoubtedly obsessive thoughts and feelings: he dared not look people in the eyes; he was a coward; he felt as if he had committed a crime; he was always afraid of getting laughed at.

Obsessive ideas and sensations of this kind are typical of sexual impotence. The cowardice of the sexually impotent person is explained by the radiation over the whole individuality of the humiliating consciousness of such an imperfection. Freud speaks very appositely of the "prefigurativeness of sexuality" for the rest of the psychical behaviour. The degree of sureness in sexual efficiency becomes the standard for the sureness in demeanour, in views, and in conduct. The motive-less consciousness of guilt, however, that seemed to play a not inconsiderable part with our patient, made one suspect the presence of deeper, suppressed, un-conscious thought-processes, which in a certain sense were really "sinful;" the analysis gradually yielded the psychical material from which I was able to infer the nature of this "sin."

It struck me above all that in his sexually coloured dreams the patient occupied himself very frequently with corpulent women whose faces he never saw, and with whom he was unable to bring about sexual union even in dreams; on the contrary, instead of an emission occurring, as might have been expected, he would be overtaken by acute dread and would wake up in alarm with such thoughts as: "This is impossible!" "This situation is unthinkable." After such anxiety-dreams he would wake up exhausted, bathed in sweat, with palpitation, and usually had "a bad day."

The fact that in the dream he never saw the face of the sexual-object I had to interpret as a dream-distortion (Freud); it serves the purpose here of making the person towards whom the libidinous dream-wish was directed unrecognisable in consciousness. The starting up in alarm signified that it was nevertheless beginning to dawn in his consciousness how "unthinkable this situation was" with the woman hinted at by the dream. The anxiety-attack is the affective reaction of consciousness against a wish-fulfilment of the unconscious.[1]

The unconscious interdiction of full sexual gratification was so strict in the patient that even in day dreams, when he indulged in his sexual phantasies, he had in a terrified way to pull himself together and somehow divert his thoughts elsewhere in the moment when he

[1]The Hungarian poet Ignotus seems to have surmised the existence of the distortion and censuring of dreams, as is evident from the following fragment of verse:

". . . A coward's dreams betray the man:
So harshly can Fate ply her flail,
That of safety he dare not even dream."

It had occurred to me long ago (see the article on "Love and Science" in Gyógyászat, 1901) that for any useful writings on individual-psychology we have to go not to scientific literature, but to belles-lettres.

was about to imagine to himself the act of cohabitation.[1]

A certain active cruelty made its appearance several times in his dreams; for instance, he bit someone's finger off, or bit someone's face. It was not hard to recognise the source of these cannibalistic inclinations in the infantile hostility against a brother, twenty years older, who in his time had behaved much too strictly and not at all kindly towards his little brothers. This propensity for cruelty, by the way, also lurked in the waking state behind the patient's "manifest" cowardice. Every time it was discovered in how cowardly a manner he had behaved in regard to this or that person (mostly a superior) he would sink into phantasies that lasted for several minutes, in which he depicted to himself in the greatest detail how he would conduct himself on the next opportunity in a similar situation, what bodily castigations and abusive language he would serve out.[2] This is an expression of the *esprit d'escalier* so frequent amongst psychoneurotics, or, as Freud terms it, "subsequentness." These high-flown plans, however, remain for the most part otiose fantasy-pictures; dread or fear always paralyses the patient's hand and tongue again and again in the

---

[1] Freud first called attention to the frequent occurrence of anxious examination-dreams in those sexually impotent, and I can fully confirm this observation. The dream phantasy of sitting for an examination very often recurs with such people as a "typical dream," and is constantly associated with the unpleasant feeling of not being ready, of making a fool of oneself, etc. This feeling is a dream-displaced affect; it belongs to the consciousness of the sexual incapacity. A synonym of cohabitation that is commonly used in vulgar Hungarian ("to shoot") is probably the reason why in the dreams of impotent patients under my treatment situations so often recur in which the chief part is played by the (mostly clumsy) use of weapons (*e. g.* rusting of the rifle, missing the target, missing fire in shooting, etc).

[2] In Ibsen's "Pretenders" the figure of the Bishop Nicholas excellently illustrates cowardice and concealed cruelty as the result of sexual impotence.

critical moment. The analysis finds a determining factor of this kind of cowardice in the infantile awe of the parents and older members of the family, which at that time restrained the child's revolt against their rebukes and bodily chastisements.

With the close physiological connection and the ideational association that obtain between the sexual function and the passage of urine I found it intelligible that the patient's inhibition also made its appearance, as it soon turned out, in regard to micturition. He was unable to discharge urine in the presence of a second person. So long as he was quite alone in a public urinal he urinated regularly, and with a good stream; at the moment when anyone entered the flow was "as if cut off," and he became unable to press out even a drop.

From this symptom, as also from his bashfulness in regard to men, I inferred that with the patient, as with most neurotics (Freud), the homosexual component was present in a higher degree than usual. I believed that the infantile source of this was to be sought in his relation to a younger brother, with whom he had slept in the same bed for years, and with whom he had lived in an offensive and defensive league against the elder brother who ill-treated them. With the expression "usual amount of homosexuality" I imply that my psycho-analyses, now quite numerous, support the theory of psycho-bisexuality, according to which there is retained from the original bisexual disposition of man not only anatomical, but also psychosexual rudiments, which under certain circumstances may obtain the supremacy.

On the ground of other similar analyses I suspected

that the corpulent woman who recurred in the dreams stood for some near relative of the patient, the mother or a sister; he indignantly rejected this imputation, however, and triumphantly told me that he had only one corpulent sister, and it was just this one that he couldn't bear; he had always been sullen and gruff towards her. When, however, one has experienced, as I have, how often a sympathy that is burdensome to consciousness is hidden behind an exaggerated harshness and ill-temper, one's suspicion is not lulled by information such as this.[1]

On one of the following days the patient had a peculiar hypnagogic hallucination, which with slight modifications he had already noticed a few times before: in the act of going to sleep he had the feeling as if his feet (which, though naked, appeared to him to have shoes on) were rising in the air, while his head sank deep down; he awakened at once with an intense feeling of dread. Having regard to the already mentioned foot- and shoe-fetishism I submitted afresh to an exact analysis the patient's free associations to this theme, with the result that the following memory-images emerged, which he had long forgotten, and which were most painful to him: The corpulent sister, whom he "couldn't stand," and who was ten years older than the patient, used to undo and do up the shoes of her then three- or four-year-old brother, and it also not infrequently happened that she would let him ride on her naked leg (covered only by a short stocking), whereupon he used to experience a voluptuous sensation in his member. (Since this is obviously a "cover-

---

[1] "I hate because I cannot love." (Ibsen).

memory" in Freud's sense, more must have passed between them). When he wanted to repeat this later on, his sister, now fourteen or fifteen years old, rebuffed him with the reproach that such conduct was improper and indecent.

I was now able to tell the patient of my assured conviction that the psychological ground for his impotence was to be sought in the wish for the repetition of those sexual acts, a wish incompatible with the "cultivated sexual-morality" (V. Ehrenfels, Freud) and hence repressed, but which lived on in the unconscious. The patient, with whom the arguments only half prevailed, adhered to his denial, but his resistance did not last much longer. He came shortly after with the news that he had thought over what I had said to him, and recollected how in his youth (from the fifteenth to the eighteenth year) he would select this infantile experience with his sister as the object of his masturbation phantasies; indeed, it was the dread of his conscience after self-gratification of this kind that had moved him to give up masturbation altogether. Since that time the childhood story had never occurred to his mind till now.

I induced the patient from the beginning to continue during the treatment his attempts at cohabitation. After the dream-analysis related above he came one day with the surprising news that on the day before (for the first time in his life) he had succeeded in this; the erection, the duration of the friction, and the orgasm had given him complete satisfaction, and, with the avidity characteristic of neurotics, he repeated the act twice again on the same evening, each time with a different woman.

I continued with the treatment and began to reduce analytically the other symptoms of his neurosis, but the patient, after he had achieved his chief aim and convinced himself of the durability of the result, lacked the necessary interest for the analysis, and so I discharged him after treating him for two months.

This therapeutic success needs explaining. From Freud's pioneering work on the evolution of sexuality in the individual (*Drei Abhandlungen*) we learnt that the child receives his first sexual impressions from the immediate environment, and that these impressions determine the direction in the later choice of the sexual-object. It may happen, however, that—as a result of constitutional causes or of external favouring factors (*e. g.* spoiling)—the incestuous object-choice becomes fixed. Cultural morality, gradually strengthened by example and education, defends itself energetically against the obtrusion of the improper wishes, and repression of these comes about. This defence to begin with succeeds completely ("Period of successful defence," Freud)—as also in our case—, but the suppressed wishes may again become active under the influence of the organic-sexual development in puberty, making necessary another corresponding stage in repression. The second repression signified for our patient the beginning of the psychoneurosis, which manifested itself in, amongst other ways, the psychosexual inhibition and the aversion to the sister. He was incapable of performing the sexual act, since every woman reminded him unconsciously of his sister; and he couldn't endure his sister because, without knowing it, he always saw in her not only the relative, but also the woman. The antipathy was a good means of protection against his becoming conscious of a feeling-stream of the opposite kind.

Still the unconscious (in Freud's sense) is only able to control the mental and bodily being of man until the analysis reveals the content of the thought-processes hidden in it. Once the light of consciousness has illuminated these mental processes there is an end of the tyrannical power of the unconscious complex. The repressed thoughts cease to be heaps and collections of non-abreacted affects; they become links in the ideational chain of normal association. It was, therefore, in our case thanks to the analysis, *i. e.* to a kind of "circumvention of the censor" (Freud), that the affective energy of the complex was no longer converted into a physical compulsion-(inhibition-) symptom, but was disintegrated and led off by thought-activity, losing its inadequate[1] significance forever.

That incestuous fixation of the "sexual hunger"[2] is to be recognized not as an exceptional, but as a relatively frequent cause of psychosexual impotence, is shewn by the quite analogous psycho-analyses by Steiner and Stekel. I am also able to bring forward a second similar case. A psychoneurotic, twenty-eight years old, (who had been treated by me and at that time was almost cured), was tormented by anxious obsessions and obsessive acts, and suffered besides from psychosexual inhibition, just like the patient whose history was related above. This symptom, however, ceased of itself in the sixth month of the analysis after we managed to make conscious infantile incest-thoughts that had been fixed on the person of the mother.

[1](This word is used in psychopathology to mean "disproportionate." Translator.)

[2]This word is used to translate the German "Libido."

When I mention that this otherwise rather "over-moral" patient also indulged in hostile phantasies against his father among his unconscious thought-processes, one will recognize in him a typical personification of the Oedipus myth, the general human significance of which has been revealed by Freud's discoveries.

The libidinous thoughts repressed in childhood, which condition psychical impotence, need not refer to the nearest relatives; it is enough that the infantile sexual-object has been a so-called "respected person," demanding in one way or another high consideration. As an example of this I may cite a patient, aged forty-five, with whom both the tormenting "cardiac anxiety" (angina pectoris nervosa) and the sexual weakness considerably improved after he was able to give an account of repressed disrespectful phantasies, the object of which was his dead foster-mother. In this case the incestuous fixation (if this designation is permitted in regard to people not related in blood) was furthered by the circumstance that the foster-mother also had not restrained her child-love within the necessary limits; she let the boy sleep in her bed till his tenth year, and for a long time tolerated without contradicting him his demonstrations of affection, which was already plainly tinged with erotism. Children are often exposed to such dangers and temptations from the side of their teachers and educators; it is not rare for them to fall a victim to masked sexual acts on the part of grown-up relatives, and not only—as might have been supposed—in the slums, but also among classes of society where the greatest possible care is lavished on children.[1]

The tragic part that the foster-mother had played in the life of this patient was shewn by the fact that, when he wanted to marry, a few years ago, the old lady, then over seventy years old, committed suicide in her despair; she threw herself out of the window of the second floor[2] just in the moment that her adopted son left the front door. The patient believed that the motive for this deed was her dissatisfaction with his choice. But his unconscious must have interpreted the suicide more correctly, for about this time appeared the cardiac pains, which one regards as converted (projected into the corporeal sphere) "heart-ache." The sexual weakness had existed with this patient since puberty, and he will perhaps attain full sexual capacity only towards the decline of masculine life.

Steiner distinguishes, besides the cases of functional impotence that are determined by unconscious complexes of infantile origin, two other kinds of psychosexual inhibition; with one of these congenital sexual inferiority, with the other certain injurious influences acting after puberty, are to be regarded as the causative agents. The value of this division is, in my opinion, more a practical than a theoretical one. From the "congenital" cases we have above all to exclude the cases of pseudo-heredity, where neuropathic parents as a result of their complaint treat the children wrongly, train them badly, and may expose them to influences

[1] See Freud's Kleine Schriften, S. 114, and also my article "Sexual-Pädagogik," Budapesti Orvosi Ujság, 1908.

[2] [In America this would be called the fourth floor, in England the third. Translator.]

that have as a result a subsequent sexual inhibition, whereas without these influences even the person afflicted through heredity would perhaps not have become sexually impotent.

Freud compares the pathogenesis of the neuroses with that of tuberculosis. The predisposition also plays an important part with the latter, but the real pathogenic agent is none the less only the Bacillus Kochii, and if this could be kept at a distance not a single soul would die of the predisposition alone. Sexual influences of childhood play the same part in the neuroses as bacteria do in infective diseases. And though one must admit that where the predisposition is very marked the ubiquitous, unavoidable impressions may suffice to determine a future functional impotence, one has nevertheless to be absolutely clear that these impressions, and not the unsubstantial "predisposition," are the specific cause (Freud) of the disorder. From this it also follows that even with "congenital sexual inferiority" psycho-analysis is not quite without hopeful possibilities.

The psychosexual impotence that is acquired after puberty also differs, in my opinion, only apparently from that constellated by unconscious complexes. When anyone, after being able for a time properly to perform the act of copulation, loses for a long period his capacity under the impression of special circumstances (*e. g.* fear of infection, of pregnancy, of being detected, too great sexual excitement, etc.), one may be confident that repressed infantile complexes are present in him also, and that the exaggeratedly long or intense, *i. e.* pathological, effect of the present harmful agent is to be ascribed to the affect that has been transferred from such complexes to the current reaction. From a practical point of view Steiner is entirely right when he brings this group into special prominence, for the cases to be reckoned here are often curable by simple tranquillisation, suggestive measures, or a quite superficial analysis (which may be equated to the old Breuer-Freud "catharsis" or "abreaction"). Still, this kind of cure has not the prophylactic value of the penetrating psycho-analysis, although one cannot gainsay its advantage in being a much lesser burden to the physician and the patient.

A superficial analysis of this kind restored his *potestas coeundi* to one of my patients, a young man who became impotent from hypochondria after acquiring his first gonorrhoea, and also to a second one, who was made impotent with his wife by the sight of her menstrual blood. Simple encouragements and suggestive tranquillisation had the same effect with a thirty-six-year-old man who, although he had previously been fairly active sexually, became impotent when he married and it was a question of marital "duty." In this case, however, I continued the analysis after restoring the sexual function, and the result of this was the discovery of the following facts: The patient, the son of a cooper, had in his fourth or fifth year masturbated the genital parts of a girl of the same age; in this he was encouraged by an undoubtedly perverse assistant of his father's, who then got the girl to manipulate the boy's prepuce with a small wooden needle, such as is used for stopping up casks with worm holes in them. In this way the needle happened to bore into the prepuce, and a medical man had to perform an operation to take it away. With all this there was considerable fright, dread, and shame. What depressed him still more, however, was that his comrades somehow got wind of the occurrence and teased him for years with the nickname "needle-prick." He became taciturn and sullen. About the time of puberty he was often frightened that the scar in his prepuce, trivial as it was, would diminish his capacity for the act, but after a little wavering the first attempts succeeded fairly well. Still, the fear of being unable to meet the higher sexual claims of married life entailed an inordinate burden for his sexuality, already weakened through an infantile complex, and after the marriage he was reduced to impotence.

The case is instructive in several respects. It shews that when potency returns after dispersing the current anxious ideas, this does not mean that this fear has been the exclusive cause of the inhibition; it is much likelier that, in this case as in all similar ones, the preconscious dread has only a "transferred field of activity," while the original source of the disorder is hidden in the unconscious. The successful treatment by suggestion would then have only "broken the point" off the symptom—as Freud says—, *i. e.* would have so far diminished the total burthen of the neuropsychical apparatus that the patient could then manage it alone.

The case also illustrates how, besides infantile incestuous fixation, other experiences of early childhood connected with the affect of pronounced shame may later determine a psychosexual inhibition.

One kind of shame deserves special mention on account of its practical importance, that, namely, which the child feels on being caught masturbating. The feeling of shame on such an occasion is often still more strongly fixed through the child receiving bodily punishment and having the fear of severe illnesses implanted in him; Freud has called our attention to the fact that the way in which the child is weaned from onanism is a typical influence in the later character- and neurosis-formation. It may be asserted with confidence that the tactless behaviour of parents, teachers, and physicians in this matter, which is so important for the child, causes more mischief than all the other noxious influences of civilisation that are so often blamed. The isolation of children in their sexual exigencies, the resulting exaggerated and false notions on everything that physiologically or ideationally has to do with sexuality, the inordinate strictness in the punishment of sexual habits of childhood, the systematic training of children to blind obedience and motiveless respect for their parents: all these are components of a method of education, unfortunately prevailing to-day, that might also be called artificial breeding of neuropaths and sexually impotent people.

I may sum up as follows my view on male psychosexual impotence: 1. Male psychosexual impotence is always a single manifestation of a psychoneurosis, and accords with Freud's conception of the genesis of psychoneurotic symptoms. Thus it is always the symbolic expression of repressed memory-traces of infantile sexual experiences, of unconscious wishes striving for the repetition of these, and of the mental conflicts provoked in this way. These memory-traces and wish-impulses in sexual impotence are always of such a kind, or refer to such personalities, as to be incompatible with the conscious thought of adult civilised human beings. The sexual inhibition is thus an interdiction on the part of the unconscious, which really is directed against a certain variety of sexual activity, but which, for the better assuring of the repression, becomes extended to sexual gratification altogether.

2. The sexual experiences of early childhood that determine the later inhibition may be serious mental traumata. When the neurotic predisposition is marked however, unavoidable and apparently harmless childhood impressions may lead to the same result.

3. Among the pathogenic causes of later psychoseuxal impotence, incestuous fixation (Freud) and sexual shame in childhood are of specially great significance.

4. The inhibiting effect of the repressed complex may manifest itself at once in the first attempts at cohabitation, and become fixed. In slighter cases the inhibition becomes of importance only later, in cohabitation accompanied by apprehension or by specially strong sexual excitement. An analysis carried to a sufficient depth, however, would probably be able in all such cases to demonstrate beside, (or, more correctly, behind), the current noxious influence that is acting in a depressing way also repressed infantile sexual memories and unconscious phantasies related to these.

5. Full comprehension of a case of psychosexual impotence is only thinkable with the help of Freud's psycho-analysis. By means of this method cure of the symptom and prophylaxis against its return is often to be obtained even in severe and inveterate cases. In mild cases suggestion or a superficial analysis may be successful.

6. The psychoneurosis of which the sexual inhibition is a part manifestation is as a rule complicated
by symptoms of an "actual-neurosis" in Freud's sense
(neurasthenia, anxiety-neurosis).

(The following sentence may be added here, extracted
from a short article written some years later by Dr.
Ferenczi ("Paraesthesias of the Genital Region in
Impotency", Internat. Zeitschr. f. Psychoanalyse, May
1913): "Apart from unconscious (onanistic) incest-
phantasies, fears of castration are the most frequent
cause of psychical impotence; most often both are the
cause (dread of castration on account of incest-wishes)".
Transl.).

CHAPTER II

INTROJECTION AND TRANSFERENCE*

I. *Introjection in the Neuroses*

THE productivity of the neurosis (during a course of psycho-analytic treatment) is far from being extinguished, but exercises itself in the creation of a peculiar sort of thought-formation, mostly ˙unconscious, to which the name 'transferences' may be given.

"These transferences are re-impressions and reproductions of the emotions and phantasies that have to be awakened and brought into consciousness during the progress of the analysis, and are characterised by the replacement of a former person by the physician."

In these sentences Freud announced, in the masterly description of a hysterical case,[1] one of his most significant discoveries.

Whoever since then, following Freud's indications, has tried to investigate psycho-analytically the mental life of neurotics, must have become convinced of the truth of this observation. The greatest difficulties of such an analysis, indeed, proceed from the remarkable peculiarity of neurotics that "in order to avoid insight into their own unconscious, they transfer to the physi-

---

*Published in the Jahrbuch der Psychoanalyse 1909.

[1] "Bruchstück einer Hysterie-analyse", in Sammlung Kleiner Schriften zur Neurosenlehre, Bd. II.

cian treating them all their affects (hate, love) that have
been reinforced from the unconscious."[1]

When, however, one becomes more familiar with
the workings of the neurotic mind, one recognises that
the psychoneurotic's inclination to transference
expresses itself not only in the special case of a psycho-
analytic treatment, and not only in regard to the
physician, but that *transference is a psychical mechanism
that is characteristic of the neurosis altogether, one that is
evidenced in all situations of life, and which underlies
most of the pathological manifestations.*

With increasing experience one becomes convinced
that the apparently motiveless extravagance of affect,
the excessive hate, love and sympathy of neurotics, are
also nothing else than transferences, by means of which
long forgotten psychical experiences are (in the unconscious phantasy) brought into connection with the
current occasion, and the current reaction exaggerated
by the affect of unconscious ideational complexes. The
tendency of hysterical patients to use exaggeration in the
expression of their emotions has long been known, and
often ridiculed. Freud has shewn us that it is rather
we physicians who deserve the ridicule, because failing
to understand the symbolism of hysterical symptoms—
the language of hysteria, so to speak—we have either
looked upon these symptoms as implying simulation, or
fancied we had settled them by the use of abstruse
physiological terms. It was Freud's *psychological* conception of hysterical symptoms and character traits
that first really disclosed the neurotic mind. Thus
he found that the inclination of psychoneurotics to

[1]Ferenczi, "Ueber Aktual-und Psychoneurosen im Sinne Freuds,"
Wiener klin. Rundschau, 1908, Nr. 48 to 51.

imitation, and the "*psychical infection*" so frequent among hysterics, are not simple automatisms, but find their explanation in unconscious pretensions and wishes, which the patient does not confess even to himself, and which are incapable of becoming conscious. The patient copies the symptoms or character traits of a person when "on the basis of an identical aetiological claim"he *identifies* himself in his unconscious with him.[1] The well-known impressionability also of many neurotics, their capacity to feel in the most intense way for the experiences of others, to put themselves in the place of a third person, finds its explanation in hysterical identification; and their impulsive philanthropic and magnanimous deeds are only reactions to these unconscious instigations—are therefore in the last analysis egoistic actions governed by the "unpleasantness (*Unlust*) principle." The fact that every sort of humanitarian or reform movement, the propaganda of abstinence (vegetarianism, anti-alcoholism, abolitionism), revolutionary organisations and sects, conspiracies for or against the religious, political, or moral order, teem with neuropaths is similarly to be explained by the transference of interest from censored egoistic (erotic or violent) tendencies of the unconscious on to fields where there can work themselves out without any self-reproach. The daily occurrences of a simple civic life also, however, offer neurotics the richest opportunity for the displacement on to permissible fields of impulses that are incapable of being conscious. An example of this is the unconscious identification of grossly sexual genital functions with those of the

[1] Freud. Die Traumdeutung, 2e Aufl., S. 107.

oral organs (eating, kissing), as was first established by Freud. In a number of analyses I have been able to prove that the partiality of hysterics for dainty feeding, their inclination to eat indigestible material (chalk, unripe fruit, etc), their peculiar search for exotic dishes, their preference or idiosyncrasy in regard to food of a certain form or consistency, that all this was concerned with the displacement of interest from repressed erotic (genital or coprophilic) inclinations, and was an indication of a lack of sexual satisfaction. (The well-known manias of pregnant women also, which, by the way, I have observed with non-pregnant women as well at the menstrual time, I have many times been able to trace to insufficient satisfactions, relative to the increased "sexual hunger"). Otto Gross and Stekel found a similar cause with hysterical kleptomania.

I am aware that in the examples brought forward I have confounded the expressions *Displacement* and *Transference*. Transference, however, is only a special case of the neurotic's inclination to displacement; in order to escape from complexes that are unpleasant, and hence have become unconscious, he is forced to meet the persons and things of the outer world with exaggerated interest (love, hate, passionate manias, idiosyncrasy) on the basis of the most superficial "aetiological pretensions" and analogies.

A course of psycho-analytic treatment offers the most favourable conditions for the occurrence of such a transference. The impulses that have been repressed, and are gradually becoming conscious, first meet "*in statu nascendi*" the person of the physician, and seek to link their unsatisfied valencies to his personality.

If we pursued this comparison taken from chemistry we might conceive of psycho-analysis, so far as the transference is concerned, as a kind of *catalysis*. The person of the physician has here the effect of a catalytic ferment that temporarily attracts to itself the affects split off by the dissection. In a technically correct psycho-analysis, however, the bond thus formed is only a loose one, the interest of the patient being led back as soon as possible to its original, covered-over sources and brought into permanent connection with them.

What slight and trivial motives suffice with neurotics for the transference of affects is indicated in the quoted work of Freud. We may add a few characteristic examples. A hysterical patient with very strong sexual repression betrayed first in a dream the transference to the physician. (I, the physician, am operating on her nose, and she is wearing a frisure à la Cléo de Mérode). Whoever has already analytically interpreted dreams will readily believe that in this dream, as well also as in the unconscious waking thought, I have taken the place of the rhinologist who once made improper advances to the patient; the frisure of the well-known demi-mondaine is too plain a hint of this. Whenever the physician appears in the patient's dreams the analysis discovers with certainty signs of transference. Stekel's book on anxiety states[1] has many pretty examples of this. The case just mentioned, however, is also typical in another way. Patients very often use the opportunity to revive all the sexual excitations they have previously noticed

[1] Stekel, Nervöse Angstzustände, 1908.

and repressed during medical examinations (in unconscious phantasies about undressing and being percussed, palpated, and "operated on"), and to replace in the unconscious the previous physicians in question by the person of the present one. One need only be a physician to become the object of this kind of transference; the mystical part played in the sexual phantasy of the child by the doctor, who knows all forbidden things, who may look at and touch everything that is concealed, is an obvious determining factor in unconscious fancying, and therefore also in the transference occurring in a subsequent neurosis[1].

With the extraordinary significance that attaches (according to Freud's conclusion which is confirmed daily) to the repressed "Oedipus-complex" (hate and love towards the parents) in every case of neurosis, one is not surprised that the "paternal" air, the friendly and indulgent manner, with which the physician has to meet the patient in psycho-analysis gets so frequently used as a bridge to the transference of conscious feelings of sympathy and unconscious erotic phantasies, the original objects of which were the parents. The physician is always one of the "revenants" (Freud) in whom the neurotic patient hopes to find again the vanished figures of childhood. Nevertheless, one less friendly remark, reminding him of a duty or of punctuality, or a tone that is only a *nuance* sharper than usual, on the part of the analysing physician is sufficient to make him incur all the patient's hate and anger that is directed against moralising persons who demand respect (parent, husband).

[1] Compare the remark about the "doctor game" in Freud's article on "Infantile Sexualtheorien," Kleine Schriften, 2e Folge, S. 171.

The ascertaining of such transferences of positive and negative affects is exceedingly important for the analysis, for neurotics are mostly persons who believe themselves incapable either of loving or of hating (often denying to themselves even the most primitive knowledge about sexuality); they are therefore either anaesthetic or else good to a fault, and nothing is more suited to shatter their erroneous belief in their own lack of feeling and angelic goodness than having their contrary feeling-currents detected and exposed *in flagranti*. The transferences are still more important as points of departure for the continuation of the analysis in the direction of the more deeply repressed thought-complexes.

Ridiculously slight resemblances also: the colour of the hair, facial traits, a gesture of the physician, the way in which he holds a cigarette or a pen, the identity or the similarity in sound of the Christian name with that of some person who has been significant to the patient; even such distant analogies as these are sufficient to establish the transference. The fact that a transference on the ground of such petty analogies strikes us as ridiculous reminds me that Freud in a category of wit shewed the "presentation by means of a detail" to be the agent that sets free the pleasure, *i. e.* reinforces it from the unconscious; in all dreams also we find similar allusions to things, persons, and events by the help of minimal details. The poetical figure "pars pro toto" is thus quite current in the language of the unconscious.

The sex of the physician is in itself a much-used bridge for the transference. Female patients very often attach their unconscious heterosexual phantasies to the fact that the physician is a man; this gives them the possibility of reviving the repressed complexes that are associated with the idea of masculinity. Still the homosexual component that is hidden in everyone sees to it that men also seek to transfer to the physician their "sympathy" and friendship—or the contrary. It is enough, however, that something in the physician seems to the patient to be "feminine" for women to bring their homosexual, and men their heterosexual interests, or their aversion that is related to this, into connection with the person of the physician.

In a number of cases I succeeded in demonstrating that the relaxation of the ethical censor in the physician's consulting room was partly determined by the lessened feeling of responsibility on the patient's part. The consciousness that the physician is responsible for everything that happens (in his own room) favours the emergence of day-dreams, first unconscious, later becoming conscious, which very often have as their subject a violent sexual assault on the part of the physician and then mostly end with the exemplary punishment of such a villain (his being sentenced, publicly degraded through newspaper articles, shot in a duel, etc.) It is just in this sort of moral disguise that the repressed wishes of people can become conscious. As another motive lessening the feeling of responsibility I recognised in a patient the idea that "the doctor can do everything," by which she understood the operative removal of any possible consequence of a *liaison*.

In the analysis the patients have to communicate all these lewd plans, just as everything else that occurs to them. In the non-analytic treatment of neurotics all this remains unknown to the physician, and as a result the phantasies sometimes attain an almost hallucinatory character and may end in a public or legal calumny.

The circumstance that other persons also are being treated psychotherapeutically allows the patients to indulge without any, or with very little, self-reproach the affects of jealousy, envy, hate, and violence that are hidden in their unconscious. Naturally the patient has then in the analysis to detach these "inadequate",[1] feeling-impulses also from the current inciting cause, and associate them with much more significant person-alties and situations. The same holds good for the more or less conscious thought-processes and feeling-impulses that have their starting-point in the financial contract between the patient and physician. In this way many "magnanimous," "generous" people have to see and admit in the analysis that the feelings of avarice, of ruthless selfishness, and of ignoble covet-ousness are not quite so foreign to them as they had previously liked to believe. (Freud is accustomed to say, "People treat money questions with the same mendacity as they do sexual ones. In the analysis both have to be discussed with the same frankness"). That the money complex, transferred to the treat-ment, is often only the cover for much more deeply hidden impulses Freud has established in a masterly characterological study ("Charakter und Analerotik").

When we bear in mind these different varieties of the transference to the physician, we become decidedly strengthened in our assumption that this is only one manifestation, although in a practical way the most important one, of the general neurotic *passion for*

---

[1] (*i. e.* disproportionate, misplaced, or inappropriate. Transl.)

transference. This passion, or mania, we may regard
as the most fundamental peculiarity of the neuroses,
and also that which goes most to explain their conversion and substitution symptoms. All neurotics suffer
from *flight from their complexes;* they take flight into
illness, as Freud says, from the pleasure that has
become disagreeable; that is to say, they withdraw
the "sexual hunger" from certain ideational complexes
that were formerly charged with pleasantness. When
the withdrawal of "sexual hunger" is less complete,
the interest for what formerly was loved or hated
disappears, being succeeded by indifference; if the
detachment of the "sexual hunger" is more complete,
then the censor does not let pass even the slight degree
of interest necessary for the exercising of attention
—the complex becomes "repressed," "forgotten,"
and incapable of being conscious. It would seem,
however, as though the mind did not easily tolerate
"sexual hunger" that has been released from its complex, and is thus "free-floating." In the anxiety
neurosis, as Freud has shewn, the deviation of the
somatic sexual excitation from the psychical field
converts the pleasure into anxiety. In the psychoneuroses we have to presuppose a similar alteration;
here *the deviation of the psycho-sexual hunger from
certain ideational complexes causes a sort of lasting unrest,*
which the patient tries to mitigate as much as possible.
He manages also to neutralise a greater or less part by
the way of conversion (hysteria) or of substitution
(obsessional neurosis). It seems, however, as if this
bond were scarcely ever an absolute one, so that a
variable amount of free-floating and complex-escaping
excitation remains over, which seeks satisfaction from

external objects. The idea of this excitation could be used to explain the neurotic passion for transference, and be made responsible for the "manias" of the neurotic. (In the *petite hystérie* these manias seem to constitute the essence of the disease).

To understand better the fundamental character of neurotics one has to compare their behaviour with that of patients suffering from dementia praecox and paranoia. The dement completely detaches his interest from the outer world and becomes auto-erotic (Jung,[1] Abraham[2]). The paranoiac, as Freud has pointed out, would like to do the same, but cannot, and so projects on to the outer world the interest that has become a burden to him. The neurosis stands in this respect in a diametrical contrast to paranoia. Whereas the paranoiac expels from his ego the impulses that have become unpleasant, the neurotic helps himself by taking into the ego as large as possible a part of the outer world, making it the object of unconscious phantasies. This is a kind of diluting process, by means of which he tries to mitigate the poignancy of free-floating, unsatisfied, and unsatisfiable, unconscious wish-impulses. One might give to this process, in contrast to projection, the name of *Introjection*.

The neurotic is constantly seeking for objects with whom he can identify himself, to whom he can transfer

[1] Jung, Zur Psychologie der Dementia Praecox, 1907. ("Lack of pleasant *rapport* in dementia praecox").

[2] Abraham, "Die psychosexuellen Differenzen der Hysterie und der Dementia praecox," Zentralbl. f. Nervenheilk. u. Psych., 1908. ("The contrast between dementia praecox and hysteria lies in the auto-erotism of the former. Turning away of 'sexual hunger' in the former, excessive investment of the object in the latter").

feelings, whom he can thus draw into his circle of interest, *i. e.* introject. We see the paranoiac on a similar search for objects who might be suitable for the projection of "sexual hunger" that is creating unpleasant feeling. So finally there appear the opposite characters of the large-hearted, impressionable, excitable neurotic, easily flaming up with love of all the world or provoked to hate of all the world, and that of the narrow-souled, suspicious paranoiac, who thinks he is being observed, persecuted, or loved by the whole world. The psychoneurotic suffers from a widening, the paranoiac from a shrinking of his ego.

When we revise the ontogenesis of the ego-consciousness on the basis of the new knowledge, we come to the conclusion that the paranoiac projection and the neurotic introjection are merely extreme cases of psychical processes the primary forms of which are to be demonstrated in every normal being.

We may suppose that to the new-born child everything perceived by the senses appears unitary, so to speak monistic. Only later does he learn to distinguish from his ego the malicious things, forming an outer world, that do not obey his will. That would be the first projection process, the primordial projection, and the later paranoiac probably makes use of the path thus traced out, in order to expel still more of his ego into the outer world.

A part of the outer world, however, greater or less, is not so easily cast off from the ego, but continually obtrudes itself again on the latter, challenging it, so to speak; "Fight with me or be my friend" (Wagner, Götterdämmerung, Act I). If the individual has unsettled affects at his disposal, and these he soon has,

he accepts this challenge by extending his "interest"
from the ego on to the part of the outer world. The
first loving and hating is a transference of auto-erotic
pleasant and unpleasant feelings on to the objects that
evoke those feelings. The first "object-love" and
the first "object-hate" are, so to speak, the primordial
transferences, the roots of every future introjection.

Freud's discoveries in the field of psychopathology
of everyday life convince us that the capacity
for projection and displacement is present also in
normal human beings, and often overshoots the mark.
Further, the way in which civilised man adjusts
his ego to the world, his philosophic and religious
metaphysics, is according to Freud only meta-
psychology, for the most part a projection of feeling-
impulses into the outer world. Probably, however,
besides projection introjection is significant for man's
view of the world. The extensive part played in
mythology by the anthropomorphising o lifeless objects seems to speak in favour of this idea. Kleinpaul's
able work on the development of speech,[1] to the
psychological significance of which Abraham[2] has called
attention, shews convincingly how man succeeds in
representing the whole audible and inaudible environment by means of the ego, no form of projection and
introjection remaining untried thereby. The way
in which in the formation of speech a series of human
sounds and noises gets identified with an object on
the ground of the most superficial acoustic analogy,
and of the slightest "aetiological claim," reminds one

[1] Kleinpaul, Das Stromgebiet der Sprache, 1893.
[2] Abraham.   Traum und Mythos, 1909.

strongly of the neurotic transference-bridges mentioned above.

The neurotic thus makes use of a path that is much frequented by the normal as well when he seeks to mollify the free-floating affects by extension of his circle of interest, i. e. by introjection, and when, so as to be able to keep unconscious various affective connections with certain objects that concern him nearly, he lavishes his affects on all possible objects that do not concern him.

In analysing a neurotic one often succeeds in tracing out historically this extension of the circle of interest. Thus I had a patient who was reminded of sexual events of childhood by reading a novel and thereupon produced a phobia of novels, which later extended to books altogether, and finally to everything in print. The flight from a tendency to masturbate caused in one of my obsessional patients a phobia of privies (where he used to indulge this tendency); later there developed from this a claustrophobia, fear of being alone in any closed space. I have been able to shew that psychical impotence in very many cases is conditioned by the transference to all women of the respect for the mother or sister.[1] With a painter the pleasure in gazing at objects, and with this the choice of his profession, proved to be a "replacement" for objects that as a child he might not look at.

In the association investigations carried out by Jung[2] we can find the experimental confirmation of this inclination of neurotics to introjection. What is characteristic for the neurosis Jung designates as the relatively high number of "complex-reactions": the

[1] See Chapter I. (Impotence).
[2] Jung Diagnostische Assoziationsstudien, 1906.

stimulus-words are interpreted by the neurotic "in terms of his complex." The healthy person responds quickly with an indifferent reaction-word that is associated by either the content or the sound. With the neurotic the unsatisfied affects seize on the stimulus-word and seek to exploit it in their own sense, for which the most indirect association is good enough. *Thus it is not that the stimulus-words evoke the complicated reaction, but that the stimulus-hungry affects of neurotics come to meet them.* Applying the newly coined word, one may say that *the neurotic "introjects" the stimulus-words of the experiment.*

The objection will be raised that extension of the circle of interest, identifying of oneself with many people—indeed with the whole human race—, and sensitiveness for the stimuli of the outer world, are attributes with which normal persons also, and especially the most distinguished representatives of the race, are endowed; that one cannot, therefore, designate introjection as the psychical mechanism that is typical and characteristic of the neuroses. Against this objection must be brought the knowledge that the fundamental differences, assumed before Freud's time, between normal and psychoneurotic do not exist. Freud shewed us that "the neuroses have no special psychical content that is peculiar to them and occurs only in them," and according to Jung's statement, neurotics suffer from complexes with which we all fight. The difference between the two is only quantitative and of practical import. The healthy person transfers his affects and identifies himself on the basis of "aetiological claims" that have a much better motive than in the case of the neurotic, and thus does not dissipate his psychical energies so foolishly as the latter does.

Another difference, to the cardinal importance of which Freud has called attention, is that the healthy person is conscious of the greater part of his introjection, whereas with the neurotic this remains for the most part repressed, finds expression in *unconscious* phantasies, and becomes manifest to the expert only indirectly, symbolically. It very often appears in the form of "reaction-formations," as an excessive accentuation in consciousness of a current of feeling that is the opposite of the unconscious one.

The fact that the pre-Freudian literature contained nothing of all these matters, of transferences to the physician, of introjections,—*ça ne les empêchait pas d'exister.* With this remark I consider answered also those critics who repudiate the positive results of psycho-analysis as not even worthy of being re-examined, but who readily accept our estimate, on which we insist, of the difficulties of this method of investigation, and use it as a weapon against the new movement. Thus I have come across among others the curious objection that psycho-analysis is dangerous because it brings about transferences to the physician, where significantly enough there was never any talk of the negative transferences,[1] but always of the erotic ones.

If, however, transference is dangerous, then, to be consistent, all neurologists, including the opponents of Freud, must give up having anything to do with

[1] The practical significance and the exceptional position of the kind of introjections that have as their object the person of the physician, and which are discovered in analysis, make it desirable that the term "transferences" given to them by Freud be retained. The designation "introjection" would be applicable for all other cases of the same psychical mechanism.

neurotics, for we get more and more convinced that in the non-analytic and non-psychotherapeutic methods of treating the neuroses also transference plays the greatest, and probably the sole important part, only that in these methods of treatment—as Freud rightly points out—merely the positive feelings towards the physician come to expression, for when unfriendly transferences make their appearance the patient leaves the "antipathetic doctor." The positive transferences, however, are overlooked by the physician, who surmises nothing, and the curative effect is attributed to the physical measures or to an obscurely conceived idea of "suggestion."

The transference shews itself most clearly in treatment by *hypnotism* and *suggestion*, as I shall try to demonstrate in detail in the following chapter of this work.

Since I have known something about transferences, the behaviour of the hysteric who after the end of a suggestion treatment asked for my photograph, in order—so she said—to be reminded of my words by looking at it, appears to me in its true light. She simply wanted to have a memento of me, as I had given so many pleasant quarters of an hour to her conflict-tortured soul by stroking her forehead, by friendly, gentle talk, and by letting her fancies have free rein in a darkened room. Another patient, with a washing mania, even confessed to me once that to please a sympathetic doctor she could often suppress her obsessive act.

These are not exceptional cases, but are typical, and they help to explain not only the hypnotism and suggestion "cures" of psychoneurotics, but also all the others by means of electrotherapy, mechanotherapy, hydrotherapy and massage.

It is not intended to deny that more reasonable conditions of living improve the nutrition and the general sense of well-being, and in this way can to some extent help to subdue psychoneurotic symptoms, but the main curative agency with all these methods of treatment is the unconscious transference, in which the disguised satisfaction of libidinous tendencies (in mechanotherapy the vibration, in hydrotherapy and massage the rubbing of the skin) certainly plays a part.

Freud summarises these considerations in the saying that *we may treat a neurotic any way we like, he always treats himself psychotherapeutically, that is to say, with transferences.* What we describe as introjections and other symptoms of the disease are really—in Freud's opinion, with which I fully agree—self-taught attempts on the patient's part to cure himself. He lets the same mechanism function, however, when he meets a physician that wants to cure him: he tries—as a rule quite unconsciously—to "transfer," and when this is successful the improvement of the condition is the result.

The plea may be raised that when the non-analytic methods of treatment follow—although unconsciously —the path automatically laid down by the sick mind they are in the right. The transference therapy would thus be, so to speak, a natural way of healing, psychoanalysis on the other hand something artificial, imposed on nature. This objection might be irrefutable. The patient does in fact "heal" his mental conflicts through repression, displacement, and transference of disagreeable complexes; unfortunately what is repressed com-

pensates itself by creating "costly replacement-forma-
tions" (Freud), so that we have to regard neuroses as
"healing attempts that have miscarried" (Freud),
where really "medicina pejor morbo." It would be
very wrong to want to imitate Nature slavishly even
here, and to follow her along a road where in the case in
question she has shewn her incapacity. Psycho-analysis
wishes to individualise, while Nature disdains this; analysis aims at making capable for life and action persons
who have been ruined by the summary repression-
procedure of that Nature who does not concern herself
with the weakly individual being. It is not enough here
to displace the repressed complexes a little further by
the help of transference to the physician, to discharge
a little of their affective tension, and so to achieve a
temporary improvement. If one wants seriously to
help the patient one must lead him by means of analysis
to overcome—opposing the unpleasantness-principle—
the *resistances* (Freud) that hinder him from gazing
at his own naked mental physiognomy.

Present-day neurology, however, will not hear of
complexes, resistances, and introjections, and quite
unconsciously makes use of a psychotherapeutic measure
that in many cases is really effective, namely transference; it cures, so to speak, "unconsciously," and
even designates as dangerous the really effective principle of all methods of healing the psychoneuroses.

The critics who look on these transferences as
dangerous should condemn the non-analytic modes of
treatment more severely than the psycho-analytic
method, since the former really intensify the transferences, while the latter strives to uncover and to
resolve them as soon as possible.

I deny, however, that transference is harmful, and surmise rather that—at least in the pathology of the neuroses—the ancient belief, which strikes its roots deep in the mind of the people, will be confirmed, that diseases are to be cured by "sympathy." Those who scornfully reproach us with explaining and wanting to cure "everything from one point" are still far too much influenced by that ascetic-religious view of life, with its depreciation of everything sexual, which for nearly two thousand years has prevented the attainment of insight into the great significance that "sexual hunger" has for the mental life of the normal and pathological.

II. *The Part played by Transference in Hypnotism and Suggestion.*

The Paris neurological school (Charcot's school) regarded stimuli acting peripherally and centrally on the nervous system (optical fixation of objects, stroking the skin of the head, etc.), as the main factors in hypnotic phenomena. The Nancy school (Bernheim's school), on the contrary, sees in these and similar stimuli only vehicles for the "administering" of ideas, and in hypnotism in particular the vehicle for introducing the idea of going to sleep. The successful administration of the sleep idea is then supposed to be able to evoke a kind of "dissociation condition of the brain" in which one is accessible with special ease to further suggestions, *i. e.* hypnosis. This was an enormous progress, the first attempt at a purely psychological explanation, freed from unjustifiable physiological phrases, of the phenomena of hypnosis and suggestion, though even this did not quite satisfy our causality criteria. It was *a priori* unlikely that fixing the eye on a shining object could be the main cause of such radical changes in the mental life as those brought about by hypnosis. It is not much more plausible, however, to assume that an idea "administered" to a waking person, the idea of sleeping, could cause such changes without the indispensable assistance of much more potent psychical forces. Everything speaks much more in favour of the view that in hypnotism and suggestion the chief work is performed not by the hypnotist and suggestor, but by the person himself, who till now has been looked upon merely as the "object" of the administering procedure. The existence of auto-suggestion and auto-hypnosis on the one hand, and the limits of producible phenomena residing in the individuality of the "medium" on the other hand, are striking proofs of what a subordinate part in the causality chain of these phenomena is really played by the intrusion of the experimentalist. In spite of this knowledge, however, the conditions of the intrapsychical elaboration of the suggestion influence remained wrapped in obscurity.

It was the psycho-analytic investigation of nervous patients by Freud's method that first yielded glimpses into the mental processes that go on in suggestion and hypnosis. Psycho-analysis allowed us to establish with certainty the fact that the hypnotist is relieved of the effort of evoking that "dissociation condition" (which effort, by the way, he would scarcely be equal to), for he finds dissociation ready, *i. e.* the existence of different layers of the mind by the side of one another (Freud's "localities," "ways of working") also in persons who are awake. Besides the certain establish-

ment of this fact, however, psycho-analysis gives previously unsurmised information also about the content
of the ideational complexes and the direction of the
affects that go to make up the unconscious layer of the
mind which is operative during hypnosis and suggestion.
It has been found that in the "unconscious" (in Freud's
sense) all the impulses are pent up that have been
repressed in the course of the individual cultural
development, and that their unsatisfied, stimulus-
hungry affects are constantly ready to "transfer"
on to the persons and objects of the outer world, to
bring these unconsciously into connection with the
ego, to "introject." If we now imagine from this
aspect the psychical state of a person to whom something is to be suggested, we note a displacement of the
earlier point of view, a displacement that is of cardinal
importance. The unconscious mental forces of the
"medium" appear as the real active agent, whereas
the hypnotist, previously pictured as all-powerful,
has to content himself with the part of an object used
by the unconscious of the apparently unresisting
"medium" according to the latter's individual and
temporary disposition.

Among the psychical complexes that, fixed in the
course of childhood, remain of extraordinarily high
significance for the whole fashioning of life later on,
the "parental complexes" rank foremost. Freud's
experience that these complexes furnish the basis for
the psychoneurotic symptoms of adults is confirmed by
all who have seriously occupied themselves with these
problems. My efforts to investigate analytically the
causes of psychosexual impotence led to the conclusion
that this condition also is in a very large number of

cases due to "incestuous fixation" of "sexual hunger" (Freud), *i. e.* to the formation of a too firm—though quite unconscious—bond between sexual wishes and the images of the nearest relatives, especially the parents; this confirms similar observations of Steiner and Stekel. We owe to Jung[1] and Abraham[2] a considerable enrichment of our knowledge concerning the lasting after-effect of parental influences. The former has shewn that psychoneuroses mostly arise from a conflict between the (unconscious) parental constellation and the striving towards personal independence, and the latter has unmasked as a symptom of the same psychical constellation the inclination to stay unmarried, or to marry near relatives; Sadger[3] also has rendered service in making these connections clear.

As psycho-analysts see things, however, it may be considered as settled that there are only quantitative differences between "normal" and "psychoneurotic" mental processes, and that the results of mental investigation of psychoneurotics are also applicable to the psychology of the normal. It is thus *a priori* likely that the suggestions which one person "gives" to another set into movement the same complexes as those seen to be active in the neuroses. I have, however, to lay stress on the fact that in reality it was not this *a priori* expectation, but actual experiences in psycho-analysis that led me to perceive this.

[1]Jung, "Die Bedeutung des Vaters für das Schicksal des einzelnen," Jahrb., Bd 1.

[2]Abraham, "Die Stellung der Verwandtenehen in der Psychologie der Neurosen," Jahrb., Bd. 1.

[3]Sadger, "Psychiatrisch-Neurologisches in psychoanalytischer Beleuchtung," Zentralbl. f. das Gesamtgebiet d. Medizin, 1908, Nr. 7 and 8.

Freud was the first to notice how in the analysis one sometimes meets with great resistances that seem to make the continuation of the work impossible, and which in fact check it until one manages to make perfectly clear to the patient that this counter-striving is a reaction to unconscious feelings of sympathy which really refer to other persons, but which at the moment have been brought into connection with the personality of the analyst.

On other occasions one observes in the patient an enthusiasm for the physician bordering on adoration, and this—like everything else—has to be submitted to analysis. It turns out here also that the physician has served as a "cover-person" for the indulgence of affects, mostly of a sexual nature, which really refer to other personalities much more significant to the patient. The analysis is very often, however, disagreeably disturbed by motiveless hate, fear and apprehension in regard to the physician, which in the unconscious relate not to him, but to persons of whom the patient is not at the time thinking. When now we go through with the patient the list of personalities whom these positive and negative affects concern, we often come across in the first place some who have played a part in the patient's immediate past (*e. g.* husband or sweetheart), then come undischarged affects from the period of youth (friends, teachers, hero fancies), and finally we arrive, mostly after the overcoming of great resistances, at repressed thoughts of sexuality, violence, and apprehension that relate to the nearest relatives, especially the parents. It thus becomes manifest that the child with its desire for love, and the dread that goes with this, lives on literally in every human being, and that all later loving, hating, and fearing are only transferences, or, as Freud terms them, "new editions" of currents of feeling that were acquired in the earliest childhood (before the end of the fourth year) and later repressed.

With this knowledge it was not making a too venturesome step further to assume that the curious authority with which we as hypnotists dispose of all the pyschical and nervous forces of the "medium" is nothing else but the expression of repressed, infantile impulses of the hypnotised person. I found this explanation much more satisfying than the assumption of a capacity on the part of an idea to provoke dissociation, which would make one feel apprehensive at one's resemblance to a god.

An obvious objection to these considerations would be that it has long been known how greatly sympathy and respect favour the bringing about of a suggestible state; this fact could not escape the competent observers and experimenters in this field. What has not been known, however, and what could only be known through the help of psycho-analysis, is first that these unconscious affects play the chief part in bringing about the action of suggestion, and secondly that in the last analysis they are shewn to be manifestations of libidinous impulses, which for the most part are transferred from the ideational complexes bearing on the relation between parent and child to the relation between physician and patient.

That sympathy or antipathy between hypnotist and medium greatly influences the success of the experiment was also previously recognised. It was not known, however, that the feelings of "sympathy" and "antipathy" are highly complex psychical organisations capable of still further analysis, and of dissection into their elements, by Freud's method. When this is done one finds in them the primary, unconscious, libidinous impulses as the substratum, and over this an unconscious and pre-conscious superstructure.

In the deepest layers of the mind the crude "unpleasantness-principle" still rules, as at the beginning of psychical developments in other words, the impulsion towards immediate motor satisfaction of "sexual hunger;" this is, according to Freud, the layer, or stage, of auto-erotism. This region in the stratification of the adult mind can no longer as a rule be directly reproduced, and has to be inferred from its symptoms. What can be reproduced already belongs for the most part to the layer (or stage) of "object-love." (Freud), and the first objects of love are the parents.

Everything points to the conclusion that an unconscious sexual element is at the basis of every sympathetic emotion, and that when two people meet, whether of the same or the opposite sex, the unconscious always makes an effort towards transference. ("In the unconscious No does not exist". . . "The unconscious can do nothing except wish," Freud writes). When the unconscious succeeds in making this transference acceptable to the conscious mind, whether it is in a pure sexual (erotic) or in a sublimated form (respect, gratitude, friendship, aesthetic admiration, etc.) a bond of "sympathy" is formed between the two persons. When consciousness refuses to accept the positive unconscious desire, then we get, according to the degree of intensity in each case, antipathy of various degrees up to loathing.[1]

As a classical witness for the reality of the "sexual attitude" towards all people I might cite Freud's patient Dora (in the *Bruchstück einer Hysterie-analyse*). In the course of the analysis, incomplete as this was, it turned out that her sexuality had not remained indifferent to a single person in her environment. The husband and wife of the family K, the governess, the brother, the mother, the father: all excited her "sexual hunger." With all this she was consciously—like most neurotics—rather prudish and negativistic than otherwise, and had no idea that sexual wishes were concealed behind her gushing friendships, her sympathies and antipathies.

Dora, however, is not exceptional, but typical. As her analysed mind stands before us she gives a true

[1]That the feeling of antipathy, of disgust, is made up of pleasantness and unpleasantness, of liking and disliking, I found to be especially well illustrated in a case of paranoiac delusion of jealousy occurring in a woman of the educated classes; the case was also investigated by Professor Freud. The original cause of her disorder was discovered to be infantile homosexuality, which had been transferred from the mother to nurses, later to young friends, and which had been allowed to function extensively. The disappointments of married life had as a result the flowing back of the "sexual hunger" into "infantile channels," but in the meantime this kind of sexual pleasure had become intolerable to her. She projected it, therefore, on to her husband (whom she had previously loved), and accused him of infidelity. Curiously enough she suspected him only in regard to quite young females, twelve or thirteen years old, or else elderly ugly ones, mostly servants, whom she found "antipathetic" or even "repulsive". Wherever she could admit her fondness to herself in a sublimated form (aesthetic liking, friendship), *e. g.* with pretty women of her own class, she could feel keen sympathy, and she also expressed no delusions in regard to them. The fact that we find a mixture of sweet and bitter "disgusting" probably has similar psychological causes, just as also the idiosyncrasy towards food and drink of a certain colour and consistence is a reaction against infantile, repressed wish-impulses, mostly of a coprophilic and urophilic nature. The impulse to spit or vomit at the sight of "disgusting" things is only the reaction to the unconscious desire to take these things into the mouth.

picture of the inner man in general, for if we go deep enough into the mental life of any human being (whether "normal" or neurotic) we can find again, apart from quantitative differences, the same phenomena.

The capacity to be hypnotised and influenced by suggestion depends on the possibility of transference taking place, or, more openly expressed, on the positive, although unconscious, sexual attitude that the person being hypnotised adopts in regard to the hypnotist; the transference, however, like every "object-love," has its deepest roots in the repressed parental complexes.[1]

Further circumstantial evidence for the correctness of this conception is obtained when one takes into consideration practical experience concerning the conditions under which a person may be hypnotised or made to receive suggestions.

It is striking how greatly the percentage for successful hypnosis differs with individual authors. One achieves a positive success in only 50 per cent, another in 80-90, or even 96 per cent of the cases. According to the unanimous conviction of experienced hypnotists, suitability for this profession presupposes a number of external and internal attributes (really only external, for the "internal" ones also must manifest themselves in movements of expression that can be noted from without and in the nature and content of speech, all of which a theatrical talent can imitate without having any feeling of conviction). Hypnosis is facilitated by an imposing appearance on the part of the hypnotist;

[1] Being convinced of the correctness of Berheim's view, that hypnosis is only a form of suggestion (suggested sleep), I attach no importance to the sharp differentiation of the two terms, and often use here the one for both.

one often thinks of an "imposing" man, further, as
having a long, and if possible black beard (Svengali);
a notable stature, thick eyebrows, a penetrating glance,
and a stern expression of countenance—though one
that arouses confidence—can compensate for the lack
of these manly attributes. It is generally recognised
that a self-confident manner, the reputation of previous
successes, the high esteem attaching to a celebrated
man of science, help in the successful effect of suggestion, even when employed also by his assistants. Such
effect is also promoted by the hypnotist being of a
higher social rank. During my military service I witnessed how an infantryman instantaneously fell asleep
at his lieutenant's command; it was a "*coup de foudre*".
My first attempts at hypnotism, undertaken in my
student days with the apprentices in my father's
publishing business, succeeded without exception;
later on I had nothing like such a high percentage of
successes, but then I had lost the absolute self-confidence that only ignorance can give.

The commands in hypnosis must be given with such
decision and sureness that contradiction should appear
to the patient as quite impossible. The "being-
startled hypnosis" may count as a borderland instance
of this kind of hypnosis, where in addition to a stern
tone grimaces and clenched fists may be of use. Being
startled—just as at the sight of the Medusa head—
may be followed in a predisposed person by his being
paralysed with fright, or by catalepsy.

There is quite another method, however, for sending
someone to sleep, the requisites being: a darkened
room, absolute stillness, gentle, friendly address in a
monotonous, slightly melodic tone (on which great

stress is laid by those experienced in the matter); light stroking of the hair, forehead, and hands may serve as adjuvant measures.

In general, therefore, it may be said that there are two ways and means at our disposal in hypnotising, or giving suggestion to, others, *i. e.* in compelling them to (relatively) helpless obedience and blind belief: *dread* and *love*. The professional hypnotists of the pre-scientific era of this therapeutic method, the real inventors of the procedures, seem, however, to have chosen instinctively with regard to every detail, for their purpose of sending to sleep, and rendering pliant, just those ways of frightening and being tender, the efficacy of which has been proved for thousands of years in the relations of parent to child.

The hypnotist with the imposing exterior, who works by frightening and startling, has certainly a great similarity to the picture impressed on the child of the stern, all-powerful father, to believe in, to obey, to imitate whom, is the highest ambition of every child.[1] And the gentle stroking hand, the pleasant, monotonous words that talk one to sleep: are they not a re-impression of scenes that may have been enacted many hundred times at the child's bed by the tender mother, singing lullabies or telling fairy-tales?

I lay no great stress on this distinction between paternal and maternal hypnosis, for it happens often enough that the father and mother change their parts.

[1] The *giant motive* that ever recurs in myths, sagas, and fairy-tales, and the universal interest in these colossal figures, has the same infantile roots, and is a symptom of the undying father-complex. This respect for "giants" appears in Nietzsche in a quite sublimated form as the demand for a "pathos of distance."

I only call attention to the way in which the situation during hypnosis tends to favour a conscious and unconscious imaginary return to childhood, and to awaken reminiscences, hidden away in everyone, that date from the time of childlike obedience.

The measures also for sending to sleep that are said to work by means of external stimulation, *e. g.* holding up a shining object, laying a ticking watch to the ear, are the same that first succeeded in fastening the attention of the child in his cradle, and are thus very effective means for awakening infantile memories and feeling-impulses.

That customs and rituals preserved since childhood also play a large part in the usual spontaneous going to sleep, and that there are auto-suggestive elements concerned in going to sleep, has recently been admitted by many, some of whom are hostile to psycho-analysis. All these considerations force one to the supposition that a preliminary condition of every successful suggestion (hypnosis) *is that the hypnotist shall figure as "grown up" to the hypnotised subject; i. e. the former must be able to arouse in the latter the same feelings of love or fear, the same conviction of infallibility, as those with which his parents inspired him as a child.*

To avoid any misunderstanding it must be pointed out with emphasis that not only is suggestibility (*i. e.* receptivity for ideas, with the inclination to blind belief and obedience,) here conceived as being genetically connected with analogous psychical peculiarities of childhood, but, further, it is our opinion that in hypnosis and suggestion "the child that is dormant in the unconscious of the adult" (Freud) is, so to speak, re-awakened. The existence of this second personality betrays itself not only in hypnosis; it is manifested at night in all our dreams, which—as we know since Freud's work—have always to do with childhood reminiscences, and by day we discover the infantile tendencies and modes of functioning of our mind in certain "erroneous performances"[1] and in all expressions of wit.[2] In our innermost soul we are still children, and we remain so throughout life. *Grattez l'adulte et vous y trouverez l'enfant.*

Whoever wants properly to appreciate this way of looking at things has, of course, fundamentally to change his accustomed views about "forgetting." Analytical experience convinces us more and more that a forgetting, a disappearing without leaving a trace, occurs as little in the mental life as does an annihilation of energy or matter in the physical world. Psychical processes seem to possess a very great capacity for persistence and, even after being forgotten for decades, can be revived as unchanged, related complexes, or can be reconstructed from their elements.

A favourable opportunity puts me in a position to support, by psycho-analytical experiences with patients that I had previously hypnotised, the view that unconditional subordination to an external will is to be explained as simply the unconscious transference to the physician of affects (love, respect) originating in childhood, and erotically tinged.

1. Five years ago I successfully hypnotised a patient who had fallen ill with an anxiety-hysteria after the proved infidelity of her fiancé. About six months ago, after the death of a nephew she had been

[1]Freud. Zur Psychopathologie des Alltagslebens.
[2]Freud. Der Witz und seine Beziehungen zum Unbewussten.

fond of, she came to me with a recurrence of her suffering, and was submitted to psycho-analysis. The
characteristic signs of transference soon shewed themselves, and when I pointed them out to the patient she
supplemented my observations with the confession that
already on the previous occasion, during the hypnotic
treatment, she had indulged in conscious erotic phantasies concerning the physician and had followed my
suggestions "out of love."

The analysis, therefore, discloses, as Freud says,
the transference that created the hypnosis. It thus
seems that I had formerly cured the patient in hypnosis
through offering her, in my friendliness, sympathy, and
words of consolation, a replacement for the unhappy
love-affair that evoked her first illness. The inclination to the faithless lover was itself only a surrogate
for the love of an elder sister, lost through the latter's
marriage, with whom she had lived in childhood in the
closest intimacy, indulging for years in mutual
masturbation. Her greatest grief, however, had been
an early estrangement from her mother, who before
then used to idolise and pamper her to an incredible
extent, and indeed all her later essays at loving seemed
to have been only surrogates of this first, infantile,
but thoroughly erotic inclination to the mother.
After the end of the hypnotic treatment her "sexual
hunger," in a way that was quite sublimated, but
which in the analysis proved to be erotic, seized on a
little eight-year-old nephew, whose sudden death evoked
the recurrence of the hysterical symptoms. The
hypnotic docility was here the result of the transference,
and the original love-object, never fully replaced, was
with my patient undoubtedly the mother.

11. An official, aged twenty-eight, came to me for the first time about two years ago with a severe anxiety-hysteria. I was already occupied with psycho-analysis, but for external reasons decided on hypnotism, and achieved with simple talking ("mother-hypnosis") a splendid temporary improvement in his emotional state. The patient soon returned, however, with a recurrence of the anxiety, and I repeated the hypnosis from time to time with the same, but always only a passing, success. As I finally decided on analysis I had the greatest difficulties with the transference, certainly increased through the hypnoses. These difficulties were only resolved when it became evident that he had identified me with his "dear mother," on the ground of superficial analogies. As a child he had felt himself drawn to the mother in an extraordinary degree, her caresses were a necessity to him, and he also admitted having experienced at that time great curiosity concerning the sexual relations of the parents; he was jealous of his father, fancied himself playing the father's part, and so on. For a time the analysis passed off quite smoothly, but when I once dismissed a remark of his a little impatiently he got a severe anxiety attack, and the course of the analysis began to be disturbed. After we had finally talked over the incident that had excited him, the analysis went deeper into the memories of similar occurrences, and now—after despatching friendships tinged with homosexuality and masochism, and painful scenes with teachers and seniors—the father-complex appeared. He saw in front of him in the flesh the "frightful, grimacing, puckered countenance of his wrathful father," and he trembled at it like an aspen leaf. At the same time,

however, a flood of memories also came that shewed how fond he was of his father, and how proud of the latter's strength and size.

These are only episodes in the analysis of a complicated case, but they shew clearly that with the hypnosis it was only his mother-complex, of which he was then still unaware, that enabled me to influence his condition. In this case, however, I should probably have been able to achieve just the same success with the other method of suggestion: intimidating, impressing, *i. e.* appealing to the father-complex.

III. The third case that I can bring forward is that of a tailor, aged twenty-six, who came for help on account of epileptic attacks, which, however, I considered were hysterical after hearing the description of them. His forlorn, submissive, and resigned appearance absolutely cried out for suggestion, and in fact he obeyed all my commands like a tractable child; he developed anaesthesias, paralyses, etc., quite at my will. I did not omit to carry out an analysis of his condition, although an incomplete one. In this I found that for years he had been somnambulistic; he used to get up at night, sit at a sewing machine, and work at an hallucinated material until he was waked. This "impulsive" occupation dated from the time when he was an apprentice to a strict master-tailor, who often hit him, and whose high demands he had tried to satisfy at any cost. This was of course only a cover-memory for his respected and feared father. His present attacks also began with an impulse to occupation. He believed he heard an inner voice saying 'Get up", and then he would sit up, take off his night-shirt, and make sewing movements, which ended in general convulsions; he could not recall afterwards the motor phenomena, knowing of them only from his wife. His father had called him every morning with the cry "Get up," and the poor fellow seemed still to be always carrying out commands that he had received as a child from his father and as an apprentice from his chief. Freud writes[1] "These subsequent effects of orders and threats in childhood may be observed in cases where the interval is as great or greater than here (1¼ decades);" he terms this occu rence "subsequent obedience."

I surmise now that this kind of "subsequentness" in the psychoneuroses in general has much in common with the *post-hypnotic command-automatisms*. In both cases actions are performed the motives of which cannot be explained, or only inadequately, since the patient is following out with them either (in the neurosis) a command repressed long ago or (in the hypnosis) a suggestion concerning which amnesia has been induced.

That children should willingly, and indeed cheerfu ly, obey their parents is really not at all obvious. One might have expected that the demands made by parents on the behaviour and conduct of children would be felt to be an external compulsion, and as something unpleasant. This is really the case in the very first years of life, so long as the child knows only auto-erotic satisfactions, but with the beginning of "object-love" it becomes different. The loved objects are introjected, taken into the ego. The child loves his parents, that is to say, he identifies himself with them in thought. Usually one identifies oneself as a child with the parent of the same sex, and fancies

[1]Freud. Jahrb. Bd., I., S. 23.

oneself into all his situations. Under such circumstances obedience is not unpleasant; the expressions of
the all-powerfulness of the father even flatter the boy,
who in his fancy embodies in himself all the power
of the father, and only obeys himself, so to speak, when
he bows to his father's will. This willing obedience
obviously only goes to a certain limit, varying with the
individual; if this is overstepped by the parents in
their demands, if the bitter pill of compulsion is not
sugared with love, a precociouss evering of the "sexual
hunger" from the parents results, and generally there
is an important disturbance of psychical development,
as especially Jung has established (in his work on the
part played by the father).

In Mereschkovszky's charming book "*Peter der
Grosse und Alexei*" (1905) the relationship is very
characteristically depicted between a cruel, tyrannical
father, who regrets every impulse of sentiment, and
the son, helplessly submissive to him, who through
his father-complex, compounded of love and hate, is
incapable of energetic revolt. The poetic historian
makes the picture of the father appear very often in
the reveries of the Crown Prince. At one time he sees
himself as a little child, with his father before his cot.
"He stretches out his arms to his father with a fond,
sleepy smile, and cries out 'Papa, Papa, my darling.'
Then he jumps up and flings himself round his father's
neck. Peter embraces him so tightly as to hurt the
child, presses him to himself, kisses his face, his neck,
his bare legs, and his whole warm, sleepy body." The
Czar, however, had later used frightfully stern educational measures when his son was growing up. His
pedagogy culminated in the following (historical)

sentence: "Give the boy no power when he is young; break his ribs so long as he is growing; when you hit him with a stick, he won't die, but will only get stronger."

And in spite of all this the Czarevitch's face glowed with bashful joy when he "gazed at the familiar, horrible and dear face, with the full, almost bloated cheeks, with the curled, pointed moustache . . . . with the cordial smile on the dainty, almost womanly tender lips; he looked into the large, dark, clear eyes, which were as frightful as they were gentle, and of which he had once dreamed as does a youth in love of a beautiful woman's eyes; he took in the odour known to him from childhood, a mixture of strong tobacco, spirits, sweat, and another, strong, but not unpleasant smell of the barracks, one that pervaded his father's working-rooms and office; he felt the touch, also known to him from childhood, of the not very smoothly shaven chin with the little cleft in the middle that formed such a curious exception, almost comical, in the gloomy countenance." Such descriptions of the father, or similar ones, are in psycho-analysis typical. The author wants to make us understand through this characterisation of the bond between father and son how it came about that the Crown Prince in his safe Italian hiding-place gave up all resistance on getting a letter from his father calling him back, and helplessly yielded himself to that cruel being (who then whipped him to death with his own hands). The Czarevitch's suggestibility is here quite correctly ascribed to his strongly marked father-complex. Mereschovszky seems likewise to have divined "transferences" when he writes: "He (the Czarevitch) transferred on to the priestly father (the confessor Jacob Ignatiew) all the love that he could not bestow on his actual father. It was a jealous, tender, passionate friendship, as though between lovers."

The feeling of awe for the parents, and the tendency to obey them, normally disappear as the child grows up, but the need to be subject to someone remains; only the part of the father is transferred to teachers, superiors, impressive personalities; the submissive loyalty to rulers that is so wide-spread is also a transference of this sort. In Alexei's case the father-complex could not fade even when he grew up, for his father really was the terrible and mighty despot that in childhood we think our fathers to be.

That the union in the father's person of parental power with the dignity attaching to a respected position can fix immovably any incestuous inclination I was able to observe with two female patients who were pupils of their own father. Passionate transference in the one and neurotic negativism in the other caused almost insuperable difficulties for the psycho-analysis. The limitless obedience in the one case and the defiant rejection of all medical efforts in the other were both determined by the same psychical complexes, by the fusion of the father and teacher complexes.

These striking cases, as well as all the other observations brought forward above, confirm Freud's view that the *hypnotic credulity and pliancy take their root in the masochistic component of the sexual instinct.*[1] Masochism, however, is pleasurably obeying, and this one learns in childhood from one's parents.

[1] Freud. Drei Abhandlungen zur Sexualtheorie, S. 18. Anm. 2.

In the case of the timid and obedient tailor we saw how the parental commands go on acting long after the years of childhood, in the manner of a post-hypnotic suggestion. I have also been able to demonstrate the neurotic analogy to the so-called "dated suggestions" (*suggestion à échéance*) in a case of morbid anxiety (the twenty-eight year old official mentioned above). He got ill on a quite trivial ground, and it was striking that he had familiarised himself rather too readily with the thought of retiring on his pension at such an early age. The analysis brought out that he had entered on this career exactly ten years before the illness, and very unwillingly, for he considered himself to have artistic gifts. At that time he had only yielded to the pressure brought to bear by his father, making up his mind, however, to get himself pensioned under the pretext of illness the moment he had served the time (ten years) that entitled him to a pension; (the inclination to malingering dated from childhood, when he had obtained in this way much tenderness from his mother and some consideration from his father). In the meantime, however, he completely forgot his resolve; he got a rather better income, and, although the conflict continued between his antipathy towards his office work and his preference for his artistic activities—which he had successfully pursued in the meanwhile,—the pusillanimity that had been instilled into him prevented him from even thinking of giving up a part of his income, a loss which his retirement would have entailed. The plan resolved on ten years ago seems to have lain dormant in his unconscious throughout the whole time, to have become mature after the given interval had elapsed, and to have cooperated "autosuggestively," so to speak, as one of the evoking causes of his neurosis. The fact, however, that the idea of dates and periods of time was able to play such a significant part in the life of this patient was at bottom a symptom of unconscious phantasies connected with infantile ponderings on the menstruation and gravidity time periods with his mother, and, amongst others, on the idea of his own situation in the womb and at birth.[1]

This case—like all others—confirms Jung's statement that "the magic binding children to their parents" is really "the sexuality on both sides."

Such far-reaching points of agreement between the mechanism of the psychoneuroses revealed analytically and the phenomena that can be produced by means of hypnosis and suggestion absolutely compel us to revise the judgement that has been passed in scientific circles on Charcot's conception of hypnosis as "artificial hysteria." Many scientists believe they have already reduced this idea to absurdity in that they are able to hypnotise ninety per cent of healthy people, considering such an extension of the "hysteria" concept as unthinkable. Psycho-analysis has led, nevertheless, to the discovery that healthy people fight with the same

---

[1] The unconscious birth-fancy was the final explanation of the following lines that he wrote in his diary during an anxiety attack, and which turned out to possess symbolic meaning: "Hypochondria surrounds my soul like a fine mist, or rather like a cobweb, just as a fungus covers a swamp. I have the feeling as though I were sticking in a bog, as though I had to stretch out my head so as to be able to breathe. I want to tear the cobweb, to tear it. But no, I can't do it! The web is fastened somewhere—the props would have to be pulled out on which it hangs. If that can't be done, one would have slowly to work cne's way through the net in order to get air. Man surely is not here to be veiled in such a cobweb, suffocated, and robbed of the light of the sun." All these feelings and thoughts were symbolic representations of phantasies concerning intra-uterine and birth events.

complexes as those from which the neurotic fall ill (Jung), that. thus some hysterical predisposition exists in every human being, which can also manifest itself under unfavourable circumstances that inflict an undue burden on the mind. The fact that so many normal people may be hypnotised can by no means be taken as an irrefragable proof of the impossibility of Charcot's conception. If, however, one is once free from this prejudice, and compares the pathological manifestations of the psychoneuroses with the phenomena of hypnosis and suggestion, one becomes convinced that the hypnotist can really shew nothing more, and nothing else, than that which the neurosis spontaneously produces: the same psychical, the same paralysis and stimulation phenomena. The impression of a far-reaching analogy between hypnosis and neurosis becomes strengthened to the point of a conviction of their inherent sameness as soon as one reflects that in both states unconscious ideational complexes determine the phenomena, and that among these ideational complexes in both cases the infantile and sexual, especially those concerned with the parents, play the greatest part. It will be the task of future investigations to see if these points of agreement extend to the details as well; our experience up to the present justifies the expectation that this will be shewn to be the case.

The certainty of this expectation is essentially supported by the undeniable existence of the so-called auto-hypnoses and auto-suggestion. These are states in which unconscious ideas, without any intended external influence, bring about all the neuro-psychic phenomena of deliberate suggestion and hypnosis. It is perhaps not too daring to assume that a far-reaching analogy must exist between the psychical mechanism of these auto-suggestions and that of psychoneurotic symptoms, which after all are the realisations of unconscious ideas. This relationship, however, must be assumed with just the same right between neurosis and foreign suggestion, since according to our conception *there is no such thing as a "hypnotising," a "giving of ideas" in the sense of psychical incorporating of something quite foreign from without, but only procedures that are able to set going unconscious, pre-existing, auto-suggestive mechanisms.* The activity of the person suggesting may then be very well compared with the action of the evoking cause of a psychoneurosis. We do not, of course, mean to deny that, in addition to this extensive resemblance, there may also exist differences between being neurotic and being hypnotised; to make these differences clear is indeed an important task for the future. I only wanted here to *point out that the high percentage of normal people that may be hypnotised can, according to the experience gained by psycho-analysis, be cited as an argument rather for the universality of the predisposition to suffer from a psychoneurosis than against the essential sameness of hypnosis and neurosis.*

Even after this discussion, which must at first produce a displeasing impression from its very novelty, the statement will probably sound paradoxical, that the *resistance* against being hypnotised or affected by suggestion is a reaction to the same psychical complexes that in other cases make transference, hypnosis, or suggestion possible; and yet Freud divined this already in his first work on psycho-analytic technique,[1] and was able to strengthen it by means of examples.

According to Freud's conception, which later experience has confirmed in all respects, an inability to be hypnotised signifies an unconscious refusal to be hypnotised. The fact that many neurotics cannot be hypnotised, or only with difficulty, is very often due to their not really wanting to be cured. They have, so to speak, come to terms with their suffering, since it yields them libidinous pleasure,[2] although by a highly unpractical and costly route, still without self-reproach, and frequently also brings other considerable advantages (termed by Freud "the secondary function of the neuroses").

The cause of a second kind of resistance lies in the relations between the hypnotist and the person to be hypnotised, in the "antipathy" to the physician. It has already been pointed out that this obstacle also is mostly created by the unconscious infantile complexes.

It may be assumed with considerable probability that the other resistances which can be demonstrated in the psycho-analytic treatment of patients similarly exert influence in attempts at hypnosis and suggestion. There are some sympathies that are unendurable. The reason for hypnosis miscarrying is in many cases, as Freud has shewn, the fear "of getting too used to the physician's personality, of losing one's independence in regard to him, or even of becoming sexually dependent on him." That with one patient an unrestrained

[1] Freud, "Zur Psychotherapie der Hysterie," IV Abschnitt in Breuer und Freud, Studien über Hysterie, 1895.

[2] Freud, Kleine Schriften, Bd. II, 1909, S. 142: "The hysterical symptom serves sexual gratification and represents a part of the person's sexual life."

inclination to transference comes to expression, in another a flight from every idea of external influence, can ultimately, I believe, be similarly traced to the parental complex, and especially to the way in which the "sexual hunger" became detached from the parents.[1]

IV. Not long ago a patient aged thirty-three, the wife of a land-proprietor, consulted me: her case may serve to illustrate these resistances. Her husband was several times awakened in the middle of the night by her moaning, and saw her restlessly turning about in every direction; "she was making sounds as if something that she was vainly trying to swallow was sticking in her throat" ran the husband's description. Finally, choking and straining movements came on, at which the patient would wake up, calmly going to sleep again soon after. The patient was the absolute opposite of a "good medium." She was one of those refractory persons who are always lying in wait for inconsistencies in the physician's remarks, who are very particular about everything he does and says, and who altogether behave in a very stubborn and almost negativistic manner. Sharpened by bad experiences with such patients, I did not even make any attempt at hypnosis or suggestion, but immediately undertook an analysis. To describe the winding ways by which I arrived at the solution of her symptom-complex would lead me too far from the subject. In the present connection I will confine myself to the explanation of her stubborn behaviour, which she shewed to me especially at the beginning of the analysis, and long before that—on

---

[1] *Infantile* (incestuous) *fixation and capacity for transference seem in fact to be reciprocal quantities.* Every psycho-analyst can entirely confirm Jung's observations on this point, but I believe that this sentence is also valid for the form of affective transference that we call suggestion.

the most trivial occasions—to her husband, with whom she often exchanged not a word for days. Her illness came on after a social gathering, at which she had interpreted as insulting the behaviour of an older lady when the latter wanted to reproach her with improperly taking the first place at the table. The appearance of inadequacy in her feeling-reaction, however, disappeared as the analysis progressed. When she was a young girl she had really improperly taken the first place at table for a short time at home, after her mother's death. The father had been left with a number of children, and after the burial a touching scene took place between him and his daughter; he promised never to marry again, at which she gave her solemn word not to marry for ten years, and to take her mother's place with the poor orphans. It happened otherwise, however. Scarcely a year had passed before her father began to insinuate that she ought to get married. She guessed what that meant, and obstinately kept every suitor at a distance. True enough, the father soon after took a young wife, and a bitter fight began between the daughter, who was displaced from every position, and her step-mother; in this fight the father openly took sides against the daughter, and the only weapon against them both that remained to her was stubbornness, which she used to the best of her powers. Up to this point the whole thing sounded like a touching story of the wicked step-mother and the faithless father; but soon came the turn of the "infantile" and the "sexual". As sign of a beginning transference I began to play a part in her dreams, and curiously enough in the not very flattering figure of a composite person put together of myself and—a horse. The associations to "horse" led to disagreeable topics; she recollected being taken by her nurse as a quite small child to a stud-farm in the barracks, and seeing many horses there (also copulation scenes between stallion and mare). She confessed further that when she was a girl she had been unusually interested in the size of the male genitals, and that she had been disappointed at the relative smallness of this organ in her husband, with whom she remained frigid. Even as a girl she persuaded a friend to agree that they would measure the dimensions of their future husbands' genital organs and tell each other. She kept her promise, but the friend didn't.

The strange circumstance that in one dream the horse appeared in a night-shirt led to the reproduction of much older childhood memories, among which, as is often the case, the overhearing of sexual acts between the parents, and especially the observation of the father's micturition, were the most important. She remembered now how often she used to fancy herself in her mother's place, how fond she used to be of playing father and mother with her dolls and friends, on one occasion going through an imaginary pregnancy with the help of a pillow stuffed under her petticoats. It turned out finally that the patient had even in childhood suffered for years from minor anxiety-hysteria: often she was not able to go to sleep till late at night from the fear that her stern father might come to her and shoot her dead with the revolver that he kept in his night-commode. The choking and straining movements in her attacks were signs of repression "from below upwards" (Freud); for a long period she was (like Freud's patient, Dora) passionately fond of sucking various objects, a large number of perverse phantasies cooperating with a strongly developed erogenous mouth-zone.

This anamnesis, although only very imperfectly reproduced, is instructive in two respects. In the first place, it shews that here stubbornness, the rejection of any idea of being influenced, which stood in the way of any attempt at treatment by suggestion, turned out in the analysis to be resistance against the father. In the second place, the case teaches one that this resistance was a derivative of a strongly fixed parental complex, an Oedipus-complex feminini generis, and that her parental complexes were interspersed with infantile sexuality. (The horse dreams of this patient also form a striking analogy with the phobia of horses in the five year old "little Hans" [Jahrbuch I.] that Freud was similarly able to trace to identification of the father with a horse.)

What I desired to establish by the facts brought forward is the view that the "medium" is really in love with the hypnotist, and has brought this tendency with her from the nursery. I will merely add that the usual state of being in love may also evince psychological phenomena that remind one of hypnosis. A man blinded with the passion of love almost helplessly does things suggested to him by his sweetheart, even if they are crimes. In the celebrated Czynsky trial the most learned experts could not decide whether the actions of the baroness concerned were determined by her being in love or by ideas "suggested" to her.

Most of the homosexuals who have told me their story stated that they had been hypnotised, or at least submitted to the influence of suggestion, by the first man with whom they had had relations. In the analysis of such a case it becomes evident, of course, that these phantasies of being hypnotised are only apologetic attempts at projection.

I will content myself with these hints, and will not continue the analogy between the state of being in love and hypnosis, lest the incorrect impression be aroused that it is here only a question of deductively expatiating on a banal resemblance. That is not at all the case. The basis on which this hypothesis is built consists of laborious individual-psychological investigations, such as we have been able to carry out since Freud's work, and if they end in a commonplace, that is in no sense an argument against their correctness.

An undeniable weakness of these considerations, it is true, is that they are based on a relatively small number of observed cases. It lies in the nature of psycho-analytic work, however, that the observation of large numbers and the statistical method are not applicable.

Nevertheless I believe I have brought together, through thorough investigation of the cases—even though these are not many—, through the fundamental agreement in all the cases, and lastly through the extent to which these observations fit in with the rest of psycho-analytic knowledge, sufficient material to support a conception of hypnosis and suggestion that differs from the previous ones.

According to this conception, the application of suggestion and hypnosis consists in the deliberate establishment of conditions under which the tendency to blind belief and uncritical obedience present in everyone, but usually kept repressed by the censor (remains of the infantile-erotic loving and fearing of the parents), may unconsciously be transferred to the person hypnotising or suggesting.[1]

[1](This chapter may be read in conjunction with that entitled "The Action of Suggestion in Psychotherapy" in the Translator's "Papers on Psycho-Analysis").

CHAPTER III

A phenomenon not rare in the evolution of science is that professional men of erudition, with all the help at their disposal, with all the implements of their knowledge and ability, combat some principle of popular wisdom which is, on the other hand, defended by the people with equal tenacity, and that finally science is forced to recognise that in essentials the popular conception, and not its own, is the correct one. It would be especially worthy of investigation to discover why it is that science, on its gradually mounting path, progresses in an irregular zigzag line, which at times comes close to the popular view of the world, and at times quite departs from it.

I mention this peculiar phenomenon for the reason that the latest investigations of dreams, those remarkable and bizarre manifestations of mental life, have laid bare facts that compel us to abandon our former views regarding the nature of dreams, and, with certain limitations, to return to the popular conceptions.

The people have never given up a belief in the significance of dreams. The oldest writings that have

*Delivered before the Königliche Gesellschaft der Aerzte, Budapest, Oct. 16, 1909; published in the Psychiatr.-Neurolog. Wochenschr., Jahrg. XII. (A translation by Professor Chase was also published in the Amer. Journ. of Psych., April, 1910, and I am indebted to President Stanley Hall for permission to reproduce the article in this series. Transl.)

been preserved to us, hewn out in stone in praise of the old Babylonian kings, as also the mythology and history of the Hindoos, Chinese, Aztecs, Greeks, Etruscans, Jews, and Christians, take the point of view held to-day by the people, that dreams can be interpreted. The interpretation of dreams was for thousands of years a special science, a particular cult, whose priests and priestesses often decided the fate of countries and called forth revolutions that changed the history of the world. This now antiquated science rested on the unshakable belief that dreams, though in a concealed way and by obscure analogies, were quite capable of being interpreted by the initiate and revealed the future, and that by these nocturnal phenomena the powers above desired to prepare mortals for approaching events of importance. In the lower ranks of the populace the dream book, that curious survival of ancient Babylonian astrology, still enjoys to-day great popularity. Although the details of the dream-books differ in the different countries, they have to be considered as products of the common folk-spirit.

On the other hand, we find on the part of the great majority of recent psychologists an almost complete contempt for the dream as a psychical function, and consequently a denial that the dream-content has any significance. Many of these investigators consider dreams to be a senseless complex of hallucinations, which blaze up in a lawless way in the brain of the sleeper. According to the view of other writers dreams are nothing but the psychical reaction to the external (objective) or internal (subjective) stimuli which the sensory end-organs of the body receive during sleep and conduct to the centres.

There were only a few who held that the mind at sleep was able to develop a complicated, significant activity, or that the dream could be maintained to have any sort of symbolic meaning. Even these authors, however, failed to make comprehensible the peculiarities of dreams without forcing their explanations into the Procrustian bed of an artificial playing with allegories.

Accordingly for centuries the army of superstitious interpreters of dreams stood over against that of the sceptics, until about ten years ago the Viennese neurologist, Professor Freud, discovered facts that make possible a unification of the two opposing conceptions, and which on the one hand helped to disclose the true nucleus in the age-old superstition, and on the other hand fully satisfied the scientific need for knowledge of the relations between cause and effect.

I may state at this point that Freud's theory of dreams and his method of interpretation approach the popular conception only in so far as it attributes sense and meaning to dreams. The newly discovered facts in no way sustain the belief of those who would ascribe dreams to interference on the part of higher powers, and see prophecies in them. Freud's theory regards dreams as mental products dependent on endopsychic occurrences, and is not calculated to strengthen the belief of those who consider the dream to be a device of higher powers or a clairvoyance of the sleeper.

It was psycho-analysis, a new method for investigating and treating psychoneuroses, that made it possible for Freud to recognise the true significance of dreams. The method takes its point of departure in the principle that the symptoms of these disorders are only the sensory images of particular thought-constellations, impregnated with feeling, which were distasteful to consciousness and therefore repressed, but which still live on in the unconscious; and in the fact that the surrogate-creations for the repressed material vanish as soon as the unconscious thought can be brought to light, and made conscious, by help of free association. In the course of this analytic work the patients' dreams were related, and Freud made their content also an object of psycho-analytic investigation. To his surprise he not only found in dream analysis a great aid to the treatment of neuroses, but he gained at the same time as a by-product a new explanation of dreams as a psychical function, more enlightening than any of the previous explanations. In many chemical processes materials are incidentally obtained by the reduction of certain chemicals that perhaps have long been thrown away as useless, but which after a time have been shewn to be valuable materials, often surpassing in value the principal products of the manufacture. This was rather the case with the explanation of dreams incidentally discovered by Freud; it opens up such outlooks for the knowledge of both the sound and the disordered mind that by comparison its particular point of departure, the treatment of certain phenomena of nervous disease, seems a scientific question of second rank.

In the short time at my disposal I cannot reproduce exhaustively Freud's theory of dreams. I must rather confine myself to the more essential explanations and the most valuable facts of the new theory, and to the verification by means of examples. Further, I do not imagine that this lecture will convince my hearers.

According to my experience conviction in matters of psycho-analysis is only to be gained through oneself. So I shall not controvert here the less important and quite superficial critics of Freud, but will rather explain in brief the most essential parts of the theory itself.

First a few words concerning the method. If we desire to analyse a dream, we proceed exactly as in the psychological investigation of psychoneurotic symptoms. Behind each obsession, no matter how illogical it may appear, are hidden coherent but unconscious thoughts, and to make these evident is the problem of psycho-analysis. Freud has shewn that the images and experiences of which the dream consists are for the most part merely disguises, symbolic allusions to suppressed trains of thought. Behind the conscious dream-content is hidden a latent dream-material, which, for its part, was aroused by coherent, logical dream-thoughts. The interpretation of the dream is nothing else than the translation of the dream from its hiero-glyphic-symbolic speech into conceptual speech, the leading back of the manifest dream-content to the logical dream-thoughts through the clues of association provided by the hidden dream-material. The means by which this is done is the so-called free association. We have the dream related to us, divide the given material into several parts or sections, and ask the dreamer to tell us all that occurs to him when he directs his attention, not to the whole dream, but to a definite part of it, to a particular event or word-image occurring in it. This association, however, must be wholly free; consequently the one thing forbidden is the dominance of critical choice among the irruptive ideas. Any half-way intelligent man can be brought to express all the thoughts associated with the fragments of the dream, whether clever or stupid, coherent or senseless, pleasant or unpleasant, suppressing the shame perhaps bound up with them. The other fragments of the dream are also worked over in this way, and so we collect the latent dream material, that is to say, all the thoughts and memories of which the conscious dream-picture is to be considered the condensation-product. It is an error to think that the activity of association when left free is devoid of any regulation by law. As soon as we disregard in the analysis the conscious goal idea of our thinking, the directive forces of the unconscious psychic activities, that is to say, the very same mental forces that functioned in the creation of the dream, prevail in the choice of associations. We have long been familiar with the thought that there is no chance in the physical world, no event without sufficient cause; on the basis of psycho-analytical experience we have to suppose just as strict a determination of every mental activity, however arbitrary it may appear. The fear is therefore unjustified that the activity of association when freed from all restraint, as it is in such an analysis, will give valueless results. The subject of the analysis, who at first reproduces his apparently senseless ideas with scornful scepticism, soon discovers, to his surprise, that the train of associations, uninfluenced by conscious aid, leads to the awakening of thoughts and memories that had long been forgotten or repressed on account of the pain they caused. Through the emergence of these, however, the fragment taken from the dream is made intelligible or capable of interpretation. If we repeat this procedure with all the parts of the dream, we see that the trains of thought radiating from the different fragments converge on to a very essential train of thought, which had been stimulated on the day before the dream night—the dream thoughts themselves. Once these are recognised, not only the single fragment, but also the dream as a whole appears coherent and intelligible. If, finally, we compare the point of departure of the dream, the dream thoughts, with the content of the naïvely related dream, we see that *the dream is nothing else than the concealed fulfilment of a repressed wish.*

This sentence contains the most essential results of Freud's investigation of dreams. The idea that dreams fulfil wishes that in the rude world of facts have to remain unfulfilled seems to partake of the language of abandoned popular science. "Dreams" are used metaphorically in most languages for "wishes," and a Hungarian proverb says just this, "swine dream of acorns, geese of maize"—which can only be regarded as an allusion to the similar direction of human dreams.

Some of the dreams of adults and most of those of children are purely wish-fulfilment dreams. The child dreams of pleasurable experiences denied him by day, of the toys that he envied his little comrades, of victorious struggles with those of his own age, of his good mother or his friendly father. Very often in his dream he seems "big," endowed with all the freedom and power of his parents for which he wishes so ardently by day. Wish dreams like these also occur to adults. The difficult examination (about which we are so anxious) seems in dreams splendidly passed; dear relatives awaken from their graves and assure us they are not dead; we appear to ourselves rich, powerful, endowed with great oratorical gifts; the most beautiful of women solicit our favour, and so on. For the most part we attain, in dreams just that which we painfully miss on waking.

The same tendency to wish-fulfilment dominates not only in nocturnal, but also in day dreams, those fancies in which we can catch ourselves at unoccupied moments or during monotonous activity. Freud has observed that women's fancies deal for the most part with things directly or indirectly concerned with sex life (of being loved, proposals, beautiful clothes), those of men predominantly with power and esteem, but also with sexual satisfaction. Fancies concerning the means of escape from a real or imagined danger and the annihilation of real or imagined enemies are also very common. These simple wish-fulfilment dreams and fancies have an obvious meaning, and need no particular labour for their interpretation.

But what is new, surprising, and incredible to many in Freud's explanation of dreams is the assertion that *all* dreams, even those which seem indifferent or even unpleasant, can be reduced to this basal form, and that it can be shewn by analysis that they fulfil wishes in a disguised way. In order to understand this we have first to make ourselves familiar with the mechanism of psychic activity in dreams.

The associative analysis of a dream is only the reversal of the synthetic work performed at night by the mind when it transforms the unwelcome thought and the unpleasant sensation that disturb sleep into wish-fulfilling dream-images. Critical consideration convinces one that this work never ceases during sleep, even when after waking we cannot recall having dreamed at all. The traditional idea that dreams disturb rest during sleep must be abandoned on the ground of these newly won results; on the contrary, since they do not allow the unpleasant, painful or burdensome thought that would disturb sleep to become conscious with its true content, but only in a changed form as the fulfilment of a wish, we are compelled to recognise dreams as the preservers of sleep.

The psychic factor watching over rest during sleep, often with the assistance of the dream disguise already mentioned, is the censor. This is the gate-keeper at the threshold of consciousness, which we see zealously at work during waking life also, especially in the psychoneuroses, and which for our problem is to be considered as either repressing all thought groupings that are in ethical or aesthetic ways distasteful, or disguising them in the form of apparently harmless symbols, symptomatic actions, or symptomatic thoughts.

The function of the censorship is to secure repose for consciousness, and to keep at a distance all psychical productions that would cause pain or disturb rest. And like the censor of political absolutism, who sometimes works at night, the psychic censorship is kept in activity during sleep, though its red pencilling is not so strongly in evidence as in waking life. Probably the censor is led to relax its activity by the idea that motor reactions are paralysed during sleep, so that thoughts cannot be expressed in deeds. Thus the fact may be explained that for the most part the images and situations emerging as wish-fulfilments in dreams are those which by day we refuse to recognise as wishes. We all shelter in our unconscious many wishes

repressed since childhood, which take the opportunity
of exercising their psychic intensity as soon as they
perceive the relaxation of the censorship at night.

It is not chance that among the wishes revealed
in dreams the greatest part is played by the strongly
repressed sexual excitations, and in particular those
of the most despised kind. It is a very great error to
believe that psycho-analysis deliberately places sexual
activity in the foreground. It cannot be denied that
whenever one attempts thoroughly to investigate the
basal facts of mental life one always strikes against
the sexual element. If, accordingly, we find psycho-
analysis objectionable for this reason, we are really
degrading the description of the unconscious facts of
human mentality by our attitude in regarding them
as obscene. The censorship of sexual matters is, as
already said, much milder in dream life than in waking
hours, so that in dreams we experience and crave for
sexual experiences without bounds, even representing
in our dreams experiences and acts that remind one
of the so-called perversions. As an example of this I
may avail myself of the dream of a patient who was
extraordinarily modest in waking life. He saw himself
enveloped in an antique peplum, fastened in front
with a safety-pin; suddenly the pin fell out, the white
garment opened in front, and his nakedness was ad-
mired by a great crowd of men. Another patient,
equally modest, told me this, which is an exhibition
dream with somewhat altered circumstances: She was
draped from top to toe in a white garment, and bound to
a pillar; around her stood foreign men, Turks or Arabs,
who were haggling over her. The scene strongly
reminds one, apart from her enveloping garment, of

an Oriental slave market; and, indeed, analysis brought out that this lady, now so modest, had read when a young girl the tales of the Arabian Nights, and had seen herself in fancy in many of the situations of the highly coloured love scenes of the Orient. At that time she imagined that slaves were exposed for sale not clothed, but naked. At present she repudiates the idea of nudity so strongly, even in dreams, that the suppressed wishes bearing on this theme can be manifested only when changed to their opposite. A third dreamer only allowed herself so much freedom in this respect as to move about amongst the other figures of her dream incompletely clad, in her stockings or with bare feet; and here analysis shewed that as a child she had over a long period greatly enjoyed removing her clothes and going about without them, so that she was nicknamed "the naked Pancri" (her name was Anna, in Hungarian Pauna). Such exhibition dreams are so frequent that Freud was able to put them in the class of his "typical" dreams, which recur with most people from time to time and have the same origin. They are based on the fact that there lives on in all of us an undying longing for the return of the paradise of childhood; this is the "Golden Age" that poets and Utopians project from the past into the future. It is a very common means of dream disguise to circumvent the censorship by presenting the wish not as such, but only in the form of an allusion in the dream. It would not be possible to understand, for example, why one of my patients dreamed so often of sexual scenes with a man by the name of Frater, who was quite indifferent to her, if we had not learned that in her youth her brother (*frater*) was her ideal and that in childhood the affection of the pair had often assumed a purely erotic form, manifesting itself by relations that she now repressed as incestuous. This repression of forbidden things often enters into dreams, especially with persons who in consequence of incomplete satisfaction of their sexual hunger are inclined to the development of morbid anxiety (Freud's anxiety neurotics). Nocturnal anxiety can become so great that the dreamer awakes with feelings of distress (*pavor nocturnus*). Anxiety, which has a physiological basis, gives in such cases an opportunity for the deeply repressed childish-perverse excitations to involve themselves in the dream, in the form of cruel, horrible scenes, which seem frightful to us, but which in a certain depth of the unconscious satisfy wishes that in the "prehistoric" ages of our own mental development were actually recognised as desires.

The great part played in such dreams by cruelties inflicted or endured must find its explanation in the sadistic idea that children have of the sex-relationship, as Freud has so prettily shewn in his "infantile sexual theories."[1]   All the cruel acts of such dreams appear in analysis as sexual events transformed into deeds of violence. Sexually unsatisfied women, for example, very commonly dream of thieves breaking in, of attacks by robbers or wild beasts, not one of the well-concealed incidents of the dream betraying the fact that the outrages to which the dreamer is subjected really symbolise sexual acts. An hysteric of my observation once dreamed that she was run down by a bull in front of which she held a red garment. There

---

[1]Freud. Sammlung Kleiner Schriften zur Neurosenlehre. 2e Folge, 1909.

was involved in this dream not only the present wish to possess such a dress, but also an unavowed sexual wish, the same one that also caused the illness. The thought of the frightfully enraged bull, which is a widespread symbol of masculine strength, came to her especially through the circumstance that a man with a so-called "bull neck" had played a certain part in the development of her sexual life.

Childhood memories make continual and always significant contributions to the creation of dreams. Freud has shewn not merely that even the earliest age of childhood is not free from sexual excitations, but rather that infantile sexuality, not yet restrained by education, is expressly of a perverse character. In infantile sexuality the oral and anal-urethral erogenous zones, the partial instincts of sexual curiosity and of exhibitionism, as well as sadistic and masochistic impulses, dominate the scene. When we consider these facts we come to the conclusion that Freud is in the right when he says that dreams express such impulses as wish-fulfilments, the fulfilment of wishes from that part of our childhood that seems long since outgrown.

There are, however, dreams of very unpleasant content which strangely enough disturb our sleep hardly at all, so that when we awaken we reproach ourselves for experiencing such terrible events with so little sympathy or feeling. This sort of dream was observed, for instance, by one of Freud's patients who in a dream was present at the funeral of a beloved nephew. An apparently unessential detail of the dream, a concert ticket, led to the explanation of the occurrence. The lady in question meant to attend a concert on the next night, where she expected to see again the man whom she had formerly loved and had not yet forgotten, and whom she had last met a long while before at the funeral of another nephew. So the dream, in order to hasten the meeting, sacrificed the other nephew. The censorship, apparently knowing that a harmless wish, not one of death, was to be fulfilled, let the funeral "pass," without attaching to it any obvious emotional excitation. This analysis may serve as an illustration of all those dreams that apparently contradict Freud's wish theory, and which have to do with very unwelcome matters or even with the non-fulfilment of wishes. If we seek out the latent dream thoughts concealed behind these dreams that are invested with painful affects, it becomes clear to us that, as Freud himself expresses it, *the non-fulfilment of a wish in a dream always means the fulfilment of some other wish.*

When we consider the dream-material gained by free association from the conscious dream elements, it becomes clear that they more usually flow from two opposite sources: from childhood memories on the one hand, and from unnoticed experiences of the "dream day," often quite indifferent, to which the person had not reacted. Indeed, according to Freud's expression, every well-articulated dream stands as it were on two legs, and is shewn by analysis to be *over-determined*, that is, to be the fulfilment of both a present and a long suppressed wish.

As an example I may relate the dream of a patient suffering from a nervous difficulty in urination. "A polished floor, wet, as though a pool lay there. Two chairs leaning against the wall. As I look around, I note that the front legs of both chairs are missing, as when one wants to play a practical joke on some one and gets him to sit down on a broken chair, so that he falls. One of my friends was also there with her affianced."

Free association on the theme of the polished floor gave the fact that on the day before her brother in a rage had thrown a pitcher to the floor, which, with the water spilled over it, looked like the floor in the dream. She also recalled a similar floor from her childhood; on this occasion her brother, then very young, had made her laugh so hard that micturition ensued. This part of the dream, which also proved to be significant for the symptom-formation of the neurosis, accordingly fulfilled infantile erotic wishes, which could now in consequence of strong censorship be presented only as allusions. The two broken chairs leaning against the wall were shewn by analysis to be a scenic presentation of the proverb "to fall to the ground between two stools." The patient had had two suitors, but the family constellation just mentioned, (the unconscious love for the brother) prevented the marriage on both occasions. And although her conscious ego, according to her repeated testimony, had long been reconciled to the idea of spinsterhood, she still seems in the depth of her soul to have regarded with some envy the recent betrothal of one of her friends. The affianced pair had in fact been calling on her the day before the dream.

According to Freud's theory we may picture to ourselves the origin of this dream in the following way: The dream-work succeeded in uniting two experiences of the day before, the breaking of the pitcher and the visit of the betrothed pair, with that train of thought, always emotionally toned, which, though already suppressed in childhood, was always in a condition to lend its affective energy to any current mental image that could be brought into even a superficial connection with it. Freud compares a dream to the promotion of a business undertaking, in which the unconscious repressed complex furnishes the capital, that is, the affective energy, while the wishes play the part of promotors.

Another source of dreams is in the sensory and sensorial nerve-stimulations to which the organism is subjected during sleep. These may be : dermal stimuli, the pressure of mattress and covering, cooling of the skin; acoustic or optical stimuli; organic sensations—hunger, thirst, an overloaded stomach, an excited condition of the sexual parts, and so on. Most psychologists and physiologists are inclined to attribute too great significance to stimuli of this sort; they think they have given a satisfactory explanation of all dreams when they say that the dream is nothing but the sum of the psychophysical reactions set free by nerve stimuli of this character. On the other hand, Freud rightly remarks that the dream does not admit these bodily stimuli as such to consciousness, but disguises and alters them in particular ways; the motive and means of this disguise are given, not through the external stimuli, but from mental sources of energy. The nervous stimuli during sleep offer, as it were, only the opportunity for the unfolding of certain immanent tendencies of the psychical life. Analysis shews that dreams caused by nervous stimulation are also wish-fulfilments, either open or concealed: the thirsty man drinks large amounts of water in his dreams; the hungry man satisfies himself; the sick man who is disturbed by the ice-packing on his head throws it away, for he thinks of himself in his dream as already well; the painful throbbing of a boil on the perinaeum leads to the dream idea of riding. So it is made possible that the hunger, the thirst, the pressure on the head, the painful inflammation, do not waken the sleeper, but are transformed into wish-fulfilments by the psychic forces.

The anxiety-dream known as "nightmare", brought on by an overloaded stomach, respiratory or circulatory disturbances, or by intoxication, permits of explanation in the same way; the unpleasant bodily sensations offer an opportunity for deeply repressed wishes to fulfil themselves, wishes which the censorship of civilisation will not allow to pass and which can break through into consciousness only in connection with feelings of anxiety and disgust.

In the process of analysis, as has already been said, we retrace, only in the reverse direction, the same path that the sleeping soul has travelled in the formation of the dream. When we compare the manifest dream, often very short, with the rich material that is brought to light during the process of analysis, and when we consider that in spite of this quantitative difference all the elements of the latent dream-content are contained in some way in the portion that is manifest to us, we must agree that Freud is right in considering this dream-condensation as the most laborious part of the dream-formation. I will try to shew this by means of an example. A patient suffering from psycho-sexual impotence brought to me on one occasion a dream composed of two fragments. In the first one the only occurrence was that instead of a Hungarian newspaper "Pesti Hirlap," which came regularly to him, he received the Vienna "Neue Freie Presse," to which as a matter of fact one of his colleagues had subscribed. The second part of the dream dealt with a brunette whom he ardently desired to marry. It turned out that in the dream he acquired not the foreign newspaper but, in the hidden sense of the dream, a foreign woman to whom in fact a colleague had "subscribed." This woman had long excited his interest, for it seemed to him that just this person would be able to get his sexuality, which was struggling with strong inhibitions, to function. The thought associations that came from this idea made it plain that he had been deceived in his hopes of another woman, with whom he had entered into the same relation. This woman, being a Hungarian, had been concealed in the dream behind the name of the paper "Pesti Hirlap." Of late he had occupied himself in seeking free sexual associations, which led to no obligations, instead of a more stable relationship. When we know the great freedom with which the dream avails itself of symbols, we are not surprised to learn that my patient also applied the word "Press" in a sexual sense. The second part of the dream shews, as though to confirm our interpretations, that the patient had often been obliged to think, not without anxiety, that relations which lasted too long, like that between him and his friend, could easily lead to a *mésalliance.* One who does not know what Freud has shewn in his monograph,[1] namely that the psychic

---

[1]Freud. Der Witz und seine Beziehung zum Unbewussten. 1909.

motive and means of presentation of wit are almost
exactly the same as those that come out in dreams,
might consider us guilty of a cheap joke in saying that
the dream succeeds in condensing in the words "Neue
Freie Presse" all the patient's thoughts and wishes
relating to the pleasures of which his illness had robbed
him and the means of benefit that he had in mind,
namely, the stimulus of the new, and the greater
freedom for which he was striving. (Novelty and
newspaper are expressed in Hungarian by the same
word "ujsag").

Highly characteristic products of the dream-condensation are the composite formations of persons,
objects, and words. These "monstrosities of the
dream world" have largely contributed to the circumstance that dreams up to our day have been regarded as mental productions without value or sense.
But psycho-analysis convinces us that when the dream
links together or fuses two features or concepts, it
furnishes a product of the same work of condensation
to which the less obvious parts of the dream owe
their disguise. One of the rules of the art of dream
interpretation says that in cases of such composite
formations the dream material of the single con-
stituents must first be sought, and then only can it be
determined on what basis of a common element or
similarity the welding together has taken place. An
example of this, which is of value theoretically, I owe
to one of my patients. The composite picture that
occurred in one of her dreams was made up of the
person of a physician and of a horse, which in addition
was attired in night clothing. Associations led from
the horse into the patient's childhood. As a girl she

had suffered for a long time from a pronounced phobia of horses; she avoided them especially on account of their evident and open satisfaction of their bodily needs. It also occurred to her that as a child she had often been taken by her nurse to the military quarters, where she had had the opportunity of observing all these things with a curiosity that was at that time still unrestrained. The night-clothing reminded her of her father, whom she had had the opportunity of seeing, while she still slept in her parents' room, not only in such costume, but in the act of satisfying his bodily needs. (This case often occurs; parents for the most part place no restraint on themselves before three- and four-year old children, whose understanding and faculty of observation they materially underestimate). The third constituent of the composite picture, the physician, awakened in me the suspicion, which proved to be well grounded, that the patient had unconsciously transferred her sexual curiosity from her father to the physician who was treating her.

The constituent parts of a composite image often have an unequal share in its formation; perhaps only a characteristic movement of one person is grafted on to the second person. I once saw myself in a dream rub my forehead with my hand just as my honoured master, Professor Freud, does when he is meditating over a difficult question. It does not require much art of interpretation to guess that this confounding of teacher and pupil, particularly in meditation, can only be ascribed to envy and ambition, when at night the intellectual censorship was relaxed. In my waking life I have to laugh at the boldness of this identification, which makes me think of the saying, "How he clears his throat, and how he expectorates, that you have learned well from him." As an example of a composite word I may mention that in a dream a German-speaking patient thought of a certain Metzler or Wetzler. No one of this name, however, is known to the patient, but on the day before the dream he was much occupied with the approaching marriage of a friend, by the name of Messer, who liked to tease (*hetzen*) the patient. The associations from Messer shewed that as a small child he had been very afraid of his grandfather, who while whetting (*wetzen*) his pocket-knife (*Taschenmesser*) had jokingly threatened to cut his penis off, a threat that was not without influence on the development of his sexuality. The names "Metzler-Wetzler" are accordingly nothing but condensations of the words *messer, hetzen* and *wetzen*.

Dream condensation stands in close relation to the work of displacement and transvaluation of the dream. This consists essentially in the fact that the psychical intensity of the dream-thoughts is shunted over from the essentials to the accessories, so that the thought-complex that is at the focus of interest is represented in the conscious dream content either not at all or by a weak allusion, while the maximum of interest in the dream is turned to the more insignificant con-stituents of the dream-thoughts. The work of con-densation and of displacement go hand in hand. The dream renders harmless an important thought, which would disturb the sleeper's rest, or be censured on ethical grounds. It goes as it were beyond such a thought, by attaching memory-images to its less essential parts until the condensed psychical intensity of the former can distract the attention from the thought of particular interest. As an example of the displaced centre of the conscious dream in comparison with the centre of the dream-thoughts I may mention the already cited dream of the aunt concerning the death of her beloved nephew. The funeral, which actually was not essential, took up the largest place in the dream, the personality that was most significant for the dream-thoughts was on the contrary present in the dream only through a distant allusion.

I was once called upon to analyse the very short dream of a woman; in it she had wrung the neck of a little, barking, white dog. She was very much astonished that she, who "could not hurt a fly," could dream such a cruel dream, and she did not remember having dreamt one like it before. She admitted that, being very fond of cooking, she had many times killed pigeons and fowls with her own hand. Then it occurred to her that she had wrung the neck of the little dog in the dream in exactly the same way as she was accustomed to do with the pigeons in order to cause them less pain. The thoughts and associations that followed had to do with pictures and stories of executions, and especially with the thought that the executioner, when he has fastened the cord about the criminal's neck, arranges it so as to give the neck a twist, and thus hasten death. Asked against whom she felt strong enmity at the present time, she named a sister-in-law, and related at length her bad qualities and malicious deeds, with which she had disturbed the family harmony, before so beautiful, after insinuating herself *like a tame pigeon* into the favour of her subsequent husband. Not long before a violent scene had taken place between her and the patient, which ended by the latter shewing

her the door with the words: "Get out; I cannot endure a biting dog in my house." Now it was clear whom
the little white dog represented, and whose neck she
was wringing in the dream. The sister-in-law is also
a small person, with a remarkably white complexion.
This little analysis enables us to observe the dream in
its displacing and thus disguising activity. Without
doubt the dream used the comparison with the biting
dog, instead of the real object of the execution fancy
(the sister-in-law), smuggling in a little white dog just
as the angel in the Biblical story gave Abraham at the
last moment a ram to slaughter, when he was preparing
to slaughter his son. In order to accomplish this the
dream had to heap up memory-images of the killing
of animals until by means of their condensed psychical
energy the image of the hated person paled, and the
scene of the manifest dream was shifted to the animal
kingdom. Memory-images of human executions served
as a connecting link for this displacement.

This example gives me the opportunity to repeat
that, with few exceptions, the conscious dream-content
is not the true reproduction of our dream-thoughts,
but only a displaced, wrongly accented caricature, the
original of which can be reconstructed only by the help
of psycho-analysis.

It is a noteworthy phenomenon of dream work that
the material of abstract thought, the concept, is capable
of being presented in the dream only to a slight extent
or not at all, that rather the dream as it were dramatises
thoughts only in optical or acoustic sense-images,
changes them to scenes enacted on a stage, and in this
way brings them to presentation. Freud strikingly
characterises the difficulty imposed on the dream by

this necessity of working only with concrete material when he says that the dream itself has to turn the thoughts of a political editorial into illustrations.

Dreams are given to using ambiguous words and interpretations of all sorts of expressions in concrete or metaphorical senses in order to make abstract conceptions and thoughts capable of presentation and so of inclusion in the dream.

The memory of every man at all educated contains a large number of proverbs, quotations, figures of speech, parables, fragments of verse, and so forth. The content of these offers very suitable material, ever present, that can be applied to the scenic presentation of a thought or to an allusion to it. I will try to make this clear by a series of examples. One of my patients related to me the following dream: "I go into a large park, walking on a long path. I cannot see the end of the path or of the garden hedge, but I think I will go on until I arrive at the end."[1] The park and hedge of the dream resembled the garden of one of her aunts, with whom she had passed many happy holidays in her youth. She remembers in connection with this aunt that they customarily shared the same room, but when her uncle was at home the young guest was "put out" into a neighbouring room. The girl at that time had only a very fragmentary conception of sex matters, and often tried by peeping through cracks in the door and through the keyhole to find out what was going on within. The wish to get to the end of the hedge symbolised in this dream the wish to get to the bottom of what was going on between the married

---

[1] (This dream was in the Hungarian language, and the sense of it depends on a play on words that is not translated by the author. Transl.)

pair. This wish was further determined by an experience of the day before.

Another patient dreamed of the corridor of the girls' boarding school in which she was educated. She saw her own clothes-closet there, but could not find the key, so that she was forced to break open the door; but as she violently opened the door, it became evident that there was nothing within. The whole dream proved to be a symbolic masturbation-phantasy, a memory from the time of puberty; the female genitals were, as so often happens, presented as a cupboard. But the supplement to the dream, "there is nothing within" (*es ist nichts darin*) means in Hungarian the same as "it is no matter" (*es ist nichts daran*), and is a sort of exculpation or self-consolation of this sufferer from a bad conscience.

Another girl, whose neurosis was brought on by the death of her brother, who, according to her view, married too early and was not happy in his marriage, dreamed continually of the dead man. Once she saw him lying in his grave, but the head was turned to one side in a peculiar manner, or the skull had grown into a bough; another time she saw him in his childhood clothes on an elevation from which he had to jump. All this symbolism was a complaint against the wife and the father-in-law of the dead man, who turned the boy's head when he was almost a child, and in the end made him "jump down" (a Hungarian idiom) and who nevertheless did not consider him their equal, for they once called him, referring to his modest origin, "one fallen from a bough" (another Hungarian idiom).

Very often falling from a great height pictures in a concrete way the threat of ethical or material fall;

with girls, sitting may mean spinsterhood (*Sitzenbleiben*) with men a large basket may mean the fear of an unsuccessful wooing (*einen Korb erhalten*). It occurs still more commonly that the human body is symbolised by a house, the windows and doors of which represent the natural openings of the body. My patient who suffered from sexual impotence made use of a vulgar Hungarian expression for coitus, namely the word for "to shoot," and very often dreamed of shooting, missing fire, the rusting of his fire-arms, and so on.

It would be an enticing problem to collect the fragments of dreams that can be explained symbolically and to write a modern dream-book, in which the explanation could be found for the separate parts of dreams. This is not possible, however, for although much typical material recurs in dreams and in most cases can be correctly interpretated without analysis, symbols may have different meanings with different individuals, and even with the same individual at different times. Accordingly, if we wish to know in any particular case all the determinants of a single dream fragment there is nothing for it but laborious analysis, for which the investigating power and the wit of the interpreter alone will not suffice, the industrious co-operation of the dreamer being indispensable.

Still greater difficulties than are created by the presentation of abstract thoughts are met with when the dream endeavours to present in a concrete way the thought-relations of the individual dream-thoughts. Freud rendered a valuable service by succeeding in making it possible to discover the whole of the concealed, formal peculiarities of the connections of the dream, with which it endeavours to present logical relations. Logical relations between two dream elements with respect to the dream-thoughts that are concealed behind them are presented in the simplest cases by temporal or spatial proximity, or by a fusion of the features of the dream.

Dreams lack a means for presenting causal connection, of the "either-or" relation of conditions, and so on, so that all these relations are brought to presentation in a very insufficient way by means of a temporal sequence of the dream elements. From this circumstance arise many embarassments for the dream interpreter, from which he can often be extricated only by the communications of the dreamer. Much, however, can be divined. For example, if one dream picture changes to another, we can divine behind this, cause and effect; but this connection the dream often presents by two completely separated dreams, one signifying the cause, the other the effect. Even the presentation of a simple negative the dream can manage only with great difficulty, so that—as we know from Freud—we can never tell in advance whether the dream-thought is to be taken in a positive or a negative way. Considering the complexities of our mental organisation it may be seen only too easily that affirmation and negation of the same thoughts and feeling-complexes are to be met with in the dream-thoughts side by side, or, rather, in succession. It may be taken as an indication of displeasure or scorn when anything in a dream is presented in a reversed form, or when the truth is presented very openly and in a striking way. The feeling of inhibition, which is so common, signifies a conflict of the will, the struggle of opposing motives.

In spite of the lack of all logical relations in the translation of the dream-thoughts into the manifest dream, the latter often seems to be possessed of sense and to be correlated. When this is the case it may result from one of two causes. We may on the one hand have to do with a dream-phantasy, that is, with the reproduction of fancies that have developed in waking life, articles read in books or magazines, fragments of novels, or bits of conversation spoken or heard by the person himself. A deeper and more general explanation for the apparently logical articulation of many dreams, however, is the fact that the rationalising tendency of mental activity, which seeks to arrange senseless material into logical trains of thought, does not rest at night. This last activity of the dream Freud calls the *secondary elaboration*. It is due to this that the originally fragmentary parts of the dream are rounded into a whole by supplementarily inserted connecting words and other little connections.

Since the dream has fundamentally condensed, displaced, disguised, and scenically presented a dream-thought, robbed it of its logical connections, and elaborated it in a secondary manner, the work of interpretation is often very difficult. We are confronted by the conscious dream-content as by a hieroglyph or by a rebus that is very difficult of solution; the result is that the explanation of many dreams needs, besides the rules of Freud's interpretation, special capacity and inclination to occupy oneself with the questions of mental life.

Not less a riddle than the dream itself is its rapid fading away after awakening. When we awake, the dream-images so toilsomely built up at night collapse like a house of cards. During sleep the mind is like an air-tight room, into which neither light nor sound can penetrate from without, but within whose own walls the slightest sound, even the buzzing of a fly, can be heard. But awakening is like opening the door to the air of the bright morning; through the doors of our senses press in the bustle and the impulses of every-day life, and the daily cares, lately soothed to sleep by wish-fancies, once more assert their domination. The censor, too, wakens from its slumber, and its first act is to declare the dream to be foolishness, to explain it as senseless, to put it as it were under guardianship. It is not always satisfied with this measure, it reacts much more strongly against the revolutionary dreams (and there is not a single dream that cannot be shewn by analysis to offend against some ethical or legal canon). The stronger method consists in the con-fiscation, the full suppression, of the dream-image. Mental confiscation is commonly called "forgetting." One wonderingly relates how distinctly one dreamed, and yet when one woke all was confused and in a few minutes it had all been forgotten. At other times one can only say that the dream was beautiful, good, bad, confused, stimulating, or stupid. Even in making this judgement often a remnant of the dream-content will shew itself, the analysis of which may lead to a later recovery of larger fragments of the dream. Behind the additional fragments of the dream thus brought to light one often finds the kernel of the dream-thoughts.

It is an important consequence of Freud's theory of dreams, that one is always dreaming, so long as one sleeps.[1] That one remembers nothing of it is no decisive objection against this consideration. My patients, for example, who at the beginning of the analysis declared that they usually had no dreams, gradually accustomed themselves to remember all their dreams by continual weakening of the internal psychic resistance against the censorship. But if in the course of the analysis one strikes a very resistant, painfully toned complex, dreams apparently cease—naturally they are only forgotten, repressed, because of their unpleasant content.

The obvious objection that these dream observations and analyses have for the most part been carried out on neurotic and thus abnormal persons, and that conclusions should not be drawn as to the dreams of healthy people, does not need to be refuted by the reply that mental health and psychoneuroses differ in only a quantitative way; the answer can also be made that the analyses of people mentally normal fully agree with the interpretations of dreams of neurotics. The communication of the analysis of one's own dreams, however, meets with almost insurmountable difficulties. Freud has not shrunk from this sacrifice—the exposure of intimate personal matters—in his *Traumdeutung*, even though regard for others makes unavoidable gaps here and there in his analyses. Similar considerations made it necessary for me to explain the interpretation of dreams not from my own dreams, but from those of my patients. For the rest, the practice of self-analysis

[1](This remark is perhaps carelessly phrased. The author probably means that unconscious psychic activity always goes on during sleep, tending to lead to the formation of dreams, not that we are always actually dreaming in the sense of consciously experiencing fully formed dreams. Transl.).

is indispensable for anyone who desires to penetrate into the unconscious processes of dream life.

The neurotic persons whose dreams I have brought forward here and there as examples also pave the way for me to say a few words about the pathological significance of dreams and their interpretation. We have seen how greatly the analysis of a neurotic may be accelerated by a successful dream analysis. The dream censorship, which is only half awake, often allows thought-complexes to penetrate to the dream consciousness that in waking life could not be brought to consciousness by free association. From the dream elements also lead out immediate and shorter ways to the repressed pathogenic material, that is, to the source of the neurotic symptoms. The becoming conscious of such complexes may be regarded as a step towards the cure.

Then, too, the diagnostic significance of dreams should not escape us, and in a time that is not too distant there ought to arise besides the physiological, also a pathological dream psychology, which should treat systematically of dreams among hysterics, obsessional patients, paranoiacs, dementia praecox patients, sufferers from neurasthenia, from the anxiety-neurosis, alcoholism, epilepsy, paralysis, etc. Many pathognostic peculiarities of dreams in these diseased conditions are already recognisable to-day.

All these more practical and special questions have been raised to importance by the unexpected theoretical consequences of this investigation of dreams. Freud has succeeded in surprising a process on the boundary line between the physiological and pathological departments of mental life, in taking it in the midst of its work, *in flagranti*, so to speak.   In this way he has brought us nearer to an understanding of the mechanism of the manifestations of neuroses and insanity in waking life.   And though it was the study of psycho-neuroses that led Freud to his investigation of dreams, the dream theory pays back with interest all that it owes to pathology.

The case could not, indeed, be other than it is. Waking life, dreams, neuroses, and psychoses are only variations of the same psychic material with different modes of functioning, and progressive insight into one of these processes must necessarily deepen and widen our knowledge of the others.

Those who expect from the new dream theory any sort of prophetic insight into the future will turn back disillusioned.   But those who value highly the solution of psychological problems that have until now been set aside as insoluble, the widening of the psychological point of view apart from any immediate practical consequences, and who are not kept back from advance by hide-bound prejudices, will perhaps supplement the presentation given here by a thorough and serious study of Freud's *Traumdeutung*.

CHAPTER IV

ON OBSCENE WORDS*

Contribution to the Psychology of the Latent Period

IN all analyses one is sooner or later faced with the question whether one should mention in front of the patient the popular (obscene) designations of the sexual and excremental organs, functions, and material, and get him to utter in an unvarnished, unaltered way the obscene words, phrases, curses, etc., that occur to his mind, or whether one can rest content with allusions to them or with the use of scientific language to denote such matters.

In one of his earlier works Freud called attention to the possibility of finding ways and means to discuss with patients even the most proscribed sexual activities (perversions) without wounding their modesty, and for this purpose he recommended the use of technical medical expressions.

At the beginning of a course of psycho-analytic treatment one avoids unnecessarily provoking resistance on the part of the patient, and in this way setting up perhaps insurmountable obstacles to the continuation of the analysis. One contents oneself, therefore, at first with allusive references or with

*Published in the Zentralbl. f. Psychoanalyse, Jahrg. I, 1911.

serious scientific terms, and can very soon talk with one's patient about the most delicate matters of sexuality, as of the instincts in general, without exciting any reaction of shame whatever. In a number of cases, however, this does not suffice. The analysis comes to a standstill, no thoughts occur to the patient, his behaviour shews signs of inhibition, indications of increased resistance manifest themselves, and this resistance ceases only when the physician manages to discover the ground for it in the fact that proscribed words and phrases have occurred to him, which he does not venture to utter aloud without the analyst's express "permission."

An hysterical patient of twenty-three, for example, who so far as consciousness was concerned was intent on the greatest honesty, and who listened without much prudishness to my explanations about her sexuality (formulated in scientific language), insisted that she had never heard or noticed anything about sexual matters; she still professed belief in the "kiss-theory" of propagation (which, by the way, is always a secondary one.) In order to display her assiduity, she bought a large work on embryology and related to me, with naïve interest and without any inhibition, her recently acquired information concerning spermatozoa and ova, male and female sexual organs and their union. On one occasion she casually told me that ever since childhood she had had the habit of shutting her eyes when at stool. She could give no reason for this eccentricity. Finally I helped her memory by asking if, by closing her eyes, she had not sought to shun the obscene writings and drawings so frequent in closets. I then had to direct attention to the obscene writings known to her, and this evoked in the patient, who up till then had been so superior and imperturbable, an intense reaction of shame, which gave me access to the deepest layers of her previously latent store of memories. The repression, therefore, evidently appertained to the wording itself of the sexual thought-complexes, and could be reversed only by uttering those "magic words."

A young homosexual, who without much ado made use of even the vulgar designations for the sexual parts and their functions, refused for two hours long to utter aloud the commoner expression for the word "flatus" which had occurred to him. He sought to avoid it by all possible circumlocutions, foreign words, euphemisms, etc. After the resistance against the word was overcome, however, he was able to penetrate much deeper into the previously barren analysis of his anal-erotism.

The hearing of an obscene word in the treatment often produces in the patient the same agitation that on some earlier occasion had been produced by accidentally overhearing a conversation between the parents, in which some coarse (usually sexual) expression had slipped out. This agitation and shock, which for a moment seriously threatens the child's respect for his parents, and which in a neurotic may remain "fixed" for life (although unconsciously), happens as a rule in the years of puberty and is really a "new edition" of the impressions made by overhearing in infancy actual sexual performances. The early confidence in parents and superior authorities, however, which the latter have sought to instil, but which has been nullified by awe, belongs to the most significant complexes of the suppressed psychical material, and if one does not shrink from—and, indeed, insists on—getting the patient to express the very wording of these thoughts (and, if necessary, to utter it oneself), it often results in unexpected disclosures and a gratifying progress in the mental dissection, which had perhaps been for some time at a standstill.

Apart from this practical importance, which, by the way, is not to be underestimated, the behaviour of the patient in this connection is also a matter of more general interest. It gives us a psychological problem.

How is it that it is so much harder to designate the same thing with one term than with another? That this is the case can be observed not only with the patient, but also with oneself. Indeed, it was the not inconsiderable inhibition which I noticed, to begin with, on mentioning such words, and against which I have even now occasionally to contend, that led me to devote more attention to this question and to investigate it by examining myself as well as my patients. By both of these ways I came to the conclusion that the popular (obscene) designations for sexuality and excretion, the only ones known to the child, are in the most intimate manner associated with the deeply repressed nuclear complex of the neurotic as well as of the healthy. (Following Freud, I call the Oedipus-complex the "nuclear complex.")

The child's thoughts about the sexual aspects of the parents, about the processes of birth and the animal functions, in a word, the "infantile sexual theories," are, as soon as they appear, clothed in the popular terminology that is the only one accessible to the child. The moral censorship and the incest-barrier, which later on covers over these theories, becomes exerted, therefore, on just this formulation of the hypotheses.

This would suffice to make comprehensible, at least in part, the resistance that is manifested against the mentioning of, and listening to, such words. As, however, this explanation did not quite satisfy me, I looked for further causes of the special quality of these word-ideas and reached a point of view that I cannot, it is true, regard as certainly correct, but which I wish to communicate here in order to prompt c ther workers to bring forward a better explanation.

An obscene word has a peculiar power of compelling the hearer to imagine the object it denotes, the sexual organ or function, *in substantial actuality*. That this is the case was clearly recognised and expressed by Freud in his discussion of the motives and conditions of obscene jokes. He writes:[1] "Through the mentioning of the obscene word the ribald jest forces the assailed person to imagine the part of the body or the function in question." I would supplement this statement by calling special attention to the fact that delicate allusions to sexual processes, and scientific or foreign designations for them, do not have this effect, or at least not to the same extent as the words taken from the original, popular, erotic vocabulary of one's mother-tongue.

One may therefore infer that these words as such possess the capacity of compelling the hearer to revive memory pictures in a regressive and hallucinatory manner. This inference, founded on self-observation,

[1]Freud. Der Witz und seine Beziehung zum Unbewussten. S. 80.

is confirmed by the statements of a considerable number of normal as well as of neurotic individuals. The causes of the phenomenon must be sought for in the hearer himself, and we have to assume that he harbours in his store of memories a number of word-sound and writing images of erotic content that differ from other word-pictures in their increased tendency to regression. On hearing or seeing an obscene word this capacity of the memory-traces in question would then come into operation.

If, now, we subscribe to Freud's conception of the ontogenetic development of the psychical mechanism out of a motor-hallucinatory reaction centre to an organ of thought (and his conception is the only one that does justice to the results of psycho-analysis and to our idea of the unconscious), we come to the conclusion that obscene words have attributes which all words must have possessed in some early stage of psychical development.

Ever since Freud's work[1] we regard as the fundamental cause of every act of mental representation the wish to put an end to an unpleasantness due to privation, by means of repeating an experience of gratification once enjoyed. If this need is not satisfied in reality, what happens in the first primitive stage of mental development is that on the appearance of the wish the perception of the previously experienced gratification becomes regressively engaged (*besetzt*) and maintained in a hallucinatory way. The idea is thus treated as equivalent to the reality (perceptual identity, as Freud terms it.) Only gradually, sharp-

[1]Freud. Die Traumdeutung. [The view in question is expounded in an article in Child Study, April and May 1916. Transl.]

ened by bitter experience of life, does the child learn
to distinguish the wish-idea from real gratification, and
to make use of his motor powers only when he has
convinced himself that he sees in front of him real
objects, and not illusions of his fantasy. Abstract
thought, thinking in words, denotes the culminating
point of this development. In this, as Freud has set
forth in detail, finer accomplishments are rendered
possible through the memory images being represented
merely by certain qualitative remains of these images,
the speech-signs.

It may be added that the capacity of representing
wishes by means of speech signs, so poor in quality,
is not acquired all at once. Apart from the fact that
it takes some time to learn to speak, it seems that
speech-signs replacing images, *i. e.* words, retain for a
considerable time a certain tendency to regression,
which we can picture to ourselves in a gradually
diminishing degree, until the capacity is attained for
"abstract" imagination and thought that is almost
completely free from hallucinatory perceptual elements.

In this line of development there may be psychical
stages of which the characteristic is that the already
perfected capacity for the more economic form of
thought by means of speech-signs is accompanied with
a still existing, strong tendency to revive regressively
the image of the object. The assumption that such
stages occur is supported by the behaviour of children
at the time of their mental development. Freud, on
investigating the psychogenesis of the pleasure afforded
by wit, recognised the significance of the child's *play
with words*. "Children," he says, "treat words as
objects."

The distinction, not yet rigorously carried out, between what is only imagined and what is real, (*i. e.* the tendency of the mind to relapse into the primary, regressive mode of functioning), may also make the special character of obscene words comprehensible, and justify the surmise that at a certain stage of development this concreteness, and with it probably a strong tendency to regression, applies still to all words. On this, indeed, rests Freud's explanation of dream images; in sleep we fall back on the original mode of mental functioning, and once more regressively revive the perceptual system of consciousness. In dreams we no longer think in words, but hallucinate.

If we now assume that this development from speech-signs, still endowed with many concrete elements, in the direction of the abstract has been subject to a disturbance, an interruption, in the case of certain words, which results in a lagging of the word-image on a lower level, then we have some prospect of approaching an understanding of the tendency to regression which is so marked when obscene words are heard.

Not only the hearing of obscene words, however, but also the utterance of them is endued with qualities that are not found in the case of other words, at least not in the same degree. Freud points out, with truth, that whoever makes an obscene joke perpetrates, in so doing, an attack (a sexual action) on the object of the aggression, and evokes the same phenomena of reaction as those which would have resulted from the action itself. When uttering an obscene word one has the feeling that it is almost equivalent to a sexual aggression: "uncovering of the individual who interests one personally."[1] The utterance of an obscene joke, therefore, shews in a higher degree what is scarcely indicated with most words, namely, the original source of all speech in pretermitted action. While other words, however, contain the motor element of the word-image only in the form of a reduced innervation impulse, the so-called "mimicry of imagery,"[2] on uttering an obscene joke we still have the definite feeling of initiating an act.

This marked investment of the vocal image of obscene words with motor elements, as also the sensorial and hallucinatory character of the heard obscene joke, may be the result of a disturbance in development. These vocal images may have remained on a level of speech development where words are still more markedly invested with motor elements. One has here to ask oneself whether this speculation, which represents only one of the many possibilities, is in any way supported by experience, and if so, what could be the cause of this developmental error, one which concerns a small group of words, and is of general occurrence among civilised people.

Psycho-analysis of normal and neurotic persons, and observation of children, if fearless investigation is made of the fate that the terms for sexual and excremental organs and functions undergo in the course of mental development, bring much confirmation of the hypothesis brought forward here. In the first place, confirmation is found throughout of the almost self-evident assumption that the specially strong aversion to repeating certain obscene words is to be ascribed

[1] Freud. Der Witz. S. 80.
[2] Ibid. S. 167.

to strong feelings of unpleasantness which have become attached to just those words through inversion of affect in the course of child development.

A young man, for example, who was on the whole normal, although he was noted for a rather exaggerated strictness in morals and was unusually intolerant of obscene words, recollected during a dream analysis that his mother caught him, when he was six and a half years old, writing down on a piece of paper a dictionary, so to speak, of all the obscene expressions he knew. The humiliation of being thus detected, especially by his mother, as well as the severe punishment that followed, resulted in a lack of interest in erotic matters for many years after and in an inimical disposition even later towards the contents of the erotic vocabulary.

The young homosexual who had displayed such strong opposition to uttering the obscene word for 'flatus" developed in infancy an extraordinary love of odour and coprophilia, and his over-lenient father did not prevent him from indulging these inclinations even on his own body (the father's). The association, inseparable from this time forward, of the idea of defilement with that of the parents resulted in an unusually strong repression of the pleasure in dirt and smell; hence also the great unpleasantness in mentioning such matters. That it was the obscene term for intestinal gas which was so much more intolerable to him than any circumlocution had its reason in childhood experiences similar to those of the "dictionary-writer" mentioned above. The intimate connection between obscenity and the parental complex was thus the strongest repressing force in both cases.[1]

In the case of the hysterical patient who used to shut her eyes when in the closet this habit could be traced back to the time of a confession at which she was severely reprimanded by the priest for artlessly mentioning the obscene term for the vagina.

Such rebukes, however, or similar ones, happen to almost every child, with the possible exception of those belonging to the lowest classes. In the fourth or fifth year of life, and considerably earlier with precocious children, (*i. e.* at a time when children are restricting their "polymorphous-perverse" impulses), a period is interpolated between the relinquishing of the infantile modes of gratification and the beginning of the true latency period, one characterised by the impulse to utter, write up, and listen to obscene words.

This fact would without doubt be confirmed by a questionnaire addressed to mothers and teachers, still more certainly by one to servants, the real confidants of children, and that this is true of children not only in Europe, but also in such a prudish country as America, I recognised, when strolling with Professor Freud in New York Central Park, from the chalk drawings and inscriptions on a beautiful marble flight of steps.

We may conceive this impulse to utter, draw, write, hear, and read obscenities as being a preliminary stage in the inhibition of the infantile desires for exposure and sexual visual curiosity. It is the suppression of

[1] The infantile interest for the sounds accompanying the emission of intestinal gas was not without influence on his choice of profession. He became a musician.

these sexual phantasies and actions, manifested in the weakened form of speech, that really connotes the beginning of the latency period proper, that period in which "the mental counter-forces against infantile sexuality, namely, disgust, shame, and morality, are formed,"[1] and the child's interest is turned in the direction of social activities (desire for knowledge).

One is hardly likely to be wrong in surmising that this suppression of obscene word-images occurs at a time when speech, and especially the sexual vocabulary, which is so strongly invested with affect, is still characterised by a high degree of regressive tendency and by a vivid "mimicry of imagery." It is, therefore, no longer so improbable that the suppressed verbal material must, in consequence of the latency period (*i. e.* the deflection of attention), remain at this more primitive developmental stage, while the rest of the vocabulary gradually becomes, for the greater part, divested of its hallucinatory and motor character by progressive exercising and training, and is rendered through this economy suitable for higher thought activities.

I know, however, from psycho-analysis of neuroses that suppressed or repressed psychical material becomes in fact through the blocking of association a "foreign body" in the mental life, which is capable of no organic growth and of no development, and that the contents of these "complexes" do not participate in the development and constitution of the rest of the individual. I might bring forward here a few surprising examples.

[1]Freud. Kl. Schr., 2e Aufl., S. 39.

Apprehension about the smallness and consequent incapacity of the copulatory organ—or, as we psycho-analysts are accustomed to say, "the complex of the small penis"—is especially common among neurotics, and far from rare among the healthy. In every case in which I have analysed this symptom the explanation was as follows: All those who suffered later in this way had in their earliest childhood occupied themselves to an unusual degree with the phantasy of coitus cum matre (or with a corresponding older person); in doing so they had naturally been distressed at the idea of the inadequacy of their penis for this purpose.[1] The latency period interrupted and suppressed this group of thoughts; when, however, the sexual impulse unfolded itself afresh in puberty, and interest was again directed towards the copulatory organ, the old distress once more emerged, even when the actual size of the organ was normal or exceeded the average. While, therefore, the penis developed in the normal way, the idea of the penis remained at an infantile level. The deflection of attention from the genital region led the individual to take no note of the changes in it.

I have similarly been able to observe among female patients a "complex of the vagina being too small" (fear that it would be torn during sexual intercourse), and have been able to explain it through the idea of the relative size of the paternal organ, an idea acquired in childhood and suppressed in the latency period. Such women are then sexually anaesthetic in consequence of the imaginary smallness of the penis in their husbands.

[1] The condition for this apprehensive phantasy is the ignorance of the extensibility of the vagina; children only know that coitus takes place in an opening through which they once passed *in toto* at birth.

As a third example of the effect of the latency period in inhibiting development in an isolated manner I may mention the "complex of the large breast": The dissatisfaction that many men feel with the dimensions of most female breasts. With one patient, whose sex hunger could be aroused only by quite enormously developed female breasts, it was established in the analysis that in his early childhood he had taken an extraordinary interest in the suckling of infants and had indulged in the secret wish that he might share with them. In the latency period these fancies disappeared from his consciousness, but when he began once more to take an interest in the opposite sex his wishes were constellated by the complex of the large breast. The idea of the breast had not developed in him during the intermediary period, and the impression of size which the organ must have made on the child, who was then so little, had become fixed. Hence he desired only women whose breasts corresponded with the old proportion of his own smallness to the size of the woman. The female breasts themselves had become relatively smaller in the intermediary period, but the fixed idea of them retained the old dimension.

These examples, which could easily be multiplied, support the assumption that the latency period actually brings about an isolated inhibition in the development of individual repressed complexes, and this makes it seem likely that the same process happens in the development of verbal images that have become latent. Apart from this inference from analogy, however, I wish to mention the fact, which has often been demonstrated from the side of experimental psychology, that young children are of a pronouncedly "visual" and "motor" reaction type. I surmise that the loss of this visual and motor character comes about not gradually, but in a series of stages, and that the advent of the latency period denotes one, and perhaps the most important one, of these stages.[1]

Little can be said at present concerning the fate of the repressed obscene verbal images during the latency period. From what I have gathered in self-analysis and in the analyses of other normal people, I think I am justified in inferring that the latency of these images, especially with men, is normally not an absolute one. The reversal of affect that occurs sees to it, it is true,

---

[1] I can bring forward two further series of observations in favour of the correctness of my supposition concerning the influence of the latency period. In a number of cases I have had the opportunity of investigating the cause of lack of capacity for visual representation and the resulting incompetency for certain subjects of school study that demand a capacity for spacial presentation (geometry, natural history). It appeared that this incapacity, which was out of correspondence with the other powers of comprehension, was not conditioned by a congenital partial weakness, but came about only after the repression of phantasies, mostly of an incestuous nature, that had been over-exuberant. To secure (Adler) the repression of certain phantasy-pictures all kind of conscious fancying, even the imaginative representation of quite indifferent objects, was instinctively avoided. (Dread of the imagination.)

Another neurotic symptom, which may be observed much more frequently, is exaggerated calm and grave precision in the carrying out of every action, of every movement, shewn also in the whole attitude and in the dread of all hurry and haste. It is usually accompanied with pronounced antipathy against those people who "let themselves go" easily, who are immoderate, hasty, lively, unthinking and frivolous. One might here speak of phobia of movement. This symptom is a reaction-formation against a strong, but suppressed, motor tendency to aggression.

Both the dread of imagining and that of movement seem to me to be exaggerations of the suppression of phantasy and the inhibition of motility that comes to everybody in the latency period, and which helps to purge the motor and hallucinatory elements even from the images that are capable of being conscious. The images, however, that are incapable of being conscious, the repressed or suppressed ones, and especially the obscene verbal images, retain, as does all repressed material, the characters of a more primitive type of imagination.

that attention is deflected so far as possible from these verbal images that are invested with unpleasantness, but a total forgetting, a becoming unconscious of them, scarcely happens in the normal.   Everyday life, intercourse with the lower classes and with servants, obscene inscriptions on benches and in public urinals, see to it that this latency gets broken through often enough and that the memory of what has been put aside gets revived, although the point of view is changed.   Nevertheless not much notice is paid to these memories for some years, and when they once more make their appearance at the time of puberty they are already invested with the character of shamefulness, perhaps also with that of foreignness (on account of their plasticity and natural vividness), which they retain throughout life.

Quite other is the historical development of these verbal images among the perverse and neurotic.

Whoever has become perverse, through his sexual constitution and experiences, will, as we might expect according to Freud's theory of sex, take possession of this source of pleasure also, and become cynical in his speech, or perhaps content himself merely with reading coarse obscenities.   There exists, indeed, a perversity of its own that consists in the uttering aloud of obscene words; I know from the analysis of several women that they have been insulted in the street by well-dressed men, who whispered obscene words to them in passing by, without any other sexual advances being made (such as offering to accompany, etc).   These are evidently mild exhibitionists and *voyeurs*, who instead of actual exposure content themselves with an act that has been weakened into the form of speech, and who in doing so select those words that (through their being forbidden, as through their motor and plastic attributes) are especially calculated to evoke the reaction of shame. This perversity might be called "coprophemia."[1]

The true neurotic turns his attention away from obscene words, either completely or almost completely. Wherever possible he passes them by without thinking of them, and when he cannot avoid them he responds with an exaggerated reaction of shame and disgust. The case mentioned above is rare, where the words get totally forgotten. Only women shew such a capacity for repression.

A very severe mental shock, however, can bring about the re-appearance of these half-buried words in the normal as well as in the neurotic. Then, just as the Olympian gods and goddesses were degraded to demons and witches after the great step in repression betokened by Christianity, so the words that once denoted the most highly treasured objects of infantile pleasure recur in the form of oaths and curses, and, characteristically, associated very often with the idea of the parents or the sacred beings and gods that correspond to them (blasphemies). These interjections that issue in vehement anger, which are often softened down to jokes also, do not at all belong, as Kleinpaul rightly insists, to conceptual speech; they do not serve the needs of conscious communication, but represent reactions to a stimulus which are nearly related to gestures. It is none the less remarkable, however, that a violent affect is only with considerable

---

[1] "Coprolalia," on the contrary, is the involuntary, obsessive expelling of obscene words, as may happen, for instance, in severe cases of tic convulsif.

difficulty saved from discharging itself along a motor
path and is turned into a oath; the affect involuntarily
makes use of the obscene words that are best suited
to the purpose from the strength of their affect and
their motor force.

Quite tragical are the cases in which obscene words
abruptly burst forth into the virtuous consciousness of
a neurotic. Naturally this can happen only in the
form of obsessive ideas, for they are so completely
foreign to the conscious emotional life of the psychoneurotic that he feels them to be merely absurd,
senseless, pathological ideas, "foreign bodies," and
can in no way recognise them as a warrantable content
of his vocabulary. If one were not prepared by what
has already been mentioned here, one would be faced
with an insoluble riddle in the fact that obsessive ideas
of obscene words, and especially of words denoting the
most despised excretions and excretory organs in a
coarse way, frequently appear in men after the death
of their father, in men, indeed, who adoringly loved
and honoured their father. Analysis then shews that
on the death, in addition to the frightful pain at the
loss, the unconscious triumph at being freed at last
from all constraint comes to expression, and the contempt for the "tyrant" who has now become harmless
displays itself in words that were most strictly forbidden to the child.[1] I have observed a similar case
with a girl whose eldest sister became dangerously ill.

An important support for my supposition that obscene words remain "infantile" as the result of inhibited development, and on this account have an

[1] As associative links between the conceptions of death and excrement one
often finds the ideas concerning the decomposition of the corpse.

abnormal motor and regressive character, would be the ethnographic confirmation. Unfortunately I have not sufficient experience on this point. What I know of the life of the lower classes, and especially of the gypsies, seems to indicate that among uncultivated people obscene words are perhaps more markedly invested with pleasure, and do not differ so essentially from the rest of the vocabulary, as compared with the state of affairs among the cultivated.

Whether further observation will support or prove incorrect the assumption of a specific infantile character of obscene verbal images, and of "primitive" attributes resulting from a disturbance in development, I think I can at least maintain after what has been said that these highly affective images have a significance in our mental life which has not up to the present received corresponding attention.

CHAPTER V

ON THE PART PLAYED BY HOMOSEXUALITY IN THE PATHOGENESIS OF PARANOIA*

IN the summer of 1908 I had the opportunity of opening up the problem of paranoia in the course of conversation with Professor Freud, and we arrived at certain tentative ideas, which for the main part were developed by Professor Freud, while I contributed to the final shaping of the train of thought with detached suggestions and criticisms. We laid down to begin with that the mechanism of projection, as explicated by Freud in the only case of paranoia at that time analysed, is characteristic of paranoia in general. We assumed further that the paranoiac mechanism stands midway between the opposite mechanisms of neurosis and of dementia praecox. The neurotic gets rid of the affects that have become disagreeable to him by means of the different forms of displacement (conversion, transference, substitution); the patient suffering from dementia praecox, on the other hand, detaches his interest from objects[1] and retracts it to his ego (auto-erotism, grandiose delusions).

The paranoiac also would make an attempt to withdraw his participation (in external interests), but it meets with only a limited success. Some of the desires get

*Published in the Jahrbuch der Psychoanalyse, Band III, 1912.

[1] Cp. Abraham, "Die psychosexuellen Differenzen der Hysterie und der Dementia praecox," Zentralbl. f. Nervenheilk. u. Psych., Juli, 1908.

happily retracted into the ego—grandiose delusions occur in every case of paranoia—but a greater part of the interest, varying in amount, cannot disengage itself from its original object, or else returns to it. This interest, however, has become so incompatible with the ego that it gets objectified (with a reversal of affect, *i. e.* with a "negative sign in front") and thus cast out from the ego. The tendency that has become intolerable, and has been withdrawn from its object, in this way returns from its love-object in the form of a perception of its own negative. The *feeling* of love is turned into the *sensation* of its opposite.

The expectation that further observation would verify the correctness of these assumptions has been fulfilled. The cases of paranoid dementia published by Maeder in the last volume of the Jahrbuch confirm Freud's assumptions to a very considerable extent. Freud himself by further studies has been able to confirm not only this leading formula of paranoia, but also certain finer details that we presuppose in the psychical mechanism of the different kinds of paranoia.

The aim of the present publication, however, is not the opening up of the whole question of paranoia (to which Professor Freud himself is devoting a larger work[1]), but only the communication of an experiential fact which the analysis of several paranoiacs has yielded, and which goes beyond the anticipated ideas mentioned above.

It has become evident, namely, that *the paranoiac mechanism* is not set in action as a defence against all possible attachments of the "sexual hunger," but, according to the observations made up to the present, *is directed only against the homosexual choice of object.*

[1] Jahrb., Bd. III. Reprinted in Sammlung kl. Schr., 3e Folge.

Homosexuality played a strikingly great part in the case of the paranoiac analysed long ago by Freud, a part not adequately appreciated by him at that time.[1] In Maeder's investigations into cases of paranoid dementia also "undoubted homosexual tendencies"[2] were discovered behind one patient's delusions of persecution.

The observation of several cases, presently to be related, seems to justify the surmise that in the pathogenesis of paranoia, homosexuality plays not a chance part, but the most important one, and that paranoia is perhaps nothing else at all than disguised homosexuality.

I

The first case occurred in the husband of my own housekeeper, a well-built man of about thirty-eight, whom I had occasion to observe exhaustively for several months.

He and his wife (who could hardly be called pretty), who had got married just before entering my service, occupied a part of my flat consisting of one room and

---

[1] "When she was alone with the servant" she "had a sensation in the lower part of the body, which made her think that the maid then had an indecent thought."—She had "hallucinations of female nudities, especially of an exposed female lap with hair, occasionally also of male genitals"—"Whenever she was in a woman's company she constantly got the torturing sensation of seeing her indecently exposed, and believed that in the same moment the woman had the same sensation about her."—"The first pictures of female laps came a few seconds after she had in fact seen a number of undressed women at the baths."—"Everything *became plain* to her as soon as her sister-in-law uttered something," etc. (Freud, Sammlung kl. Schr., S.124).

[2] Jahrb., Bd. II, S. 237.

the kitchen.[1]   The husband worked all day (he was an
employee in the post-office), came home punctually
in the evening, and in the first part of his time with me
gave no grounds for complaint.   On the contrary, he
impressed me by his extraordinary diligence and his
great politeness to myself.   He always found something
in my rooms to clean and embellish.   I would come
across him late at night putting fresh polish on the doors
or floors, burnishing the top window-panes that could
hardly be reached, or arranging some ingenious novelty
in the bathroom.   He was most desirous of giving me
satisfaction, obeyed all my instructions with military
smartness and punctuality, but was extremely sensitive
to any criticism on my part, for which, it is true he
rarely gave any occasion.

One day the housekeeper sobbingly told me that she
lived very unhappily with her husband.   He was drinking
a great deal latterly, came home late, and constantly
scolded and abused her without cause.   At first I did
not want to interfere in this domestic affair, but when
I accidentally heard that he was beating his wife (which
fact the woman had concealed from me for fear of
losing her place), I spoke to him seriously and insisted
he should abstain from alcohol and treat his wife well,
all of which he tearfully promised me.   When I offered
to shake hands with him I could not prevent his im-
petuously kissing my hand.   I ascribed this at the
time, however, to his emotion and to my "paternal"
attitude (although I was younger than he).

After this scene peace prevailed in the house for a
time.   A few weeks later, however, the same scenes were

---

[1] It is customary here in Budapest to get a reliable married couple to look
after one's residence.

repeated, and when I now looked at the man more carefully I saw evident signs of chronic alcoholism. On this I interrogated the woman and learnt from her that she was constantly being accused by her husband of marital infidelity, without the slightest ground. The suspicion naturally occurred to me at once that the husband was suffering from alcoholic delusions of jealousy, the more so since I knew the housekeeper to be a very respectable and modest person. I managed once more to get the husband to give up drinking, and to restore peace in the house for a while.

The state of affairs, however, soon changed for the worse. It became clear that we had to deal with a case of alcoholic paranoia. The man neglected his wife, and stayed in the public-house drinking till midnight. On coming home he beat his wife, abused her incessantly, and accused her of flirting with every male patient who came to see me. I learnt subsequently that he was even at this time jealous also of me, but his wife, from a comprehensible anxiety, concealed this from me. I was naturally unable to keep the couple any longer, but I allowed the woman, at her request, to retain her position until the quarter was up.

It was now that I learnt all the details of these domestic scenes. The husband, whom I called to account, absolutely denied having beaten his wife, although this had been confirmed by people who had witnessed it. He maintained that his wife was a lascivious woman, a sort of vampire that "sucked out a man's force;" that he had relations with her five or six times every night, that this was never enough for her, however, so that she committed adultery with every possible man. During this explanation the emotional scene described above was repeated; he took possession again of my hand, and kissed it amid tears. He said he had never known anyone dearer or kinder than I.

As his case began to interest me from a psychiatric point of view also, I learnt from the woman that the man had had sexual relations with her only two or three times since they were married. Now and then he would make preparations in this direction—mostly *a tergo*—and then push her away, declaring in abusive language that she was a whore, and that she could do it with anyone she liked, but not with him.

I began to play an increasingly important part in his delusions. He wanted to force his wife, under the threat of stabbing her, to confess she had had sexual relations with me. Every morning when I went out he burst into my bedroom, sniffed the bed-clothes, and then beat his wife, asserting he had recognised her odour in the bedding. He tore from her a head-kerchief I had brought back for her from a holiday, and stroked it several times a day; he was not to be parted from a tobacco-pipe that I had made him a present of. If I was in the water-closet he listened all the time in the ante-room, then related to his wife with obscene words what he had heard, and asked her "if it pleased her.' He then hurried into the closet immediately after me, to see whether I had "properly rinsed everything away."

All this time he remained the most zealous servant you could think of, and was exaggeratedly amiable towards me. He turned to account my absence from Budapest and without instructions repainted the water-closet, even adorning the walls with coloured sketches.

The fact that they had been discharged was kept private from him for a time. When he heard of it he became sad, abused and hit his wife, and threatened that he would put her in the street and stab me, "her darling." Even now he remained well-behaved and devoted so far as I personally was concerned. When I learned, however, that he was sleeping at night with a well-ground kitchen knife at his side and on one occasion seriously looked like forcing his way into my bedroom, I felt I could not wait the two or three days till their notice was up. The woman notified the authorities, who took him to the insane asylum after having him medically certified.

There is no doubt that this was a case of alcoholic delusions of jealousy. The conspicuous feature of homosexual transference to myself, however, allows of the interpretation that this jealousy of men signified only the projection of his own erotic pleasure in the male sex. Also, the disinclination for sexual relations with his wife was probably not simply impotency, but was determined by his unconscious homosexuality. The alcohol, which might well be called a *censure-poison*, had evidently for the most part (though not quite) robbed his homosexuality, which had been spiritualised into friendliness, assiduity and complaisance, of its sublimations, and so caused the crude homosexual erotism that thus came to the surface—intolerable as such to the consciousness of a man of ethical high standing—to be simply imputed to his wife. In my opinion the alcohol played here only the part of an agent destroying sublimation, through the effect of which the man's true sexual constitution, namely the preference for a member of the same sex, became evident.

It was only subsequently that I received a complete confirmation of this. I learnt that he had been married before, years ago. He lived only a short time in peace with this first wife also, began to drink soon after the wedding, and abused his wife, tormenting her with jealousy scenes, until she left him and got a divorce.

In the interval between these two marriages he was said to have been a temperate, reliable, and steady man, and to have taken again to drink only after the second marriage. Alcoholism was thus not the deeper cause of the paranoia; it was rather that in the insoluble conflict between his conscious heterosexual and unconscious homosexual desires he took to alcohol, which then by destroying the sublimations brought the homosexual erotism to the surface, his consciousness getting rid of this by way of projection, of delusions of jealousy.

The destruction of the sublimation was not complete. He was still able to let a part of his homosexual tendency function in a spiritualised form, as a faithful, compliant servant of his master, as a smart subordinate in his office, and as a competent worker in both positions. Where the circumstances made high claims on his capacity for sublimation, however,—for instance, in his occupation with the bedroom and closet—he was compelled to saddle his wife with his desires, and by jealousy scenes to assure himself that he was in love with her. The boasting about his colossal potency in regard to his wife was similarly a distortion of the facts that served to calm his mind.[1]

II

I shall cite as a second case that of a lady, still young, who after living for years in moderate harmony with her husband, and bearing him daughters, began to suffer from delusions of jealousy not long after giving birth to a son; alcohol played no part in her case.[2]

She began to find everything in her husband suspicious. A cook and one chambermaid after another were dismissed, and finally she got her way and had only male servants in the house. Even that didn't help. The man, who was everywhere regarded as a model husband, and who assured me on his word of honour that he had never been unfaithful to her, could not go a step or write a line without being watched, suspected, and even abused by his wife. Curiously enough she was suspicious of her husband only with either very young females, about twelve or thirteen years old, or quite old, ugly ones, while she was not

---

[1] The one-sided agitation of temperance reformers tries to veil the fact that in the large majority of cases alcoholism is not the cause of neuroses, but a result of them, and a calamitous one. Both individual and social alcoholism can be cured only by the help of psycho-analysis, which discloses the causes of the "flight into narcosis" and neutralises them. The eradication of alcoholism only seemingly signifies an improvement in hygiene. When alcohol is withdrawn, there remain at the disposal of the psyche numerous other paths to the "flight into disease". And when then psychoneurotics suffer from anxiety-hysteria or dementia praecox instead of from alcoholism, one regrets the enormous expenditure of energy that has been applied against alcoholism, but in the wrong place.

[2] I have briefly narrated the case in another connection: see Chapter II.

jealous of society women, friends, or good-class govern-esses, even when they were attractive or pretty.

Her conduct at home became more and more odd, and her threats more dangerous, so that she had to be taken to a sanatorium. (Before doing this I got the patient to consult Professor Freud, who agreed with my diagnosis and approved of psycho-analysis being tried).

The patient was so remarkably distrustful and perspicacious that it was not easy to establish a *rapport* with her. I had to take the ground that I was not quite convinced of her husband's innocence, and in this way induced the otherwise inaccessible patient to part with the delusional ideas that she had till then kept to herself.

Among these were pronounced delusions of grandeur and of connection. Between the lines of the local newspaper were innumerable insinuations of her supposed moral depravity, and of her ridiculous position as a betrayed wife; the articles were written by journalists at the orders of her enemies. Personal-ities of the highest standing (*e. g.* of the episcopal court) knew of these goings on, and the fact that the royal manœuvres took place every year just in the neighbourhood of her home was not unconnected with certain secret intentions of her enemies. The enemies turned out in the course of further conversation to be the dismissed servants.

I then gradually learnt from her that it was against her will, and only at her parents' wish, especially her father's, that she had looked favourably on her hus-band's courtship. He seemed to her at the time too common, too coarse. After the marriage, however, she said she got used to him. A curious scene took place in the house after the birth of the first daughter. The husband was supposed to have been dissatisfied that she had not borne a son, and she felt quite conscience-pricked about it also; on this she began to doubt whether she had done right to marry this man. At this time she began to be jealous of an extra servant-girl, aged thirteen and said to be very pretty. She was still in bed after the confinement when she summoned the little girl and made her kneel down and swear by her father's life that the master had done nothing to her. This oath calmed her at the time, and she thought she might have made a mistake.

After a son was at last born, she felt she had fulfilled her duty to her husband and was now free. She began to behave discordantly. She became jealous of her husband again, and on the other hand would behave towards men in a remarkable manner. "Only with the eyes, however," she said, and if anyone took the hints she gave, she always vigorously rebuffed him.

This "harmless playfulness," on which her enemies similarly put a false construction, soon disappeared from view, however, behind the jealousy scenes, which went from bad to worse.

In order to make her husband impotent as regards other women, she got him to perform coitus several times every night. Even so, when she left the bedroom for a moment (to attend to bodily needs) she locked the room behind her. She hurried back at once, but if she found any disarrangement of the bed-clothes she became suspicious that the discharged cook, who might have got a key made, had been with him in the interval.

The patient, as we see, realised the sexual insatiability

that the alcoholic paranoiac mentioned above had only invented and could not carry out. (A woman can, to be sure, increase sexual relations at will, even without real pleasure, much more easily than a man). The sharp watching of the state of the bed-clothes was also repeated here.

The patient's behaviour in the sanatorium was full of contradictions. She coquetted with all the men, but would not let any of them approach her. On the other hand she made close friendships and enmities with all the female inhabitants of the house, and her conversations with me turned for the most part on these. She willingly took the luke-warm baths prescribed for her, but used the opportunity given by the bathing to collect detailed observations on the shapes and figures of the other female patients. She described to me with every sign of disgust and abhorrence the wrinkled abdomen of an elderly patient who was very ill. As she narrated her observations on prettier patients, however, the lascivious expression of her face was unmistakable. One day when she was alone with these younger ones she got up a "calf exhibition;" she stated that she won the first prize in the competition (narcissism).

I tried, with great circumspection, to learn something about the homosexual component of her sexual development by asking her whether, like so many young girls, she had been passionately fond of her girl friends. She divined my intention immediately, however, snubbed me severely, and maintained that I wanted to talk her into all sorts of abominations. I managed to calm her, whereupon she confessed to me under a pledge of secrecy that when she was a child she performed mutual masturbation for years with a little girl, whom she had seduced. (The patient had only sisters, no brothers). More than this, indications of over-strong sexual fixations to the mother and nurses could be inferred from the patient's communications, which were becoming more and more scanty.

The comparative peacefulness of the patient was for the first time seriously disturbed by her husband's visit, and the delusions of jealousy flared up anew. She accused her husband of having used her absence to do all sorts of disgraceful things, and her suspicion was particularly directed against the aged house-porteress, who, as she had heard, had helped in the house-cleaning. In sexual relations she became more insatiable than ever. If her husband refused this, she threatened to kill him, and on one occasion actually threw a knife at him.

The slight traces of transference to the physician, which were present at the beginning, also gave way in these stormy times to a more and more vehement resistance, so that the prospects of the analysis sank to nothing. We found ourselves compelled, therefore, to provide for her in a more distant institution where she could be more strictly watched.

This case also of delusional jealousy only becomes clear when we assume that it was a question of the projection on to the husband of her pleasure in her own sex. A girl who had grown up in almost exclusively feminine surroundings, who as a child was too strongly attached to the female nurses and servants and in addition to this had for years enjoyed sexual relations with a girl comrade of her own age, is suddenly forced into a *mariage de convenance* with a "coarse man."

She reconciles herself to it, however, and only once shews indignation against an especially crude piece of unkindness on her husband's part, by letting her desires turn towards her childhood ideal (a little servant girl). The attempt fails, she cannot endure the homosexuality any longer, and has to project it on to her husband. That was the first, temporary attack of jealousy. Finally, when she had done her "duty" and borne her husband the son he demanded, she felt herself free. The homosexuality that had been kept in bounds until then takes stormy possession in a crude erotic way of all the objects that offer no possibility for sublimation (quite young girls, old women and servants), though all this erotism, with the exception of the cases where she can hide it under the mask of harmless play, is imputed to the husband. In order to support herself in this lie, the patient is compelled to shew increased coquetry towards the male sex, to whom she had become pretty indifferent, and indeed to demean herself like a nymphomaniac.

III

One day I was asked by a lawyer to examine and declare sane one of his clients, the recorder of the town X, who was being unjustly persecuted by his compatriots. Soon after the man in question announced himself. It made me suspicious to begin with that he handed me a mass of newspaper cuttings, documents, and pamphlets, numbered and sorted in the most exemplary order, all of which he had written himself. A glance at the papers convinced me that he was a paranoiac with delusions of persecution. I made an appointment to examine him on the next day, but the perusing of his papers alone shewed me the homosexual root of his paranoia.

His disputes had begun with his writing to a captain that his vis-à-vis, an officer of the . . . regiment, *"shaved himself at the window, partly in his shirt, with a bare chest."* "In the second place he lets his gloves dry at the window on a line, as I have seen done in small Italian villages." The patient asked the captain "to effect a redress of this nuisance." He replied to the çaptain's disclaimer by attacking him. Then followed a notification to the colonel, in which he begins to speak of the "drawers" of the man opposite; he complains again also of the gloves. In printing of an enormous size he emphasises the fact that the matter would be indifferent to him if it were not that he wanted to let his sister occupy the rooms giving on to the street. "I believed I was fulfilling a chivalrous duty to the lady." At the same time an extreme sensitiveness and every sign of megalomania is noticeable in the papers. In the later ones the drawers get mentioned oftener and oftener. The expression "protection of ladies," underlined, frequently appears.

In a subsequent application he adds that he had forgotten to mention that the lieutenant was accustomed to dress himself in the evening at the brightly-lit window without pulling down the blinds. "That would make no difference to me" (this in small letters): *"In the name of a lady, however, I must beg for protection against such a sight."*

Then came memorials to the commander-in-chief, to the ministry of war, to the cabinet, etc, and in all of them the words in small print, "shirt, drawers,

naked chest," etc,—and only these—had been subsequently underlined in red. (The patient was the
owner of a newspaper, and could get everything printed
according to his heart's desire).

From a document of the commander-in-chief it
appeared that the patient's father and brother had been
insane and had ended in suicide. The father was, as
the patient expressed it, a "country lawyer and orator"
(the patient was also a lawyer), the brother was a
lieutenant. It was further to be gathered that the
patient was a follower of Kneipp;[1] indeed he appeared
once at the Supreme Court of Justice with bare feet
in sandals, for which he was reprimanded (exhibitionism).

Then he transferred the affair on to the code of
honour basis,[2] but always slipped out in the critical
moment, appealing to some paragraph or other in the
duelling code, of which he was complete master.   Here
the half-deliberate exaggeration crept in that he spoke
as if his letter had been an insult to the officer by a *deed*.
In other places he said (in huge print) that he had
cited facts to the officer in the most considerate way
possible.   He ascribes to the military authorities the
opinion of himself that he was "an old woman, who
has nothing else to do but discover objects of her curiosity."   He quoted innumerable examples of how officers
abroad were punished for insulting a girl in the street.
He demanded protection for defenceless women in

[1] (Kneipp was the founder of a pseudo-religious sect, one of whose tenets
was that the members should wear the same foot-gear as that worn in the
time of Christ. Transl.)

[2] (This refers to the custom still prevailing in Hungary, and elsewhere, of
regarding certain matters as affairs of honour involving the necessity of a
duel if suitable satisfaction be not provided.   Transl.)

general against brutal assaults, etc. In one of his applications he complained that the above-mentioned captain had "angrily and ostentatiously turned his face away from him."

The number of law-suits in which he was involved increased like an avalanche. What annoyed him most was that the military authorities ignored his memorials. Civilians he dragged before the civil courts; soon he transferred the matter to the political sphere, egged on in his newspaper the military and municipal authorities against each other, and exploited the "Pan-Germans" against the Hungarian civil authorities. In a short time about a hundred "comrades" came forward, who applauded him both publicly and by letter.

Then followed a curious episode. One day he complained to the new colonel that another officer had called "For shame, you miserable Saxon!" after *his sister* in the street. The sister was supposed to confirm this in a letter, which was certainly written by the patient himself.

He then turned to newspaper articles, in which he set difficult riddles with "dangerous" places indicated with dots. He mentioned, for instance, a French proverb that in German ran "das L. . . T. . . ". I had considerable trouble to discover that this signified "Lächerliche tötet."[1]

A NEW COMPLAINT AGAINST THE CAPTAIN (Nr I) mentioned "grimaces, gestures, movements, challenging glances." He wouldn't have bothered about it, but it concerned a lady. The officer was like a boy. He and his sister would make the matter plain to him regardless of everything. This was followed

[1] "Ridicule kills."

by new attacks on honour with retreat of the patient, who with legal niceties appealed to the duelling code.

Then follow threatening letters in which he, in his sister's name, talks a lot about "self-help;" long explanations; a hundred quotations about duelling, etc.: for instance, "Not bullets or swords is it that kill, but the seconds." The words "man," "men," "manly,' recur again and again. He writes hymns of praise to himself, and gets fellow-citizens to sign them. In one place he ironically states that perhaps one would like him, in the service of love, "to kiss the hands and feet of those gentlemen."

Now comes the fight with the municipal authorities, to whom the military had applied. Forty-two municipal councilmen demanded that he be punished. He picked out one of these, named Dahinten, and bitterly persecuted him in public. Encouraged by the cries of approval and the backing up of a Vienna yellow journal, he canvassed for the position of vice-Lord Lieutenant of a county—and blamed everyone at the injustice of his not getting this.

Then he wanted to restore the *good relations between the civil and military authorities*, always underlining these words.

Finally the matter reached a superior civil authority, who got the patient's mental state examined into. He came to me in the hope I would declare him to be sane.

Previous experiences with paranoiacs made it easy for me to infer from these facts alone the extraordinarily important part played by homosexuality in this case. The appearance of the delusion of persecution, perhaps long hidden, was evoked by the sight of a half-naked officer, whose shirt, drawers, and gloves also seem to have made a great impression on the patient. (Let me recall the part played by the bed-clothes in the two cases mentioned above). No female person was *ever* accused or complained of, he constantly fought and wrangled only with men, for the most part officers or high dignitaries, superiors. I interpret this as projection of his own homosexual delight in those persons, the affect being preceded by a negative sign. His desires, which have been cast out from the ego, return to his consciousness as the perception of the persecutory tendency on the part of the objects that unconsciously please him. He seeks until he has convinced himself that he is hated. He can now indulge his own homosexuality in the form of hate, and at the same time hide from himself. The preference for being persecuted by officers and officials was probably conditioned by the fact of his father having been an official and his brother an officer; I surmise that these were the original, infantile objects of his homosexual phantasies.

The false, magnified potency of the alcoholic delusional patient and the hypocritical nymphomania of the jealous paranoiac correspond with the exaggerated chivalry here and with the delicate feeling that he demands from men towards women. I have found this with most manifest homosexual men. This high esteem is one reason why homosexuals, like many psychically impotent men, are unable to take a woman as an object of love. Homosexuals esteem women, but love men. Thus also our paranoiac, only that his love has been transformed through reversal of affect into persecutory delusion and hate.

The fact that he put his sister in the foreground as

the insulted person was probably also in part conditioned by passive-homosexual phantasies in which he identifies himself with this sister. His complaint that he was regarded as an old woman, who was seeking for the objects of her curiosity in nude officers and their underlinen, speaks in favour of this view. When, therefore, he continually complains of insults on the part of the men who persecute him, he means unconsciously sexual assaults of which he would like to be the object himself.

It is neat to see in this case how the laboriously built up social sublimations of homosexuality collapse, probably under the pressure from the overgrowth of infantile phantasies, perhaps also as a result of other exciting causes which are unknown to me, and how the childish-perverse basis of these spiritualisations (*e. g.* peeping mania, exhibitionism) breaks through in the delusions.

As a control to my conception of this case I noted the patient's reactions to a hundred stimulus-words of Jung's scheme, and analysed the associations. The instructive part of this analysis is that it yielded meagre results. The paranoiac so thoroughly gets rid of the affects disturbing him that he believes they do not concern him, and that is why he relates in his actions and speech everything that the hysteric from fear of his conscience represses deeply. It is further striking, and evidently characteristic of true paranoia, that of Jung's "complex-signs" disturbed reproduction is hardly met with. The patient recalls excellently even the reactions to the "critical" stimulus-words that touch the complexes. Projection guards the paranoiac so well from affects that he has no need of the hysterical amnesia. Nearness of a complex seems to betray itself here rather through talkativeness and personal relation. The reactions are in any case throughout egocentric. Sound and rime reactions are very frequent, as are witty ones. So much for the form. I shall narrate here for the sake of example, some individual reactions, together with the analysis relating to them.

S. W.[1] Cooking. R. cook. A. Cooking makes women quarrelsome. A woman gets inflamed, heated, at the fire. My mother was also heated. I wouldn't let her cook to-day. A man can stand much more. Goethe says, to be sure: "Seven men would not stand what one woman can." My mother had six children. *A man would be more suitable for bearing children.* (In this reaction we find the forbearance towards women and the over-estimation of men, with a phantasy: for a man to bear children).

S. W. River. R. I should like to bathe in a river. A. I am passionately fond of bathing; I bathed in the river with my cousin every day until October. He shot himself, on account of over-strain. I avoid over-strain, and that's why I don't have much to do with women. (Attempt to explain on hygenic grounds his sexual avoidance of women. The cousin was an officer).

S. W. Salt. R. Reminds me of the salt of marriage. A. I am an enemy of married life. In it there is daily "friction." (He perhaps means also the compulsion to coitus in marriage).

S. W. Writing. R. I like the writing of the Berlin

[1]S. W. ═Stimulus-word. R. ═Reaction. A. ═Analysis.

artist who has died, the founder of the Kunstgewerbe
. . . Eckmann was his name. A. Striking, enormously large handwriting like his pleases me. Like
that of my father's. Mine resembles my father's, but
it is not so pretty. My letters, however, are also
large ones. (Esteem for his father and his physical
superiority expresses itself, as so often, in the tendency
to copy his handwriting. Pleasure in the size of the
letters may also be taken symbolically).

S. W. Cork. R. "Brings out the popping effect
of champagne." A. Nature hasn't given women any
of this. Hence their fading. My father, however, was
handsome even as an old man.

S. W. Hitting. R. That is what my opponents
deserve, to put it mildly. A. What I should best like
would be to turn a hose on them till they were soaking.
That would be fine. Fire-brigades interested me even in
childhood. (Fire-hose is one of the universal symbols
for the male organ).

S. W. Pure. R. To the pure all things are pure.
A. I was always a cleanly child, and was praised for
this by my uncle. My elder brother was dirty. (Exaggerated or precocious intolerance for dirt and disorder on a child's part is a symptom of homosexual
fixation—Sadger).

IV

The fourth case I wish briefly to relate was not one
of pure paranoia, but one of dementia praecox with
marked paranoiac aspects.

It concerned a country teacher, still young, who—so
his rather elderly-looking wife told me—had been

tormented for about a year with thoughts of suicide, believed himself to be persecuted and accused by everyone, and brooded alone for hours at a time.

I found the patient, who was in bed, awake, but with his head hidden away under the clothes. I had hardly exchanged a few words with him when he asked me if as a doctor I had to keep my patient's secrets. After I affirmed this he told me, amidst signs of intense dread, that he had three times performed cunnilingus with his wife. He knew that humanity had condemned him to death for this crime, that his hands and feet would be chopped off, his nose would decompose, and his eyes be plucked out. He shewed me a defective place in the ceiling, which, however, had been walled up, through which they must have watched his crime. His greatest enemy, the school-director, was informed of everything by means of complicated mirrors and electro-magnetic apparatus. Through his perverse deed he had become a woman, for a man performed coitus with his penis, not with his mouth. They would cut off his penis and testicles, or else his whole "Kürbiskopf" (literally block-head, but kürbis is also a vulgar Hungarian expression for testicles).

I happened to touch my nose, and he said "Yes, my nose is decomposing, you want to say." I said on entering the room "Are you Herr Kugler?" Coming back to this he explained: "The whole story is told in my name; I am *Die* Kugel-er (= Kugl-er), *i. e.* a *die-er*, a man-woman.[1] The d'or of the Christian name Sándor signified to him gold (French or = gold), *i. e.* he was made sexless[2] On one occasion he wanted to jump

[1] (Die and er are German for she and he respectively. Transl.)
[2] (Gold in German happens to be of the neuter gender. Transl.)

out of the window, but the word "Hunyad" occurred to him ("huny" is Hungarian for to shut, "ad" for to give), *i. e.* he is *closing* his eyes (he dies), so that his wife may *give* herself to another (sexually). So that no one should think this of him he stayed alive. They might even think when he was alive that he wanted to *shut an eye* if his wife "gave" herself to another.

He was filled with a terrible sense of guilt on account of his perverse act. Such perversity had always been foreign to him, and now also he abhors it. His enemy must have caused it, perhaps through suggestion.

On closely questioning him I learnt that he had sacrificed himself for his director ("A handsome, imposing man"); the latter was also very pleased with him and often said, "I could do nothing without you; you are my right hand." (This reminds one of the "better half"). For the past five years the director had tormented him, disturbing him with documents when he was most deeply engrossed at his work in explaining a poem to the class, etc.

At the question "Can you speak German" (tud németül in Hungarian) he dissected and translated the word németül (=German) into the syllables:

> ném=nimm (German for take)
> et=und (German for and)
> ül=sitz (German for seat) (ül is Hungarian for
to sit),

i. e. I meant by my question that he should take his penis in his hand, and, as a punishment for this, sit (be imprisoned in a hole). By this he expressly meant his own penis, which according to his enemies' accusation he wanted to insert into another hole, *i. e.* other strange women.

He swore that he adored his wife. His father had been a poor man-servant (this was true) and very stern with him. In student days he constantly sat at home and read poetry aloud to his mother. His mother had always been very kind to him.

We have here to do with a man who had happily sublimated his homosexuality for a long time, but who since the disappointment with the previously adored director hated all men, and in order to find reason for this hate had to explicate every expression, every gesture, every word, in terms of the wish to be persecuted. He soon got to hate me also: everyone of my words and gestures he explained in a hostile way, and dissected, translated, and distorted every word until it was turned into a hostile insinuation.

The patient's mother told me her son had always been a good child. Instead of playing with other children, he read aloud books, especially poetry, to his mother, and explained to her their contents. The father was a simple workman, and was sometimes rather harsh with the boy, whom he often annoyed by disturbing the reading.[1]

There is no doubt that the patient thought very little of his father, to whom he was intellectually superior, and longed for a more imposing one. This he found later in the person of the school-director, his superior, whom he served for years with tireless zeal, but who did not satisfy the patient's expectations (doubtless too high). He wanted now to give his love

[1]Hence the traumatic effect of the later disturbing of his lecture by the director.

ack to his wife, but in the meantime, however, she had become for him a "neutral quantity." The heterosexual exaggeration and the cunnilingus might have veiled his eyes to the lack of desire for his wife, but the longing for the male sex did not cease; it was only cast out from the ego-consciousness and returned to this as a projection with a negative prefix; he became a persecuted being.

*   *   *   *   *   *   *   *

In addition to those here narrated I have made an "analytic anamnesis" with three other paranoiacs.[1] In each of these projected homosexual desires played the most important part, but as I learnt nothing essentially new from these cases I did not made any exact notes of them.

The histories here published, however, *justify the surmise that with paranoia it is essentially a question of the re-occupa ion of homosexual pleasurable objects with unsublimated "sexual hunger," against which the ego defends itself by help of the projection mechanism.*

The establishment of this process would naturally bring us face to face with a larger problem, that of the "choice of neurosis" (Freud); with the question, namely, what conditions have to be fulfilled for the normal preponderance of heterosexuality, a homosexual neurosis, or paranoia to proceed from the infantile bisexuality, or ambisexuality.[2]

[1]One with delusions of jealousy and two querulants. One of the latter, an engineer, introduced himself to me with the complaint, "certain men in some unknown way sucked the masculine power from his genitals."

[2]I suggest that the term *ambisexuality* be used in psychology instead of the expression "bisexual predisposition." This would connote that we understand by this predisposition, not the presence of male and female material in the organism (Fliess), nor of male and female sex hunger in the mind, but the child's psychical capacity for bestowing his erotism, originally objectless, on either the male or the female sex, or on both.

CHAPTER VI

ON ONANISM[*]

A part of the neurotic disturbances caused by onanism is certainly of a purely psychical nature and can be traced to the apprehension that, in the earliest years of childhood (at the time of infantile masturbation), had been brought into an indissoluble associative connection with the idea of self-gratification (fear of castration with boys, fear of having the hands cut off with girls). A great many cases of hysteria and obsessional neurosis prove in the analysis to be the psychical result of this infantile apprehension, which—on the awaking of object-love—becomes accompanied with apprehension of incestuous onanistic phantasies. The adult dread of masturbation is thus composed of infantile (castration-) dread together with juvenile (incest-) dread, and the symptoms resulting from the conversion and substitution of this dread may be removed by means of analysis.

I have no doubt, however, that onanism is also able directly to evoke certain nervous and psychical disturbances, although it cannot be pointed out too often that this significance of onanism is as a rule much less

*Contribution to the Symposium on Onanism held by the Vienna Psycho-Analytical Society. Published in the Diskussionen der Vereinigung, Heft II. 1912.

than that of psychoneurotic symptoms caused by rough frightening and repression.

In a series of cases in which the analysis had made conscious the dread of castration- and incest-thoughts, and had thereby removed psychoneurotic symptoms, in which, however, abstinence from onanism was not total even during and after the treatment, the patients shewed on the day following masturbation a typical disturbance in their psychical and somatic condition which I will term One-Day-Neurasthenia. The chief complaints of the patients were: marked fatigability and leaden weight in the legs, especially on getting up in the morning; insomnia or disturbed sleep; over-sensitiveness to light and sound stimuli (sometimes definite sensations of pain in the eye and ear); gastric disturbances; paraesthesias in the lumbar region, and sensitiveness to pressure along the nerves. In the psychical sphere: great emotional irritability; ill-humour and fault-finding; incapacity or diminished capacity for concentration (aprosexia). These disturbances lasted the whole forenoon, gradually receded in the early hours of the afternoon, and only towards evening was there complete restoration of the bodily state, with calm in the sphere of the emotions and recovery of full intellectual capacity.

I wish expressly to remark that these symptoms did not coincide with any relapse in, or worsening of, the psychoneurotic symptoms, and that I did not manage in a single case to reach these symptoms psychoanalytically or to influence them in this way. Honesty, therefore, demands that psychological speculations should be disregarded here, and that the symptoms

described be recognised as physiological results of
onanism.

This observation supports, so I think, Freud's views
regarding the genesis of neurasthenia. The masturbatory actual-neurosis may be conceived as a becoming
chronic, a summation, of the symptoms of the onanistic
one-day neurasthenias.

Many observations tell in favour of the conclusion
that masturbatory activity is really able to bring about
physiological effects that do not pertain to the normal
act of coitus, and theoretical considerations are not in
disaccord with it.

There are men who have frequent sexual intercourse
with their wives, in spite of a diminution in "sexual
hunger," but who replace in their imagination the
person of their wife by another, and, therefore, so to
speak, perform onanism per vaginam. When such
men occasionally have sexual relations with someone
else who gives them complete satisfaction, they remark
a very great difference between their state after the
coitus that was helped by phantasy and after the
coitus that gave satisfaction in itself. If the other person fulfilled the conditions of their sexual hunger, they
felt invigorated after the act, enjoyed a short sleep, and
on both the same and the next day were unusually
competent and efficient. After the onanistic coitus,
however, there surely followed a one-day neurasthenia,
with all the symptoms described above. Especially
typical in such cases was the occurrence, immediately
after the intercourse, of pain in the eyes when light
fell on them, weight in the legs, and—apart from the
psychical irritability—a pronounced hyperaesthesia of
the skin, especially sensitiveness to tickling. On the

ground of the accompanying feelings of heat and
pulsation I interpret the insomnia as the result of
vasomotor excitability.

Theoretical considerations also yield no sound
objection to the supposition that normal coitus and
masturbation are processes that are to be estimated
differently not only psychologically, but also physiologically. Whether the onanism is performed by
rubbing with the hand or through friction of the
member against the vagina of a non-satisfying sexual
object two processes are essentially altered in comparison with normal intercourse. With onanism the
normal fore-pleasure is absent, whereas the share
taken by the phantasy is enormously increased. Now
I do not believe that fore-pleasure is a purely psychological process. When a satisfying sexual object is
gazed at, touched, kissed, embraced, the optic, tactile,
oral, and muscular erogenous zones are actively excited,
and they automatically pass over a part of this excitation to the genital zone; the process takes place to begin
with in the sense organs, or sensorial centres, and the
phantasy is only secondarily drawn into sympathetic
enjoyment. With onanism, however, all the sense
organs are silent, and the conscious phantasy, together
with the genital stimulation, have to procure the whole
sum of excitation. The forcible retaining of a picture,
often imagined with hallucinatory sharpness, during a
sexual act that normally is almost unconscious is no
slight task; it is certainly great enough to explain a
resulting fatigability of the attention.

The excitability of the sense organs after onanism
(and in neurasthenia) is not so easily explained. Too
little is known for this purpose of the nervous processes

in normal coitus. Through the stimulation of the
erogenous zones in coitus a state of preparedness of the
genital organ is aroused in the first place; in the friction
that succeeds, the genito-spinal reflex then plays
the chief part; it ends in a summation of genital stimuli,
and finally—synchronously with ejaculation—in an
explosive radiation of the excitation over the whole
body. I surmise that the sensual pleasure, which, like
all common feelings, cannot be localised, arises through
the genital stimulation (when it has accumulated enough
or reached a certain tension) explosively radiating
beyond the spinal centre into the whole sphere of feeling,
thus into the cutaneous and sensorial centres as well.
If this is the case, it is probably not a matter of indifference whether the wave of lust finds a sphere of feeling
that is prepared by fore-pleasure, or one that is unex-
cited and, so to speak, cold. It is therefore very far
from obvious that the nervous processes in coitus and
masturbation should be physiologically identical, and
indeed the considerations just mentioned even give a
hint of the direction in which one would have to look
for the causes of the vasomotor, sensory, sensorial,
and psychical over-stimulation that remains after
onanism. It is possible that the wave of lust normally
dies away altogether, but that with masturbation a
part of the excitation cannot reach a proper level; this
amount of excitation remaining over would explain
the one-day neurasthenia—perhaps neurasthenia altogether.[1]

---

[1] "One-Day Neurasthenia" sometimes happens even after quite normal
coitus, *e. g.* when as an exception the intercourse takes place in the forenoon,
when the sexual hunger is usually less. The sexual hunger increases in
the late hours of the afternoon, a fact that certainly is not without bearing on the evening improvement in the neurasthenic's condition.

The discoveries of Fliess concerning the relations between nose and genitalia should also not be forgotten. The vasomotor over-excitation in masturbation can cause chronic disturbances in the erectile tissue of the nasal mucous membrane, which may then lead to the most diverse forms of neuralgia and functional disturbances. In some of my cases of masturbatory neurasthenia the patient's condition perceptibly improved after cauterisation of the genital points in the nose. Extensive investigations will have to be undertaken on this matter.

Whereas in the preceding remarks I wanted to warn against regarding the results of masturbation exclusively from the psychological point of view, I fear that in the question of ejaculatio praecox it is the opposite mistake that is made. To judge from my experience, precocious emission of semen often happens with people to whom coitus is for one reason or another disagreeable, who thus have an interest in finishing the business as quickly as possible. Now we know that onanists—warped by their phantasy—are only too soon dissatisfied with their sexual object, and it is to be supposed that unconsciously they would like to shorten the act. By these remarks I do not mean to say that local causes (changes around the ductus ejaculatorii) are in no case to be held responsible for the ejaculatio praecox.

I only wish to add a remark about the genesis of the tooth-pulling symbolism of onanism in dreams and neuroses. We all know that tooth-pulling in dreams symbolises onanism. Freud and Rank have shewn this with irrefragable examples and have also drawn attention to colloquial German, which professes the same symbolism. The same symbol, however, is very often met with among Hungarians who certainly did not know of those German expressions, and yet the Hungarian language has no similar synonym for masturbation. On the other hand the symbolic identification of tooth-pulling and castration could in all the cases be made probable through analysis. Dreams use tooth-pulling as a symbol for castration, *i. e.* the punishment in the place of the onanism.

In the formation of this symbol of onanism—apart from the external similarity of tooth and penis, tooth-pulling and cutting off a penis—a certain temporal factor may not be without significance. Castration and tooth-pulling (falling out of the teeth) are the first operative interventions with the possibility of which the child is seriously threatened. It is then not hard for the child to repress the more disagreeable of the two interventions (castration) out of the phantasy, and on the other hand to emphasise symbolically the tooth-pulling that resembles it. This is probably the way in which sexual symbolism altogether has come about.

There exists, by the way, even a tooth-neurosis of its own (excessive dread of anything being done to the teeth, *e. g.* by a dentist; continual boring and probing into the cavities of hollow teeth; obsessions concerned the teeth, etc). In the analysis this neurosis proves to be a derivative of onanism, or fear of castration.

CHAPTER VII

TRANSITORY SYMPTOM-CONSTRUCTIONS DURING THE ANALYSIS*

(Transitory Conversion, Substitution, Illusion, Hallucination, "Character-Regression," and "Expression-Displacements.")

I T is in the transference that the physician, as well as the patient, receives the really convincing impressions as to the correctness of the analytical explanation of symptoms. So long as the psychical material afforded through free association is the only proof that the patient has of the correctness of the analytical explanations, they may seem to him remarkable, surprising, even illuminating; he still does not attain a conviction of their indubitable correctness, the feeling that they are the only explanations possible, however honestly he may try to become convinced, or even if he forces conviction on himself with all his strength. It definitely looks as if one could never reach any real convictions at all through logical insight alone;[1] one needs to have lived through an affective experience, to have—so to speak—felt it on one's own body, in order to gain that degree of certain insight which deserves the name of "conviction." The

---

*Published in the Zentralblatt für Psychoanalyse, Jahrg. II, 1912.

[1] (The author is evidently speaking of psychological truths, not of physical ones. Transl.).

physician also who has only learned analysis from books, without having submitted his own mind to a thorough analysis and gathered practical experience with patients, cannot convince himself of the truth of its results; at the most he gains a more or less high degree of confidence, which may at times closely approach conviction, but behind which there always still lurks a suppressed doubt.

I wish here to bring forward a number of symptoms that I have seen arise with my patients during the treatment and pass away through analysis, which contributed in converting into certainty my impression of the truth of the Freudian mechanisms, and aroused or strengthened the patients' confidence in the matter.

Free association and the analytic scrutinising of the incoming thoughts is not infrequently interrupted in hysterics by the abrupt appearance of somatic phenomena of a sensory or motor nature. One might at first sight be inclined to regard these conditions as disagreeable disturbances of the analytic work, and to treat them accordingly. If, however, one takes really seriously the principle of everything that happens being strictly determined, one has to seek an explanation for these phenomena also. If one makes up one's mind to do so, and thus submits these symptoms also to analysis, it becomes plain that they really are representations, in symptom form, of unconscious feeling and thought-excitations which the analysis has stirred up from their inactivity (state of rest, equilibrium) and brought near to the threshold of consciousness, but which before becoming quite conscious—in the last moment, so to speak—have been forced back again on account of their painful character (to consciousness), whereby their sum of excitation, which can no longer be quite suppressed, becomes transformed into the production of somatic symptoms. A symptom that has been brought about in this way does not only represent a certain sum of excitation, but it proves to be determined in a qualitative manner also. For if attention be directed to the nature of the symptom, to the kind of motor or sensory state of stimulation or of paralysis, to the organ in which it occurs, to the occurrences and thoughts that immediately preceded the formation of the symptom, and an effort be made to discover its meaning, this somatic symptom is shewn to be a symbolic expression for an unconscious thought-or emotion-excitation that has been stimulated through the analysis. If one now translates the symptom for the patient from symbolic to conceptual language, it may happen, even when he had no idea of this mechanism beforehand, that he at once declares with great astonishment that the sensory or motor state of stimulation or paralysis has disappeared as suddenly as it had appeared. Observation of the patient shews unmistakably that the symptom only ceases when the patient has recognised our explanation to be the correct one, not when he has merely understood it. In so doing the patient very often betrays the fact of being "detected" through smiling, laughing, blushing, or some other sign of embarrassment; not infrequently he himself confirms the correctness of our surmise or brings at once memories of his past that strengthen our supposition.

I had to interpret one of the dreams of an hysterical patient as a wish-phantasy; I told her that this dream betrayed her dissatisfaction with her situation, her

desire for a better educated and more agreeable husband
in a more distinguished position, and especially the
wish for more beautiful clothes.   At this moment the
patient's attention was deflected from the analysis by
the sudden onset of toothache.   She begged me to give
her something to ease the pain, or at least to get her a
glass of water.   Instead of doing so, I explained to the
patient that by the toothache she was perhaps only
expressing in a metaphorical way the Hungarian saying
"My tooth is aching for these good things."[1]   I said
this not at all in a confident tone, nor had she any idea
that I expected the pain to cease after the communication.   Yet, quite spontaneously and very astonished,
she declared that the toothache had suddenly ceased.

Subsequent questioning of the patient established
the fact that she had striven to blind herself to the
trying situation in which she found herself on marrying
beneath her station.   The interpretation of the dream
disclosed her unfulfilled wishes in such a manner that
she could scarcely escape its truth.   She managed
nevertheless in the last moment to let the "unpleasant-
ness-censor" prevail, to drive the recognition of my
interpretation into the sphere of bodily feeling by means
of the association-bridge "My tooth aches for it,"
and thus to transform into toothache the painful insight.

The unconscious utilisation of this current expression
was perhaps the final, but not the only condition of the
symptom-formation.   Psychical space, just as physical
space, has several dimensions, so that the site of a point
in it can only be determined exactly by means of
several coordinate axes.   Put into psycho-analytical

[1] (Compare the English expression: "My mouth waters for, etc." Transl.)

language, that is: every symptom is over-determined. Ever since childhood the patient in question had fought against an unusually strong inclination to masturbation, and with masturbators the teeth have a special symbolic significance.[1] The factor of bodily predisposition also has always to be considered in cases of this sort.

On another occasion the same patient brought her repressed infantile-erotic phantasies to expression in the form of a declaration of love addressed to the physician, and received by way of reply—instead of the hoped-for response—an explanation of the transference character of this access of feeling. Thereupon she immediately felt a curious paraesthesia in the mucous membrane of the tongue, crying out: "My tongue suddenly feels as though it were scalded (*abgebrüht*)." At first she rejected my explanation that with the word "abgebrüht" she was only expressing her disappointment at the declining of her love advances, but the sudden and startling disappearance of the paraesthesia after my explanation gave her food for thought, and she presently admitted that I had been right in my surmise. In this case also the preference for the tongue as the site of symptom-formation was determined by several conditions, the analysis of which made possible the penetration into the deeper layers of the unconscious complexes.

It is very common indeed for patients to express a suddenly appearing mental suffering by transitory cardiac pains, the feeling of bitterness by a bitter feeling in the tongue, and care by a sudden sense of pressure on the head. One neurotic used to utter his aggressive intentions directed against me (more correctly: against

[1] (See Ch. VI, p. 163. Transl.)

his father) in the form of sensations which he felt on those parts of the body where his unconscious wanted to injure me: the feeling as though he had suddenly received a blow on the head turned out to be a murderous intention, a pricking in the cardiac region to be one of stabbing. (Consciously he is a masochist and his aggressive phantasies can enter consciousness only in the form of the self-borne talion punishment—an eye for an eye: a tooth for a tooth.) Another patient regularly felt a peculiar sense of giddiness as soon as we came to talk about matters that severely tested his lack of self-confidence. The analysis led to infantile experiences in which, while at a considerable height, he felt himself so helpless that he became giddy. The sudden appearance of heat or cold sensations may signify emotional stirrings (with a corresponding name) in the patient or, conversely, may represent the idea that the patient surmises the existence of such feeling in the physician.

A "frightful sleepiness" overcame one patient every time that she wanted to escape by a short cut the analysis which was getting disagreeable to her. Another one used this means to indicate her unconscious erotic phantasies, which were associated with this sleepy condition; she was one of those persons who could endure sexual phantasies only when they were without self-reproach, *e. g.* only in the form of an imaginary rape.

These *transitory conversions* are also to be observed, though much less often, in the sphere of motility. By this I do not mean the "symptomatic actions" in the sense of Freud's Psychopathology of Everyday Life, which are higher, combined and coordinated actions, but isolated, and sometimes painful, spasms in indivi-

dual muscles or suddenly appearing states of weakness
resembling paralysis.

A neurotic who wanted to remain homosexual, and
who sought by every possible means to escape from the
heterosexual erotism that was powerfully pressing
forward, got a cramp in the left leg every time in the
analysis that he managed to suppress phantasies which
threatened to produce an erection. He discovered for
himself the symbolic identification "Leg=Penis, Cramp
=Erection." Drawing in of the belly-wall with or
without the feeling of retraction of the penis occurred
with one patient every time that he took more liberties
with the physician than his infantile cowed unconscious
would allow him. Analysis shewed the cramp to be a
defensive measure against the feared punishment—
castration. Not infrequently a convulsive clenching
of the fist is revealed to be an inclination to assault,
a contraction of the masseters to be a refusal to speak
or a desire to bite.

Transitory states of weakness in the whole muscula-
ture or in certain groups of muscles are sometimes to be
explained as symptoms of moral weakness or as a not
wanting to carry out some action. The conflict
between two tendencies of equal strength can express
itself, as in dreams, in an inhibition of certain movements.

In the analysis of these passing conversion-symptoms
one learns as a rule that something of the kind has
already happened before in the patient's life; one has
then to search for the causes that evoked them on the
previous occasion. There occur, however, also transitory symptoms that seem to the patient to be quite new,
and which, according to him, have never been ex-

perienced before the analysis; even in such cases it nevertheless remains for the most part undecided whether they had not merely escaped the patient's introspection, which was less trained before the analysis. *A priori*, however, one cannot dismiss the possibility that the analysis, penetrating into the disagreeable layers of the mind and disturbing its apparent rest, can force the patient to make use of quite new possibilities of symptom-formation. In ordinary life or in a non-analytic treatment the thought-connections would have come to a stop far enough from the disagreeable areas.

Transitory obsessional phenomena may also occur in the treatment. There is something similar to an obsession in every association, however senseless, that is a conscious substitute for an intelligent but repressed idea ("Replacement-associations," according to Freud). Apparently senseless ideas of a true obsessional character are sometimes produced, however, which definitely obsess the patient's thinking and yield only to an analytic explication. An obsessional patient, for instance, suddenly interrupted the free association with the thought: He couldn't understand why the word "window" should mean just a window; why the letters w-i-n-d-o-w, which after all are only senseless sounds and tones, should signify a corporeal object. He could not be brought to give any further free associations: the idea of the meaning of the word window so strongly dominated him that he was unable to produce any new thought. For a while I allowed myself to be deceived by the intelligent patient, took up his idea, and discussed the theory of speech-formation. But I soon saw that the patient was not interested in the explanation, the idea remaining in its obsessional form. Then it occurred to me that it might be a piece of resistance and I wondered how it was to be resolved. I reflected on what had preceded this obsessional association in the analysis, and recalled that just before it occurred I had explained to the patient the meaning of a symbol and that he had seemed to accept my explanation with an acquiescing "yes." I now expressed my surmise that the patient had not been able to agree with this explanation, but had repressed his contradiction. The repressed incredulity then returned in the distorted guise of the thought "why should the letters w-i-n-d-o-w signify a window." This should really run: "Why does the symbol just explained signify just that object?" With this explanation the interruption was removed.

Indirect contradiction, which here quite unconsciously formed an obsession, evidently has its source in similar conscious reactions of small children who through their lack of courage and self-confidence are compelled to adopt this mediate speech when they want to contradict an adult[1].

Another obsessional patient let his incredulity be recognised in a different way. He began not to understand any foreign words that I used, and then, as I faithfully translated them for him for a while, he maintained that he could not longer understand his mother-tongue. He behaved absolutely like a dement. I then explained to him that with this lack of under-

---

[1] I said once to a boy, aged five, that he need not be afraid of a lion, for the lion would run away if only he would look him straight in the eyes. His next question was: "And a lamb can sometimes eat up a wolf, can't it?" "You didn't believe my story about the lion," said I. "No, not really—but don't be cross with me for it," answered the little diplomatist.

standing he was unconsciously expressing his disbelief. Really it was me (my remarks) that he wanted to mock, but he repressed this inclination and acted like an idiot, as if to say: If I were to accept this nonsense, I would be a fool. From now on he understood my explanations perfectly well.[1]

A third obsessional patient was curiously obsessed by the Slavonic term for doctor ("Lekar"). The obsessional impulse came from the German homonym of the word, (=licker) a term of abuse which the patient, a man of high ethical principles, could bring out only indirectly.

In rare and exceptional cases true *hallucinations* are evoked in the analysis hour. (Much more often, of course, come memories of especial clearness and vividness in respect to which, however, the patient can none the less still behave in an objective way, *i. e.* he can correctly estimate their unreality).

One of my patients shewed a special capacity for hallucinations, constantly making use of them when the analysis came upon certain things that were painful to her. On such occasions she would suddenly drop the thread of the free associations and produce instead pure hallucinations with a fearful content: she sprang up, crouched in a corner of the room, and with signs of acute dread made convulsive movements of defence and protection, after which she soon got calm again. When she came to herself she could tell

---

[1]Analytical experience make it highly probable that many intelligent children at the stage of repression marked by the latency period, before they have gone through the "great intimidation," regard adults as dangerous fools, to whom one cannot tell the truth without running the risk of being punished for it, and whose inconsistencies and follies have therefore to be taken into consideration. In this children are not so very wrong.

me exactly the content of the hallucinated processes, and it turned out that they were phantasies presented in a dramatic or symbolic form (fights with wild animals, rape scenes, etc.), which were connected with the associations immediately preceding the hallucinations; the analysis of them mostly brought to light new memory material, affording her great relief. The hallucinatory-symbolic representation was thus merely the last means of escaping the conscious recognition of certain pieces of insight. It could also be neatly observed in this case how the associations gradually approached conscious knowledge, and then suddenly glided away in almost the last moment, allowing the excitement to regress on to the sense area.

It is not rare for transitory *illusionary deceptions* (especially of the sense of smell) to appear in the analysis hour. In one case an illusionary "change in the perceptual world" could be observed in the analysis. I was just striving to make clear to a patient her excessive ambition, arising from narcissistic fixation, and said to her that she might be happier if she could properly appreciate this, renounce a part of the phantasies of self-importance, and be content with smaller successes. In this moment she called out, her face glowing: "It is wonderful, now I suddenly see everything, the room, the bookcase, so 'concretely' clear in front of me; everything has bright and natural colours and is so plastically arranged in space." On further questioning I learnt that for years she had not been able to see so "concretely," the outer world appearing to her dull, faded, and flat. The explanation was as follows: As a spoilt child she obtained the satisfaction of all her desires; since she had been grown up the perfidious world had not been so considerate to her wish-fancies, whereupon "she had not been pleased with the world;" she projected this feeling into the optical sphere by seeing the world since then changed in the way described. The prospect of reaching new possibilities of happiness through renouncing a part of the wish-fulfilments was similarly projected into the optical sphere, and expressed itself there as illumination and more vivid reality of the perceptual world. These variations in optical excitability may be conceived as "autosymbolic phenomena" in Silberer's sense, as symbolic self-perception of psychical processes of the "functional category." In this case, by the way, it would be more correct to speak of transitory disappearance of a symptom than of transitory creation of one.

Transitory *character-regressions* during the treatment I should call a pretty frequent occurrence, the essence of which consists in certain character traits temporarily losing their sublimations and suddenly regressing on to the primitive, infantile level of instinct life from which they had taken their origin.

It is not rare, for instance, with certain patients for an acute need for passing water to develop in the analysis hour. Many hold out until the end of the sitting, others suddenly get up and have to leave the room—sometimes with signs of anxiety—in order to attend to the need. In cases where the natural explanation of the occurrence could be excluded (and my communication concerns only such), I was able to establish the following psychical origin of the vesical excitation: It was always with very ambitious and vain patients, who did not admit their vanity to themselves, and who felt their ambitiousness wounded in the most sensitive way by the psychical material brought out in the analysis hour, also feeling discouraged by the physician, without having made this wounding of their ego completely conscious, or logically working it over and overcoming it. With one of these patients the parallelism between the more or less wounding content of the analytic conversation and the desire to micturate was so noticeable that I could at will evoke the latter by dwelling on a theme that was plainly disagreeable to the patient. Analytic talking out on this theme can reverse the "character-regression" or hinder its reappearance.

An occurrence of this sort allows the process of regression, established by Freud, to be observed—as it were *in flagranti*. It shews that a sublimated character trait can in the event of denial (of gratification)— assuming the corresponding sites of fixation in the psychical development—really fall back on to the infantile level at which the satisfaction of the not yet sublimated impulse met with no hindrance. The saying "*on revient toujours à ses premiers amours*" finds here its psychological confirmation; the person who is disappointed in his ambition reaches back towards the auto-erotic foundation of this passion.[1]

Temporary *rectal troubles* (diarrhoea, constipation) often reveal themselves in the analysis as regressions of the anal character. One patient suffered from acute diarrhoea towards the end of the month, when she had to send to her parents means of support that in her unconscious she only unwillingly parted with. Another

---

[1] (Ambitiousness is unconsciously associated with urethral erotism. Transl.)

compensated himself for the physician's fees by producing large quantities of intestinal gas.

When a patient feels himself unkindly treated by the physician he takes to onanism, if there is a corresponding auto-erotic fixation. He brings in the form of this transference the confession of his childhood masturbation. As a child he gave up self-gratification only in exchange for object-love (love of the parents). If he feels himself disappointed in this kind of love he relapses. Even patients who cannot remember ever having masturbated may one day come with a confession of dismay that they have suddenly had to give in to an irresistible impulse to self-gratification.

(These sudden regressions to anal, urethral, and genital auto-erotism also explain why the disposition of these erotisms to function in anxiety states [*e. g.* dread of examinations] is so strong. The fact also that in his fearful dread a man being hanged relaxes both sphincters and ejaculates semen may be due, apart from direct nervous stimulation, also to a final convulsive regression to the pleasure sources of life. I once saw a nephritic patient aged seventy, who was tortured by acute headache and cutaneous irritation, carrying out movements of onanism in his despair.)

With male neurotics who feel themselves unkindly treated by the physician *homosexual obsessions* may appear, which often refer to the person of the latter. This is a proof, which might almost be called experimental, that friendship is essentially sublimated homosexuality, which in case of denial is apt to regress on to its primitive level.

Expression displacements. I noticed with one patient that he yawned with striking frequency. I then remarked that the yawning accompanied just those analytic conversations whose content, since it was important to him although disagreeable, would more suitably have evoked interest than boredom. Another patient who came to treatment soon after this brought me what I believe to be the solution of this peculiar phenomenon. She also yawned often and at inappropriate times, but in her case the yawning was sometimes accompanied with a flow of tears. That gave me the idea that these patients' yawning might be a distorted sigh, and in both cases the analysis confirmed my surmise. The censorship effected in both cases the repression of certain disagreeable emotional states that were aroused through the analysis (pain, grief), but it was unable to bring about a complete suppression, only a displacement of the movements of expression, one that was enough, however, to conceal from consciousness the real character of the emotional state. On turning my attention, after these observations, to the movements of expression with other patients as well, I found that there are other forms of "expression displacements." One patient, for instance, had to cough every time he wanted to avoid saying something to me; the intended, but suppressed, speech then came through nevertheless in the form of a cough. We see that the displacement from one emotional expression to another takes place along the line of physiological vicinity (yawning—sighing; talking—coughing). A cough may also represent a consciously or unconsciously intended, and then suppressed, laugh, in which case the displaced expression of the emotional state —as with a pure hysterical symptom—contains also the punishment for the satisfaction of pleasure. Neurotic women often cough when they are being medically examined, *e. g.* auscultated; this also I believe may be regarded as a displacement of the movements of laughter elicited by unconscious erotic phantasies. After what has been said it will cause no surprise if I add that in one case I was able to interpret a temporary hiccough as representing a sob of despair. These symptoms that only appear transitorily in the analysis also throw light on the chronic hysterical symptoms of the same kind (spasms of laughter and of crying). Really incredible—but none the less true—is the occurrence of an "expression displacement" to which Professor Freud called my attention. Many patients produce a rumbling in the stomach when they have concealed some associations. The suppressed speech is turned into a ventriloquism (*Bauchreden*).

Besides the didactic value for physicians and patients, discussed at the beginning of the paper, these "transitory symptom-formations" possess a certain practical and theoretical significance. They offer us points of attack for dealing with the patient's strongest resistances, concealed as transferences, and are thus of practical, technical value for the analysis. And in giving us the opportunity to watch symptoms of disease arise and disappear before our eyes, they throw light on these processes in general. They enable us to form theoretic conceptions of the dynamics of disease, at least with many kinds of disease.

We know from Freud that a neurotic disorder comes about in three stages: the infantile fixation (a disturbance in the development of the sexual hunger) constitutes the foundation of every neurosis; the second stage is that of the repression, which remains still without symptoms; the third that of the outbreak of the disorder, the symptom-formation.

The experiences gathered here of "transitory symptom-formations" make it probable that in the great neuroses, as in these neuroses *en miniature*, symptoms are formed only when repressed portions of complexes threaten, for internal or external reasons, to enter into associative connection with consciousness, *i. e.* to become conscious, and when thereby the equilibrium of a previous repression is disturbed. The "unpleasantness" censorship watching over the calm of consciousness then manages in the last moment, so to speak, to deflect the excitation from the progressive path, *i. e.* its path into consciousness, and—since the driving back into the old repression situation does not succeed well— to let a part of the excitation and of the unconscious psychical structures find at least a distorted expression in symptoms.

CHAPTER VIII

STAGES IN THE DEVELOPMENT OF THE SENSE OF REALITY*

THE development of the mental forms of activity in the individual consists, as Freud has shewn, in the resolution of the originally prevailing pleasure-principle, and the repression mechanism peculiar to it, by the adjustment to reality, *i. e.* by the testing of reality that is based on judgement. Thus arises out of the "primary" psychical stage, such as is displayed in the mental activities of primitive beings (animals, savages, children), and in primitive mental states (dreams, neurosis, phantasy), the secondary stage of the normal man in waking thought.

At the beginning of its development the new-born babe seeks to attain a state of satisfaction merely through insistent wishing (imagining), whereby it simply ignores (represses) the unsatisfying reality, picturing to itself as present, on the contrary, the wished-for, but lacking, satisfaction; it attempts, therefore, to conceal without effort all its needs by means of positive and negative hallucinations. "It was only the non-appearance of the expected satisfaction, the disappointment, that led to the abandonment of this attempt at satisfaction by the hallucinatory method. Instead, the psychical apparatus had to decide to represent the actual circumstances of the outer world

*Published in the Internat. Zeitschr, f. ärztl. Psychoanalyse, 1913.

to itself, and to strive to alter reality. With this a new principle of mental activity was initiated; not what was pleasant was any longer imagined, but what was real, even though it should be unpleasant."[1]

The significant essay in which Freud displayed to us this fundamental fact of psychogenesis is confined to the sharp differentiation between the pleasure and the reality stages. Freud also concerns himself here, it is true, with transitional states in which both principles of mental functioning coexist (phantasy, art, sexual life), but he leaves for the present unanswered the question whether the development of the secondary form of mental activity from the primary takes place gradually or in a series of steps, and whether such stages of development are to be recognised, or their derivatives demonstrated, in the mental life of the normal or abnormal.

An earlier work of Freud's, however, in which he affords us deep insight into the mental life of obsessional patients,[2] calls attention to a fact from which as a starting point one may attempt to bridge over the gap between the pleasure and the reality stages of mental development.

Obsessional patients who have submitted themselves to a psycho-analysis—so it runs in that work—admit to us that they cannot help being convinced of the omnipotence of their thoughts, feelings, and wishes, good and bad. However enlightened they may be, however much their academic knowledge and their reason may strive to the contrary, they have the feeling

[1]Freud. "Formulierungen über die zwei Prinzipien des psychischen Geschehens." Jahrb. Bd. III. S.1.
[2]Freud. "Bemerkungen über einen Fall von Zwangsneurose." Jahrb. Bd. I. S. 411.

that their wishes in some inexplicable way get realised. Of the truth of this state of affairs any analyst can convince himself as often as he likes. He will learn that the weal and woe of other people, indeed their life and death, seem to the obsessional patient to depend on certain thought processes and actions, in themselves harmless, on which he engages. The patient has to think of certain magical formulas, or carry out a certain action; otherwise a great misfortune will befall this or that person (mostly a near relative). This conviction, though felt to be superstitious, is not shaken even by repeated experiences to the contrary.[1]

Leaving aside the fact that analysis reveals such obsessive thoughts and actions to be the substitutes of wish-impulses that are logically correct, but which on account of their intolerableness have been repressed,[2] and turning our attention exclusively to the peculiar manifestation of this obsessional symptom, we must admit that it constitutes a problem in itself.

Psycho-analytical experience has made it clear to me that this symptom, the feeling of omnipotence, is a projection of the observation that one has slavishly to obey certain irresistible instincts. The obsessional neurosis constitutes a relapse of the mental life to that stage of child-development characterised, amongst other things, by there being as yet no inhibiting, postponing, reflecting thought-activity interposed between wishing and acting, the wish-fulfilling movement following spontaneously and unhesitatingly on the

[1] This article was finished before use could be made of Freud's article on "Animismus, Magie und Allmacht der Gedanken" (Imago, Jahrg. II, Heft I), which deals with the same topic from other points of view.

[2] Freud. Sammlung kleiner Schriften zur Neurosenlehre. 1906. S. 45 und 86.

wishing—an averting movement away from something disagreeable, or an approach towards something agreeable.[1]

A part of the mental life, more or less removed from consciousness, thus remains with the obsessional patient—as the analysis shews—on this childhood level in consequence of an arrest in development (fixation), and makes wishing equivalent to acting because—just on account of the repression, of the distraction of attention—this repressed portion of the mental life was not able to learn the difference between the two activities, while the ego itself, which has developed free from repression and grown wise through education and experience, can only laugh at this equating of the two. Hence the inner discordance of the obsessional patient, the inexplicable occurrence of enlightenment and superstition side by side.

Not being quite satisfied with this explanation of the feeling of omnipotence as an autosymbolic phenomenon,[2] I put to myself the question: Whence then does the child get the boldness to set thinking and acting as equivalents? Whence comes the feeling of obviousness with which it stretches out its hand after all objects, after the lamp hanging above him as after the shining moon, in the sure expectation of reaching it with this gesture and drawing it into the domain of its power?

---

[1] It is well known that small children almost reflexly stretch out their hands after every object that shines or in any other way pleases them. They are to begin with also incapable of foregoing any "naughtiness" that yields them any kind of pleasure, whenever the stimulus causing this appears. A young boy who had been forbidden to bore his finger into his nose answered his mother, "I don't want to, but my hand does and I can't prevent it."

This is what Silberer terms the self-perceptions that are symbolically represented.

I then recalled that according to Freud's assumption "a piece of the old grandiose delusion of childhood was honestly confessed" in the omnipotence phantasy of the obsessional patient, and I tried to trace out the origin and fate of this delusion. In this way I hoped also to learn something new about the development of the ego from the pleasure to the reality principle, since it seemed to me probable that the replacement (to which we are compelled by experience) of the childhood megalomania by the recognition of the power of natural forces composes the essential content of the development of the ego.

Freud declares an organisation that is a slave to the pleasure principle, and which can neglect the reality of the outer world, to be a fiction, one, however, which is almost realised in the young infant, when one only takes into account the maternal care.[1] I might add that there is a stage in human development that realises this ideal of a being subservient only to pleasure, and that does so not only in imagination and approximately, but in actual fact and completely.

I mean the period of human life passed in the womb. In this state the human being lives as a parasite of the mother's body. For the nascent being an "outer world" exists only in a very restricted degree; all its needs for protection, warmth, and nourishment are assured by the mother. Indeed, it does not even have the trouble of taking the oxygen and nourishment that is brought to it, for it is seen to that these materials, through suitable arrangements, arrive directly into

[1] Jahrb. Bd. III. S. 2. Footnote. See also the controversy between Bleuler and Freud on this question (Bleuler, "Das autistische Denken." Jahrb. Bd. IV.).

its blood-vessels. In comparison with this an intestinal worm, for example, has a good deal of work to perform, "to change the outer world," in order to maintain itself. All care for the continuance of the foetus, however, is transferred to the mother. If, therefore, the human being possesses a mental life when in the womb, although only an unconscious one,— and it would be foolish to believe that the mind begins to function only at the moment of birth—he must get from his existence the impression that he is in fact omnipotent. For what is omnipotence? The feeling that one has all that one wants, and that one has nothing left to wish for. The foetus, however, could maintain this of itself, for it always has what is necessary for the satisfaction of its instincts,[1] and so has nothing to wish for; it is without wants.

The childhood megalomania of their own omnipotence is thus at least no empty delusion; the child and the obsessional patient demand nothing impossible from reality when they are not to be dissuaded from holding that their wishes must be fulfilled; they are only demanding the return of a state that once existed, those "good old days" in which they were all-powerful. (*Period of unconditional omnipotence*).

With the same right by which we assume the transference of memory traces of the race's history on to the individual, indeed with more justification than this, we may assert that the traces of intra-uterine psychical processes do not remain without influence

---

[1] As a result of disturbances, such as through illness or injury of the mother or of the umbilical cord, etc., necessity can face a human being already in the mother's body, can rob him of his omnipotence and compel him to the effort of "changing the outer world," *i.e.* of performing work (an example being the inspiration of amniotic fluid when in danger of suffocation.)

on the shaping of the psychical material produced after birth. The behaviour of the child immediately after birth speaks for this continuity of the mental processes.[1]

The new-born child does not accommodate himself uniformly as regards all his needs to the new situation which is visibly disagreeable to him. Immediately after the delivery he begins to breathe, so as to restore the provision of oxygen that has been interrupted by the tying of the umbilical vessels; the possession of a respiratory mechanism, formed already in intra-uterine life, at once enables him actively to remedy the oxygen privation. If, however, one observes the remaining behaviour of the new-born child one gets the impression that he is far from pleased at the rude disturbance of the wish-less tranquillity he had enjoyed in the womb, and indeed that *he longs to regain this situation*. Nurses instinctively recognise this wish of the child, and as soon as he has given vent to his discomfort by struggling and crying they deliberately bring him into a situation that resembles as closely as possible the one he has just left. They lay him down by the warm body of the mother, or wrap him up in soft, warm coverings, evidently so as to give him the illusion of the mother's warm protection. They guard his eye from light stimuli, and his ear from noise, and give him the possibility of further enjoying the intra-uterine absence of irritation, or, by rocking the child and crooning to him monotonously rhythmical lullabies, they reproduce the slight and monotonously rhythmical stimuli that

[1]Freud has incidentally pointed out that the sensations of the child during the birth act probably evoke the first anxiety affect of the new being, which remains prefigurative for all later anxiety and anxiousness.

the child is not spared even in utero (the swaying movements of the mother when walking, the maternal heart-beats, the deadened noise from without that manages to penetrate to the interior of the body).

If we try, not only to feel ourselves into the soul of the new-born babe (as the nurses do), but also to think ourselves into it, we must say that the helpless crying and struggling of the child is apparently a very unsuitable reaction to the unpleasant disturbance that the previous situation of being satisfied has suddenly experienced as a result of the birth. We may assume, supported by considerations which Freud has expounded in the general part of his *Traumdeutung*,[1] that the first consequence of this disturbance is the hallucinatory re-occupation of the satisfying situation that is missed, the untroubled existence in the warm, tranquil body of the mother. The first wish-impulse of the child, therefore, cannot be any other than to regain this situation. Now the curious thing is that—presupposing normal care—this hallucination is in fact realised. From the subjective standpoint of the child the previously unconditional "omnipotence" has changed merely in so far, that he needs only to seize the wish-aims in a hallucinatory way (to imagine them) and to alter nothing else in the outer world, in order (after satisfying this single condition) really to attain the wish-fulfilment. Since the child certainly has no knowledge of the real concatenation of cause and effect, or of the nurse's existence and activity, he must feel himself in the possession of a magical capacity that can actually realise all his wishes by simply imagining

[1] Freud. Die Traumdeutung. 3e Aufl., S. 376.

the satisfaction of them. (*Period of magical-hallucin-atory omnipotence*).

That the nurse guesses the hallucinations of the child aright is shewn by the effect of her actions. As soon as the first nursing measures are carried out the child calms itself and goes to sleep. *The first sleep, however, is nothing else than the successful reproduction of the womb situation (which shelters as far as possible from external stimuli)*, probably with the biological function that the processes of growth and regeneration can concentrate all energy on themselves, undisturbed by the performance of any external work. Some considerations, which cannot be presented in this connection, have convinced me that also every later sleep is nothing else than a periodically repeated regression to the stage of the magical-hallucinatory omnipotence, and through the help of this to the absolute omnipotence of the womb situation. According to Freud, one has to postulate for each system subsisting by the pleasure-principle arrangements by means of which it can withdraw itself from the stimuli of reality.[1] Now it seems to me that sleep and dreams are functions of such arrangements, that is to say, remains of the hallucinatory omnipotence of the small child that survive into adult life. The pathological counter-part of this regression is the hallucinatory wish-fulfilment in the psychoses.

Since the wish for the satisfying of instincts manifests itself periodically, while the outer world pays no attention to the occurrence of the occasion on which the instinct is exerted, the hallucinatory representation of the wish-fulfilment soon proves inadequate to bring

[1]Freud. Jahrb., Bd. III, S. 3.

about any longer a real wish-fulfilment. A new condition is added to the fulfilment: the child has to give certain *signals*—thus performing a motor exertion, although an inadequate one—so that the situation may be changed in the direction of his disposition, and the "ideational identity" be followed by the satisfying "perceptual identity."[1]

The hallucinatory stage was already characterised by the occurrence of uncoordinated motor discharges (crying, struggling) on the occasion of disagreeable affects. These are now made use of by the child as magic signals, at the dictation of which the satisfaction promptly arrives (naturally with external help, of which the child, however, has no idea). The subjective feeling of the child at all this may be compared to that of a real magician, who has only to perform a given gesture to bring about in the outer world according to his will the most complicated occurrences.[2]

We note how the omnipotence of human beings gets to depend on more and more "conditions" with the

[1] Freud. Die Traumdeutung. Loc. cit.

[2] When I search in pathology for an analogy to these discharges I have always to think of *genuine epilepsy*, that most problematical of the major neuroses. And although I fully admit that in the question of epilepsy the physiological is difficult to separate from the psychological, I may call attention to the fact that epileptics are known to be uncommonly "sensitive" beings, behind whose submissiveness frightful rage and domineeringness can appear on the least occasion. This characteristic has up to the present usually been interpreted as a secondary degeneration, as the consequence of repeated attacks. One should, however, think of another possibility, namely whether the epileptic attacks are not to be considered as regressions to the infantile period of *wish-fulfilment by means of uncoordinated movements*. Epileptics would then be persons with whom the disagreeable affects get heaped up and are periodically abreacted in paroxysms. If this explanation proves to be useful we should have to localise the place of fixation for a later affliction of epilepsy in this stage of uncoordinated wish-manifestions.— The irrational stamping of the feet, clenching of the fists, and grinding of the teeth, etc, that are to be seen in outbursts of anger would be a milder form of the same regression in otherwise healthy persons.

increase in the complexity of the wishes. These efferent manifestations soon become insufficient to bring about the situation of satisfaction. As the wishes take more and more special forms with development, they demand increasingly specialised signals. To begin with are such as, imitations of the movement of sucking with the mouth when the infant wants to be fed, and the characteristic expressions by means of the voice and abdominal pressing when it wants to be cleansed after excreting. The child gradually learns also to stretch out its hand for the objects that it wants. From this is developed later a regular gesture-language: by suitable combinations of gestures the child is able to express quite special needs, which then are very often actually satisfied, so that—if only it keeps to the condition of the expression of wishes by means of corresponding gestures—the child can still appear to itself as omnipotent: *Period of omnipotence by the help of magic gestures.*

This period also has a representative in pathology; the curious jump from the world of thought into that of bodily processes, which Freud has discovered hysterical conversion to be,[1] becomes more intelligible to us when we view it as a regression to the stage of gesture-magic. Psycho-analysis shews us in fact that hysterical attacks present with the help of gestures the repressed wishes of the patient as fulfilled. In the mental life of the normal the countless number of superstitious gestures, or such as are in some other way considered efficacious (gestures of cursing, blessing, praying) is a remainder of that developmental period of the sense of reality in which one still felt mighty

[1] See Freud's works in the Studien über Hysterie, 1895.

enough to be able to violate the regular order[1] of the universe. Fortune-tellers, soothsayers, and magnetisers continually find belief in the assertion of such complete power of their gestures, and the Neapolitan also averts the evil eye with a symbolic gesture.

With the increase in the extent and complexity of the wants goes naturally an increase, not only of the "conditions" that the individual has to submit to if he wishes to see his wants satisfied, but also of the number of cases in which his ever more audacious wishes remain unfulfilled even when the once efficacious conditions are strictly observed. The out-stretched hand must often be drawn back empty, the longed-for object does not follow the magic gesture. Indeed, an invincible hostile power may forcibly oppose itself to this gesture and compel the hand to resume its former position. Till now the "all-powerful" being has been able to feel himself one with the world that obeyed him and followed his every nod, but gradually there appears a painful discordance in his experiences. He has to distinguish between certain perfidious things, which do not obey his will, as an outer world, and on the other side his ego; *i. e.* between the subjective psychical contents (feelings) and the objectified ones (sensations). I once called the first of these stages the *Introjection Phase* of the psyche, since in it all experiences are still incorporated into the ego, and the later one the *Projection Phase.*[2] One might also, following this terminology, speak of the omnipotence stage as the introjection stage, the reality stage as the projection stage, of the development of the ego.

[1]This being of course quite unsuspected.
[2]Ch. II.

Still even the objectifying of the outer world does not at once destroy every tie between the ego and the non-ego. The child learns, it is true, to be content with having only a part of the world, the ego, at his disposal, the outer world, however, often opposing his wishes, but there still remains in this outer world qualities that he has learned to know in himself, *i. e.* ego qualities. Everything points to the conclusion that the child passes through an *animistic period* in the apprehension of reality, in which every object appears to him to be endowed with life, and in which he seeks to find again in every object his own organs and their activities.[1]

The derisive remark was once made against psycho-analysis that, according to this doctrine, the unconscious sees a penis in every convex object and a vagina or anus in every concave one. I find that this sentence well characterises the facts. The child's mind (and the tendency of the unconscious in adults that survives from it) is at first concerned exclusively with his own body, and later on chiefly with the satisfying of his instincts, with the pleasurable satisfactions that sucking, eating, contact with the genital regions, and the functions of excretion procure for him; what wonder, then, if also his attention is arrested above all by those objects and processes of the outer world that on the ground of ever so distant a resemblance remind him of his dearest experiences.

Thus arise those intimate connections, which remain throughout life, between the human body and the objective world that we call *symbolic*. On the one hand the child in this stage sees in the world

[1] On the subject of animism see also the essay "Ueber Naturgefühl" by Dr. Hanns Sachs (Imago, Jahrg. I.)

nothing but images of his corporeality, on the other
he learns to represent by means of his body the
whole multifariousness of the outer world. This
capacity for symbolic representation is an important
completion of the gesture-language; it enables the
child not only to signalise such wishes as immediately
concern his body, but also to express wishes that relate
to the changing of the outer world, now recognised as
such. If the child is surrounded by loving care, he
need not even in this stage of his existence give up the
illusion of his omnipotence. He still only needs to
represent an object symbolically and the thing, believed
to be alive, often really "comes" to him; for the
animistically thinking child must have this impression
at the satisfaction of his wishes. From the uncertainty
regarding the arrival of the satisfaction it gradually
dawns on him, to be sure, that there are also higher,
"divine" powers (mother or nurse), whose favour he
must possess if the satisfaction is to follow closely on
the magic gesture. Still this satisfaction also is not
hard to obtain, especially with indulgent surroundings.

One of the bodily means that the child makes use of
for representing his wishes, and the objects he wishes
for, attains then an especial significance, one that
ranges beyond that of all other means of representation—speech, namely. Speech is originally[1] imitation,
i. e. vocal representation, of sounds and noises that are
produced by things, or which can be produced by their
help; the executive capacity of the speech organs allows
the reproduction of a much greater multiplicity of

[1] See Kleinpaul, Leben der Sprache (1893), and Sperber, "Uber den
Einfluss sexueller Momente auf Entstehung und Entwicklung der Sprache,"
Imago, 1912.

objects and processes of the outer world than was possible with the help of gesture-language, and in a much simpler manner. Speech symbolism thus gets substituted for gesture symbolism: certain series of sounds are brought into close associative connection with definite objects and processes, and indeed gradually identified with these. From this accrues the great progress: there is no longer a necessity for the cumbrous figurative imagination and the still more cumbrous dramatic representation; the imagination and representation of the series of sounds that we call words allow a far more specialised and economic conception and expression of the wishes. At the same time conscious thinking makes speech symbolism possible by becoming associated to thought processes that are in themselves unconscious, and lending them perceptual qualities.[1]

Now conscious thought by means of speech signs is the highest accomplishment of the psychical apparatus, and alone makes adjustment to reality possible by retarding the reflex motor discharge and the release from unpleasantness. In spite of this the child knows how to preserve his feeling of omnipotence even in this stage of his development, for his wishes that can be set forth in thoughts are still so few and comparatively uncomplicated that the attentive *entourage* concerned with the child's welfare easily manages to guess most of these thoughts. The mimic expressions that continually accompany thinking (peculiarly so with children) make this kind of thought-reading especially easy for the adults; and when the child actually formulates his wishes in words the *entourage*, ever ready to help, hastens to fulfil them as soon as possible. The

[1]See Freud, Traumdeutung, III Aufl., S. 401 and Jahrb., Bd. III, S. I.

child then thinks himself in possession of magic capacities, is thus in the *period of magic thoughts and magic words.*[1]

It is this stage of reality development to which the obsessional patients seem to regress when they are not to be dissuaded from the feeling of the omnipotence of their thoughts and verbal formulas, and when, as Freud has shewn, they set thinking in the place of acting. In superstition, in magic, and in religious cults this belief in the irresistible power of certain prayer, cursing, or magical formulas, which one has only to think inwardly or only to speak aloud for them to work, plays an enormous part.[2]

This almost incurable megalomania of mankind is only apparently contravened by these neurotics with whom behind the feverish search for success one at once comes across a feeling of inferiority (Adler), which is well-known to the patients themselves. An analysis that reaches to the depths reveals in all such cases that these feelings of inferiority are in no sense something final, an explanation of the neurosis, but are themselves the reactions to an exaggerated feeling of omnipotence, to which such patients have become "fixed" in their early childhood, and which has made it impossible for them to adjust themselves to any subsequent renunciation. The manifest seeking for greatness that these people have, however, is only a "return of the repressed," a hopeless attempt to reach once more, by means of changing the outer world, the omnipotence

---

[1] The psychological explanation of "magic" naturally does not exclude the possibility of this belief containing also the foreshadowing of physical facts (telepathy, etc.)

[2] This "omnipotence" ("Motor power") is highly characteristic also of obscene words. See Chapter IV.

that originally was enjoyed without effort.

We can only repeat: All children live in the happy delusion of omnipotence, which at some time or other— even if only in the womb— they really partook of. It depends on their "Daimon" and their "Tyche" whether they preserve the feelings of omnipotence also for later life, and become *Optimists*, or whether they go to augment the number of *Pessimists*, who never get reconciled to the renunciation of their unconscious irrational wishes, who on the slightest provocation feel themselves insulted or slighted, and who regard themselves as step-children of fate—because they cannot remain her *only* or *favourite* children.

Freud dates the end of the domination of the pleasure-principle only from the complete psychical detachment from the parents. It is also at this epoch, which is extremely variable in individual cases, that the feeling of omnipotence gives way to the full appreciation of the force of circumstances. The sense of reality attains its zenith in Science, while the illusion of omnipotence here experiences its greatest humiliation: the previous omnipotence here dissolves into mere "conditions." (Conditionalism, determinism.) Nevertheless, we possess in the doctrine of the freedom of the will an optimistic philosophical dogma that can still realise phantasies of omnipotence.

The recognition that our wishes and thoughts are conditioned signifies the maximum of normal projection, *i. e.* objectification. There is also, however, a psychical disorder, paranoia, which has the characteristic, among others, that in it even the person's own wishes and thoughts are expelled into the outer world, are projected.[1]   It seems natural to locate the fixation-point of this psychosis in the period of the final renunciation of omnipotence, *i. e.* in the projection phase of the sense of reality.

The stages in the development of the sense of reality have here been presented up to now only in terms of the egoistic, so-called "ego-instincts," which serve the function of self-preservation; reality has, as Freud has established, closer connections with the ego than with sexuality, on the one hand because the latter is less dependent on the outer world (it can for a long time satisfy itself auto-erotically), on the other hand because it is suppressed during the latency period and does not come at all into contact with reality.   Sexuality thus remains throughout life more subjected to the pleasure-principle, whereas the ego has immediately to experience the bitterest disappointment after every disregarding of reality.[2]   If we now consider the *feeling of omnipotence in sexual development* that characterises the pleasure stage, we have to observe that here the "period of unconditional omnipotence" lasts until the giving up of the auto-erotic kinds of satisfaction, a time when the ego has already long adjusted itself to the increasingly complicated conditions of reality, has passed through the stages of magic gestures and words, and has already almost attained the knowledge of the omnipotence of natural forces. Auto-erotism and narcissism are thus the omnipotence stages of erotism, and, since narcissism never comes to

[1] See Freud, "Die Abwehr-Neuropsychosen" (Kl. Schr. z. Neurosenlehre, S.45), "Psychoanalytische Bemerkungen über einen autobiographisch beschriebenen Fall von Paranoia," Jahrb., Bd. III, and Chapter V of this book.

[2] Freud. Jahrb., Bd. III, S. 5.

an end at all, but always remains by the side of object-erotism, it can thus be said that—in so far as we confine ourselves to self-love—in the matter of love we can retain the illusion of omnipotence throughout life. That the way to narcissism is at the same time the constantly accessible way of regression after every disappointment in an object of love is too well-known to need proof; auto-erotic—narcissistic regressions of pathological strength may be suspected behind the symptoms of Paraphrenia (Dementia praecox) and Hysteria, whereas the fixation-points of the Obsessional Neurosis and of Paranoia should be found in the line of development of "erotic reality" (the compulsion to find an object).

These relations, however, have not yet been appropriately studied with all the neuroses, so that we have to be content with Freud's general formulation concerning the *choice of neurosis*, namely, that the variety of the subsequent disorder is decided by "which phase in the development of the ego and the sexual hunger is affected by the determining inhibition of development."

One may nevertheless venture to add to this sentence a second one; we suspect that the wish-constituent of the neurosis, *i. e.* the varieties and aims of the erotism that the symptoms present as fulfilled, depends on where the fixation-point is in the phase of the development of the sexual hunger, while the mechanism of the neuroses is probably decided by what stage in the development of the ego the individual is in at the time of the determining inhibition. It is very well thinkable that with the regression of the sexual hunger to earlier stages of development the level of the reality-sense that was dominant at the time of fixation also becomes renascent in the mechanisms of the symptom-formation. Since, that is to say, this earlier kind of "reality-testing" is incomprehensible to the present ego of the neurotic, there is nothing to prevent its being placed at the disposal of the repression, and used for the presentation of censured feeling- and thought-complexes. Hysteria and the obsessional neurosis, for example, would according to this conception be characterised on the one hand by a regression of the sexual hunger to earlier stages of development (auto-erotism, Oedipusism), and on the other hand in their mechanisms by a relapse of the reality-sense to the stage of magic gestures (conversion) or of magic thoughts (omnipotence of thought). I repeat: It will need much longer laborious work before the fixation-points of all neuroses can be established with certainty. I wish here only to point to one possibility of a solution, one, it is true, that to me is plausible.

What we may conceive about the *phylogenesis* of the reality-sense can at present be offered only as a scientific prediction. It is to be assumed that we shall some day succeed in bringing the individual stages in the development of the ego, and the neurotic regression-types of these, into a parallel with the stages in the racial history of mankind, just as, for instance, Freud found again in the mental life of the savage the characters of the obsessional neurosis.[1]

In general the development of the reality-sense is represented by a succession of repressions, to which mankind was compelled, not through spontaneous "strivings towards development," but through neces-

[1]Freud. "Ueber einige Uebereinstimmungen im Seelenleben der Wilden und der Neurotiker," Imago, Jahrg I, 1912.

sity, through adjustment to a demanded renunciation. The first great repression is made necessary by the process of birth, which certainly comes about without active cooperation, without any "intention" on the part of the child. The foetus would much rather remain undisturbed longer in the womb, but it is cruelly turned out into the world, and it has to forget (repress) the kinds of satisfaction it had got fond of, and adjust itself to new ones. The same cruel game is repeated with every new stage of development.[1]

It is perhaps allowable to venture the surmise that it was the geological changes in the surface of the earth, with their catastrophic consequences for primitive man, that compelled repression of favourite habits and thus "development." Such catastrophes may have been the sites of repression in the history of racial development, and the temporal localisation and intensity of such catastrophes may have decided the character and the neuroses of the race. According to a remark of Professor Freud's, racial character is the precipitate of racial history. Having ventured so far beyond the knowable, we have no reason to shrink before the last analogy and from bringing the great step in individual repression, the latency period, into connection with the last and greatest catastrophe that smote our primitive ancestors (at a time when there were certainly human beings on the earth), *i. e.* with the misery of the glacial period, which we still faithfully

---

[1] If this thought is logically pursued, one must make oneself familiar with the idea of a tendency of perseveration, or regression-tendency, also dominating organic life, the tendency to further development, adaptation, etc., depending only on external stimuli.

recapitulate in our individual life.[1]

The impetuous curiosity to know everything that
has just seduced me into enchanted vistas of the past,
and led me to bridge over the yet unknowable by the
help of analogies, brings me back to the starting-point
of these considerations: to the theme of the acme and
decline of the feeling of omnipotence. Science has to
repudiate this illusion, or at least always to know when
she is entering the field of hypotheses and fancies. In
fairy-tales, on the contrary, phantasies of omnipotence
are and remain the dominating ones.[2] Just where we
have most humbly to bow before the forces of Nature,
the fairy-tale comes to our aid with its typical motives.
In reality we are weak, hence the heroes of fairy-tales
are strong and unconquerable; in our activities and our
knowledge we are cramped and hindered by time and
space, hence in fairy-tales one is immortal, is in a
hundred places at the same time, sees into the future
and knows the past. The ponderousness, the solidity,
and the impenetrability of matter obstruct our way
every moment: in the fairy-tale, however, man has
wings, his eyes pierce the walls, his magic wand opens
all doors. Reality is a hard fight for existence; in the

---

[1] Cases where development precedes the real needs seem to contradict
the conception that only external compulsion, and never spontaneous
impulse, leads to the giving up of accustomed mechanisms (development).
An example for this would be the development of the respiratory mechanism
already in utero. This happens, however, only in ontogenesis, and is here
to be regarded as a recapitulation of a compulsory process of development
in the history of the race. The playful practising of animals (Gross) also
are not the preliminary stages of a future racial function, but repetitions of
phylogenetically acquired capacities. They thus allow of a purely historical-
causal explanation, and we are not compelled to regard them from the point
of view of finality.

[2] Cp. Riklin, Wunscherfüllung und Symbolik im Märchen. (Schriften
zur angewandten Seelenkunde, Heft 2).

fairy-tale the words "little table, be spread" are sufficient. A man may live in perpetual fear of attacks from
dangerous beasts and fierce foes; in the fairy-tale a magic
cap enables every transformation and makes us inaccessible.   How hard it is in reality to attain love that can
fulfil all our wishes! In the fairy-tale the hero is irresistible, or he bewitches with a magic gesture.

Thus the fairy-tale, through which grown-ups are so
fond of relating to their children their own unfulfilled
and repressed wishes, really brings the forfeited situation of omnipotence to a last, artistic presentation.

CHAPTER IX

A LITTLE CHANTICLEER*

A lady, a former patient of mine who had retained her interest in psycho-analysis, called my attention to the case of a little boy, which she surmised would be of general interest.

The case was that of a five-year-old boy, Árpád by name, who according to the unanimous reports of all his relatives had developed up to the age of three and a half in quite a regular way both mentally and physically, and was said to have been a perfectly normal child; he spoke fluently and shewed considerable intelligence.

All at once he became quite different. In the summer of 1910 the family went to an Austrian spa, where they had also spent the previous summer, and took rooms in the same house as in the year before. Immediately after the arrival the child's demeanour changed in a curious way. Hitherto he had taken an interest in all the goings on, both indoors and out of doors, that might attract the attention of a child; from now on he was interested in only one thing, and that was the fowl-house in the courtyard of the dwelling. Early in the morning he hastened to the poultry, watched them with tireless interest, imitated their sounds and movements, and cried when he was forcibly removed from the fowl-run. But even when he was away from it he did nothing else but crow and cackle. He did this unintermittingly for hours at a time, and answered to questions

*Published in the Internat. Zeitschr. f. ärztl. Psychoanalyse, 1913.

only with these animal cries, so that his mother was seriously concerned lest her child would lose his power of speech.

This peculiar behaviour of little Árpád lasted throughout the whole duration of the summer stay. When the family returned to Budapest he began once more to speak in a human way, but his talk was almost exclusively of cocks, hens, and chickens, at the most with geese and ducks besides. His usual game, repeated endlessly every day, was as follows: He crumpled up newspaper into the shape of cocks and hens, and offered them for sale; then he would take some object (generally a small flat brush), call it a knife, carry his "fowl" to the sink (where the cook really used to kill the poultry), and cut the throat of his paper hen. He shewed how the fowl bled, and with his voice and gestures gave an excellent imitation of its death agony. Whenever fowls were offered for sale in the courtyard little Árpád got restless, ran in and out of the door, and gave no peace until his mother bought some. He wanted to witness their slaughter. Of live cocks, however, he was not a little afraid.

The parents asked the child endless times why he was so afraid of cocks, and Árpád always related the same story: He had once gone out to the hen-coop, had micturated into it, whereupon a fowl or a capon with yellow feathers (sometimes he said with brown) came and bit his penis, and Ilona, the servant, had dressed the wound. Then they cut the cock's throat, so that he died.

Now, as a matter of fact, the parents remembered this occurrence, which had happened in the *first* summer spent in the spa, when Arpád was only two and a half years old.   One day the mother had heard the little one shrieking fearfully, and learnt from the servant that he was frightened of a cock which had snapped at his penis.   Since Ilona was no longer in the family's service it could not be ascertained whether on that occasion Arpad had really been hurt or (as the mother's memory went) had merely been bandaged by Ilona to calm him.

The curious part of the matter was that the psychical after-effect of this experience had set in with the child after a latent period of a whole year, on the second visit to the summer residence, without anything having happened in the meanwhile to which the relatives could ascribe this sudden recurrence of the fear of fowls and the interest in them.   I did not, however, let the negative nature of this evidence restrain me from putting a question to the child's *entourage*, one sufficiently justified by psycho-analytical experience, namely, whether in the course of the latent period the child had not been threatened—as so often happens—with the cutting off of his penis on account of voluptuous playing with his genitals.   The answer, given unwillingly, was to the effect that at the present time, it was true, the boy was fond of playing with his member, for which he often got punished, that it was also "not impossible" that someone might have "jokingly" threatened to cut it off, further that Árpád had had this bad habit "for a long time," but whether he already had it in the latent year was no longer known.

In what comes presently it will be seen that in fact Arpád had not been spared this threat at a later date, so that we are entitled to regard the assumption as probable that it was the threat experienced in between which had so greatly excited the child on re-visiting the scene of the first terrifying experience, in which the well-being of his member had similarly been endangered. A second possibility is of course not be excluded, namely, that the first fright already had been exaggerated by a still earlier threat of castration, and that the excitement on re-visiting the hen-coop is to be ascribed to the increase of "sexual hunger" that had come about in the meantime. Unfortunately it was no longer possible to reconstruct these time relationships, and we have to be content with the probability of the causal connection.

Personal investigation of the boy yielded nothing striking or abnormal. Immediately on entering my room his attention was attracted by a small bronze mountain cock among the numerous other objects lying about; he brought it to me and asked "will you give it to me?" I gave him some paper and a pencil and he immediately drew a cock (not unskilfully). Then I got him to tell me the story about the cock. But he was already bored and wanted to get back to his toys. Direct psycho-analytic investigation was therefore impossible, and I had to confine myself to getting the lady who was interested in the case and, being a neighbour and friend of the family, could watch him for hours at a time, to note down his curious remarks and gestures. I was able to establish so much for myself, however, that Arpad was mentally very alert and also not untalented; his mental interest and his talent, were, it is true, peculiarly centered round the feathered folk of the fowl-run. He clucked and crowed in a masterly way. Early in the morning he woke the family—a true Chanticleer—with a lusty crow. He was musical, but sang only popular songs in which cock, fowl, or the like came, being especially fond of the song:

> "To Debreczen I must run,
> There to buy a turkey-cock,"

then the songs: "Chicken, chicken, come, come, come," and

> "Under the window are two chickens,
> Two little cocks and a hen."

He could draw, as was remarked above, but he confined himself exclusively to birds with a large beak, drawing these with considerable skill. One thus sees the directions in which he was seeking to sublimate his pathologically strong interest in these creatures. The parents had finally to put up with his hobbies, seeing that their interdictions did no good, and bought for him various toy birds made of unbreakable material with which he carried out all sorts of fanciful games.

Árpád was in general a pleasant little fellow, but very defiant whenever he was reprimanded or beaten. He hardly ever cried, and never begged for forgiveness. Apart from these character traits, however, there were no traces of true neurotic traits to be recognised. He was easily frightened, dreamt a great deal (of fowls, of course) and often slept badly (*Pavor nocturnus*).

Árpád's curious sayings and actions, which were noted down by the lady observer, mostly display an unusual pleasure in phantasies about the cruel torturing of poultry. His typical game, imitating the slaughter of fowls, I have already mentioned; to this should be added that even in his bird dreams it was mostly "killed" cocks and hens that he saw. I will here give a literal translation of some of his characteristic sayings:

"I should like to have a live plucked cock," he once said quite spontaneously. "He must have no wings, no feathers, and no tail, only a comb, and he must be able to walk like that."

He was playing in the kitchen with a fowl that had just been slaughtered by the cook. All of a sudden he went into the next room, fetched a curling-tongs out of a drawer, and cried: "Now I will stick this dead fowl's blind eyes." The slaughtering of poultry was quite a festival for him. He could dance round the animals' bodies for hours at a time in a state of intense excitement.

Someone, pointing to the slaughtered fowl, asked him: "Would you like it to wake again?" "The devil I would; I would knock it down again at once myself."

He often played with potatoes or carrots (which he said were fowls), slicing them into small pieces with a knife. He could hardly be restrained from throwing to the ground a vase that had fowls painted on it.

The affects displayed in regard to fowls, however, were by no means simply those of hate and cruelty, but were plainly ambivalent. Very often he would kiss and stroke the slaughtered animal, or he would "feed" his wooden goose with maize, as he had seen the cook do; in doing this he clucked and peeped continuously. Once he threw his unbreakable doll (a fowl) in the oven because he could not tear it, but then pulled it out again at once, cleansed it and caressed it. The animal figures in his picture book, however, had a worse time of it; he tore them in pieces, was then naturally unable to bring them back to life, and got very upset.

If such symptoms were observed in an adult insane patient, the psycho-analyst would not hesitate to interpret the excessive love and hate concerning poultry as a transference of unconscious affects that really referred to human beings, probably near relatives, but which were repressed and could only manifest themselves in this displaced, distorted way. He would further interpret the desire to pluck and blind the animals as symbolising castration intentions, and regard the whole syndrome as a reaction to the patient's fear of the idea of his own castration. The ambivalent attitude would then arouse in the analyst the suspicion that mutually contradictory feelings in the patient's mind were balancing each other, and on the basis of numerous experiential facts he would have to surmise that this ambivalence probably referred to the father, who—although otherwise honoured and loved—had at the same time to be also hated on account of the sexual restrictions sternly imposed by him. In a word, the analytic interpretation would run: The cock signified in the syndrome the father.[1]

In little Árpád's case we can spare ourselves the trouble of making any interpretation. The work of repression was not yet able entirely to conceal the significance of his peculiarities; the original thing, the repressed tendencies, could still be discerned in his talk, and indeed it became evident at times with a startling openness and crudity.

[1] In a very large number of analyses of dreams and neuroses the figure of the father is discovered behind that of an animal. See Freud, Schriften etc. Ch. 1, and Internat. Zeitschr. f. Psychoanalyse, Jahrg. I, Heft 2.— Professor Freud tells me that one of his next works in "Imago" will make use of this identity to explain totemism. (This has since appeared in book form under the title "Totem und Tabu." Transl.)

His cruelty was often displayed in regard to human beings also, and was strikingly often directed against the genital region of adults. "I'll give you one in the faeces, in your behind," he was fond of saying to a boy somewhat older than himself. Once he said, still more plainly, "I'll cut your middle out." The idea of blinding occupied him pretty often. He once asked his neighbour: "Can one make a person blind with fire or with water?" (He was also highly interested in the genitals of poultry. With every fowl that was slaughtered they had to enlighten him about the sex—whether it was a cock, a hen, or a capon.)

He ran to the bed of a grown-up girl and called out: "I'll cut your head off, lay it on your belly, and eat it up." Once he said quite suddenly: "I should like to eat a potted mother (by analogy: potted fowl); my mother must be put in a pot and cooked, then there would be a potted mother and I could eat her." (He grunted and danced the while). "I would cut her head off and eat it this way" (making movements as it eating something with a knife and fork).

After cannabalistic desires of this sort he would at once get an attack of remorse, in which he masochistically yearned for cruel punishments. "I want to be burnt," he would then call out: "Break off my foot and put it in the fire." "I'll cut my head off. I should like to cut my mouth up so that I didn't have any."

There can be no doubt that by fowl, cock, chicken he meant his own family, for he said once quite spontaneously: "My father is the cock!" On another occasion: "Now I am small, now I am a chicken. When I get bigger I shall be a fowl. When I am bigger still I shall be a cock. When I am biggest of all I shall be a coachman." (The coachman who drove their carriage seemed to impress him even more than did his father).

After this independent and uninfluenced admission of the boy we can better understand the enormous excitement with which he was never tired of watching the goings on in the fowl-yard. He could conveniently observe in the hen-coop all the secrets of his own family about which no information was vouchsafed to him at home; the "helpful animals" shewed him in an unconcealed way everything he wanted to see, especially the continual sexual activity between cock and hen, the laying of eggs, and the creeping out of the young brood. The dwelling conditions at Árpád's are such that he had beyond all question been a ear-witness to similar proceedings (between the parents). The curiosity in this way aroused he then had to satisfy by insatiable gazing at animals.

We are also indebted to Árpád for the last confirmation of my assumption that the morbid dread of cocks was ultimately to be traced to the threat of castration for onanism.

One morning he asked the neighbour: "Tell me, why do people die?" (Answer: Because they get old and grow tired). "Hm! So my grandmother was also old? No! She wasn't old, and yet she died. Oh, when there's a God why does he always let me fall down. And why does he make people have to die?" Then he began to get interested in angels and souls, upon which he was given the explanation that they are only fairy-tales. At this he got quite rigid with fright and said: "No! That's not true! There are angels. I have seen one who carries the dead children to heaven." Then he asked, horrified: "Why do children die?"

"How long can one live?" It was only with great difficulty that he calmed down.

It turned out then that early on the same day the chamber-maid had suddenly lifted his bed-clothes and found him manipulating his penis, whereupon she threatened to cut it off. The neighbour tried to quiet him and told him that no harm would be done to him; every child did things of that sort. Upon which Árpád cried out indignantly: "That's not true! Not every child! My papa has never done anything like that."

Now we understand better his unquenchable rage towards the cock who wanted to do with his member what the grown-ups threatened to do, and his awe for this sexual animal which dared to do everything that filled him with terror; we also understand the cruel punishments that he pronounced on himself (on account of the onanism and the sadistic phantasies).

To complete the picture, so to speak, he began later on to occupy himself greatly with religious thoughts. Old, bearded Jews filled him with great respect, mixed with dread. He begged his mother to invite these beggars into the house. When one actually came, however, he would hide and watch him from a respectable distance; as one of these was going away the boy let his head hang down and said, "Now I am a beggar-fowl." Old Jews interested him, so he said, because they come "from God" (out of the temple).

In conclusion another utterance of Árpád's may be given which shews that he had not watched the goings on of the fowls so long for nothing. He told his neighbour one day in all seriousness: "I shall marry you and your sister and my three cousins and the cook, no, instead of the cook rather my mother." He wanted therefore, to be a real "cock of the roost."

CHAPTER X

I

The Symbolic Representation of the Pleasure and Reality Principles in the Oedipus Myth*

SCHOPENHAUER writes[1]: "Every work has its origin in a happy thought, and the latter gives the joy of conception; the birth, however, the carrying out, is, in my own case at least, not without pain; for then I stand before my own soul, like an inexorable judge before a prisoner lying on the rack, and make it answer until there is nothing left to ask. Almost all the errors and unutterable follies of which doctrines and philosophies are so full seem to me to spring from a lack of this probity. The truth was not found, not because it was unsought, but because the intention always was to find again instead some preconceived opinion or other, or at least not to wound some favourite idea, and with this aim in view subterfuges had to be employed against both other people and the thinker himself. *It is the courage of making a clean breast of it in face of every question that makes the philosopher. He must be like Sophocles' Oedipus, who, seeking enlightenment concerning his*

*Published in Imago, 1912.
[1]Letter to Goethe, dated November the 11th, 1815.

*terrible fate, pursues his indefatigable enquiry, even when
he divines that appalling horror awaits him in the answer.
But most of us carry in our hearts the Jocasta, who begs
Oedipus for God's sake not to enquire further; and we
give way to her, and that is the reason why philosophy
stands where it does.*[1] Just as Odin at the door of hell
unceasingly interrogates the old prophetess in her
grave, disregarding her opposition and refusals and
prayers to be left in peace, so must the philosopher
interrogate himself without mercy.   This philosophical
courage, however, which is the same thing as the
sincerity and probity of investigation that you attribute
to me, does not arise from reflection, cannot be wrung
from resolutions, but is an inborn trend of the mind."

The deep and compressed wisdom of these remarks
deserves to be discussed, and to be compared with the
results of psycho-analysis.

What Schopenhauer says about the psychical attitude
requisite for scientific (philosophical) production sounds
like the application of Freud's formula about the "principles of psychical happenings"[2] to the theory of
Science.   Freud distinguishes two such principles: the
pleasure-principle, which in the case of primitive beings
(animals, children, savages), as in that of the more
primitive mental states (in dreams, wit, phantasy,
neurosis, psychosis) plays the leading part and allows
processes to come about that only strive for the shortest
way of gaining pleasure, while the psychical activity
of acts that might create feelings of unpleasantness
(*Unlust*) is withdrawn (repression); then the reality-
principle, which presupposes a higher development and

[1] Not underlined in the original.
[2] Freud. Jahrb. d. Psychoanalyse, Bd. III, S. 1.

growth of the psychical apparatus, and has as its characteristic that "in place of the repression, which excluded a number of the incoming ideas as creative of unpleasantness (*Unlust*), impartial judgement appears, which has to decide whether a given idea is true or false, *i. e.* in harmony with reality or not, and which decides by comparison with the memory-traces of reality."

Only one kind of thought activity remains free from the tests of reality, even after the inauguration of the higher principle, and subject solely to the pleasure-principle, namely, phantasy, while it is Science that is most successful in overcoming the pleasure-principle.[1]

Schopenhauer's opinion, quoted above, on the mental disposition requisite for scientific activity would therefore run somewhat as follows if converted into Freud's terminology: the thinker may (and should) give his phantasy play, so as to be able to taste the "joy of conception"—new ideas are of course not to be had in any other way[2]—, but in order that these phantastic notions may evolve into scientific ideas they must first be submitted to a laborious testing by reality.

Schopenhauer recognised with acute perception that the greatest resistances raised against unprejudiced testing of reality, even in the case of a scientist, are not of an intellectual, but of an affective nature. Even the scientist has human failings and passions: vanity, jealousy, moral and religious bias tending to blind him to a truth that is disagreeable to him; and he is on y too inclined to regard as true an error that fits his personal system.

[1] Freud. Loc. cit., S. 4.
[2] See on this point Robitschek, "Symbolisches Denken in der chemischen Forschung," Imago, Jahrg. I, Heft 1.

Psycho-analysis can only complement Schopenhauer's postulate in a single point. It has found that the inner resistances may be fixed in the earliest childhood and may be completely unconscious; it therefore demands of every psychologist who enters on the study of the human mind that he should thoroughly investigate beforehand his own mental constitution—inborn and acquired—down to the deepest layers and with all the resources of the analytic technique.

Unconscious affects, however, may falsify the truth not only in psychology, but also in all other sciences, so we have to formulate Schopenhauer's postulate as follows: Everyone who works in Science should first submit himself to a methodical psycho-analysis.

The advantages that would accrue to Science from this deepened self-knowledge on the part of the scientist are evident. An enormous amount of power for work, which is now wasted on infantile controversies and priority disputes, could be put at the disposal of more serious aims. The danger of "projecting into Science as a generally valid theory peculiarities of one's own personality" (Freud[1]) would be much less. The hostile manner also in which, even nowadays, new unusual ideas or scientific propositions are received when put forward by unknown authors, unsupported by any authoritative personality, would give way to a more unprejudiced testing by reality. I will go so far as to maintain that, if this rule of self-analysis were observed, the development of the various sciences, which today is an endless series of energy-wasting revolutions and reactions, would pursue a much smoother, yet a more profitable and an accelerated course.

[1]Freud. "Ratschläge, etc." Zentralbl. f. Psychoanalyse, Jahrg. II.

It cannot be regarded as chance that the Oedipus myth immediately occurred to Schopenhauer when he wished to illustrate by a simile the correct psychical attitude of the scientist in mental production and the inner resistances that arise against this correct way of working.   Had he been—as we analysts are—convinced of the strict determination and determinability of *every* psychical act, this thought would surely have made him reflect.   For us, who are the fortunate possessors of the Freudian psychology (which like a mental Dietrich provides a ready key to so many locks that have till now been considered impossible to open), it is not at all difficult to retrieve this piece of analysis. This idea that occurred to Schopenhauer indicates his unconscious perception of the fact that of all inner resistances by far the most significant is the resistance against the infantile fixation on hostile tendencies against the father and on incestuous ones towards the mother.

These tendencies, which through the civilised education of the race and of the individual have become intensely disagreeable, and have therefore been repressed, draw with them into the repression a large number of other ideas and tendencies associated with these complexes, and exclude them from the free interchange of thought, or at all events no longer allow them to be treated with scientific objectivity.

The "Oedipus complex" is not only the nuclear complex of the neuroses (Freud); the kind of attitude adopted towards it also determines the most important character traits of the normal man, and in part also the greater or lesser objectivity of the scientist.   A man of science who is prevented by the incest barrier from admitting to himself nascent inclinations of love and disrespect towards blood-relations will—so as to assure the repression of these inclinations—also not want, nor be able, to test in their reality with the impartiality demanded by Science the actions, works, and thoughts of other authorities as well as the paternal one.

To decipher the feeling and thought content that lies behind the wording of the Oedipus myth was thus beyond even the power of a Schopenhauer, otherwise so discerning. He overlooked the fact—as did the whole civilised world until Freud—that this myth is a distorted wish-phantasy, the projection of repressed wish-excitations (father-hate, mother-love) with an altered pleasure-prefix (abhorrence, shuddering awe) on to an external power, "fate." This reconstruction of the real meaning of the myth, its interpretation as a "material phenomenon" (Silberer), was thus alien to the philosopher. While writing this letter he was himself dominated—so I believe—by affects that would have debarred this insight.

The actual occasion that led Schopenhauer to choose this comparison of himself with Oedipus may be divined from the other parts of the letter. The neglected philosopher saw himself recognised for the first time by a man of Goethe's greatness and standing. He answered him with expressions of gratitude that we are not accustomed to from the proud, self-confident Schopenhauer: "Your Excellency's kind letter has given me great pleasure, because everything coming from you is for me of inestimable value, a sacred possession. Further, your letter contains the praise of my work, and your approval outweighs in my estimation that of any other."

That sounds absolutely like the enthusiastic gratitude of one man to an older respected one in whom he hopes to find the long-sought protector, *i. e.* to find again the father. Besides God, King, and national heroes, heroes of the spirit like Goethe are also *"revenants"* of the father for countless men, who transfer to them all the feelings of gratitude and respect that they once shewed to their bodily father. The subsequent quotation of the Oedipus myth, however, may well have been an unconscious reaction against this—perhaps rather extravagant—expression of gratitude towards the father, a reaction that allowed some display of the hostile tendencies that go to make up the fundamentally ambivalent feeling-attitude of a son towards his father. In favour of this view speaks the fact that towards the end the letter becomes more and more proud and self-confident. Schopenhauer there asks Goethe to secure the publication of his chief work (Die Welt als Wille und Vorstellung), and now speaks to him as to an equal; he lays a eulogising emphasis on the unusual value of his book, the remarkable nature of its contents, and the beauty of its style, closing with a few cool, business-like lines, which might perhaps be called brusque. "I will ask you please to give me a quite decisive answer without delay, because in case you do not accept my proposal I will commission someone who is going to the Leipsic fair to seek a publisher there for me."

Perhaps it was just the aid of the attention that had been deviated from the concrete meaning that enabled Schopenhauer to decipher in this letter the "functional symbolism" (which for some time escaped even psychoanalysts) of certain details of the Oedipus myth.

Silberer gives the name of functional symbol-phenomena to those pictures occurring in dreams, phantasies, myths, etc, in which not the content of thought and imagination, but the way of functioning of the mind (*e. g.* its ease, difficulty, inhibition, etc) is indirectly represented.[1]

If we allow Schopenhauer's comparison and translate it into analytical-scientific language, we have to say that the two chief personages of Sophocles' tragedy also symbolise the two principles of mental activity. Oedipus, "who, seeking enlightenment concerning his terrible fate, pursues his indefatigable enquiry, even when he divines that appalling horror awaits him in the answer," represents the reality-principle in the human mind, which permits none of the emerging ideas, even those that produce pain, to be repressed, but bids all to be equally tested as to their intrinsic truth. Jocasta, "who begs Oedipus for God's sake not to enquire further," is the personification of the pleasure-principle, which, regardless of objective truth, wants nothing else than to spare the ego pain, to gain pleasure wherever possible, and, so as to reach this goal, bans to the unconscious whenever possible all ideas and thoughts that threaten to set free pain.

Encouraged by Schopenhauer's interpretation and its striking analytical confirmation, I venture to go a step further and to raise the question whether it is pure chance that in both the Oedipus myth and the Edda Saga, also cited by our philosopher, the reality-principle is represented by men (Oedipus, Odin) and the pleasure-principle by women (Jocasta, Erda). The

[1]Cp. Silberer's throughout original and pregnant works on symbolism, especially those in the Jahrb. d. Psychoanalyse, Bd. I-III.

psycho-analyst is not accustomed to fly hastily to the idea of "accident," and would incline rather to attribute to the Greek and Teutonic peoples, as well as to Sophocles and Schopenhauer, an unconscious knowledge of the bisexuality of every human being. Schopenhauer actually says that most human beings carry in them Oedipus and Jocasta. In accord with this interpretation is the observation of daily experience that in general in women the tendency to repression—the pleasure-principle, therefore—prevails; in men the capacity for objective judgement and for tolerating painful insight—the reality-principle, therefore.

An eye made keen by individual-psychological experience will certainly be able to discover and solve many more significant symbols in Sophocles' tragedy. I will only point out two very striking ones, both of the category of "somatic symbol-phenomena"(Silberer), in which, therefore, bodily states are mirrored. To start with, there is the name of the tragic hero Oedipus, which in Greek means "swell-foot." This apparently senseless and odd denomination at once loses this character when we know that in dreams and jokes, as well as in the fetishistic worship of the foot or in the neurotic dread of this member, it symbolises the male organ.

The fact that this member is described in the hero's name as swollen is sufficiently explained by its erectibility. It cannot surprise us, by the way, that the myth completely identifies with a phallus the man who achieved the monstrous feat of sexual intercourse with the mother, a feat no doubt conceived as superhuman.

The other somatic symbol-phenomenon is Oedipus' self-blinding as a punishment for his unconscious committed sins. It is true that the tragedian gives the explanation for this punishment: "For why was I to see, When to descry No sight on earth could have a charm for me?"[1] he makes Oedipus (not quite unequivocally) cry out. But certain psycho-analytical experiences, in which the eyes regularly have to be interpreted as symbols of the genital organs, give me the right to interpret the self-blinding as a displacement of the really intended self-castration of Oedipus, the talion punishment more comprehensible in this connection. To the horrified question of the Chorus, however;

Rash man, how could'st thou bear to outrage so
Thine eyes? What Power was it, what wrought on thee?

the hero answers:

> Apollo, Apollo fulfils,
> O friends, my measure of ills—
> Fills my measure of woe.

In other words, it was the sun (Phoebus Apollo), the most typical father-symbol;[2] the hero was no longer to look him in the eyes, a consideration that may have given a second determining factor for the distortion of the castration punishment to blinding.[3]

[1](I quote throughout from Sir George Young's translation of the Oedipus Tyrannus. Transl.)

[2]Freud. "Nachtrag zur Analyse Schrebers," Jahrb. d. Psychoanalyse, Bd. III.

[3]These symbol interpretations will be at once evident to the practised psycho-analyst, since he can find them confirmed in his dream analyses countless times. While reading through this article, however, I received from Dr. Otto Rank the information that the correctness both of the interpretation of the name Oedipus here attempted and that of the sexual-symbolic explanation of self-binding could be determined with certainty from comparative mythological studies. In his work that has just appeared, "Das Inzest-motiv in Dichtung und Sage," these interpretations are substantiated with a rich collection of facts, which makes it possible for the non-analyst also to accept them.

If we have once assimilated these interpretations, it must amaze us to see how the folk-soul should have managed to fuse together in this myth the knowledge (distorted, it is true) of the most significant content, the nuclear complex of the unconscious (*i. e.* the parental complex), with the most general and comprehensive formula of mental activity. Our amazement gives way to understanding, however, when we have learnt from Otto Rank's fundamental mytho-psychological works to grasp the way in which the creative folk-soul works. Rank shewed in a beautiful example[1] that the individual poet "by means of his own complex-tones succeeds in clarifying and emphasising certain attributes of a transmitted material," but that the so-called folk-productions are also to be regarded as the work of numerous or countless individuals, who originate, transmit, and decorate the tradition. "Only in this case," he says further, "the story goes through a series of similarly disposed individual minds, each of which works in the same direction, at the production of general human motives and the polishing of many disturbing accessory works."

After the double interpretation of the Oedipus myth we may imagine the crystallising process of our myth, described by Rank, somewhat as follows:

Significant but unconscious psychical contents (aggressive phantasies against the father, sexual hunger for the mother with erection-tendencies, dread lest the father would avenge the sinful intent with the punishment of castration) procured, each for itself, indirect symbolic representatives in the consciousness of all men. Men with special creative capacities, poets,

[1]Rank. "Der Sinn der Griselda-Fabel," Imago. Jahrg. I, Heft 1.

give expression to these universal symbols. In this way the mythical motives of exposure by the parents, victory over the father, unconscious intercourse with the mother, and self-blinding, might have arisen in individuals independent of one another. In the course of the passage of the myths through countless poetic individual minds, one that Rank has made probable, condensation of the separate motives led secondarily to a greater unity, which then proved to be durable and which was fashioned anew in much the same form by all peoples and at all times.[1]

It is probable, however, that in this, as also in every other myth, and perhaps indeed with mental productivity in general, parallel with the tendency to give expression to psychical contents there is also an unconscious aim at bringing to presentation the mental ways of functioning that are operative in mastering these contents.[2] Only this latter fusion then yields the perfected myth, which without foregoing any of its effect on men is transmitted unchanged for hundreds of years. So was it with the Oedipus myth, in which not only the most deeply repressed feeling and thought complexes of mankind are represented in images, but also the play of the mental forces that were operative in the attempt to master these contents, differing according to sex and individuality.

For the correctness of this interpretation let some passages from the tragedy itself bear witness:

[1] See on this point Rank, Der Mythus von der Geburt des Helden, (Schriften zur angewandten Seelenkunde, Heft V).

[2] Silberer, to whom we owe the formulation of the idea of functional symbolism, cites a long series of myths and fairy-tales that can be resolved into both material and functional symbol-phenomena. ("Phantasie und Mythos," Jahrb. d. Psychoanalyse, Bd. II .

Oedipus: - And how can I help dreading
   My mother's bed?

Jocasta: But why should men be fearful,
  O'er whom Fortune is mistress, and fore-
   knowledge
  Of nothing sure? *Best take life easily,*[1]
  As a man may. For that maternal wedding,
  Have you no fear; for many men ere now
  Have dreamed as much; but he who by
   such dreams
  Sets nothing, has the easiest life of it.

   * * * * *

Jocasta (to OEDIPUS, *who, enquiring after the frightful truth, summons the only witness of the crime*):
   Why ask who 'twas he spoke of?
  Nay, never mind—never remember it—
  'Twas idly spoken!

Oedipus: Nay, it cannot be
  That having such a clue I should refuse
  To solve the mystery of my parentage!

Jocasta: For heaven's sake, if you care for your own
   life,
  Don't seek it! I am sick, and that's enough!

   * * * * *

Jocasta: But I beseech you, hearken! Do not do it!
Oedipus: I will not hearken—not to know the whole.
Jocasta: I mean well; and I tell you for the best!
Oedipus: What you call best is an old sore of mine.
Jocasta: *Wretch, what thou art O might'st thou never*
   know!

   * * * * *

[1]The passages in Italics are not underlined in the original.

Oedipus: *Break out what will, I shall not hesitate,*
           Low though it be, to trace the source of me.

    *   *   *   *   *

*Shepherd (who was ordered to kill the new-born Oedipus,
but who exposed him to the open):*
         O, I am at the horror, now, to speak!
Oedipus: And I to hear. But I must hear—no less.

"The Jocasta in us," as Schopenhauer says, the
pleasure-principle, as we express it, wishes thus that
a man "should best take life easily, as a man may,"
that he "set no store by" (suppresses) the things that
disturb him, *e. g.* that with the most superficial motiva-
tion he should refuse to accord any significance to
phantasies and dreams about the death of his father and
sexual intercourse with his mother, pay no attention
to disagreeable and dangerous talk, not search after
the origin of things, but above all it warns a man
against recognising who he is.

The reality-principle, however, the Oedipus in the
human soul, does not allow the seductions of pleasure
to keep him from penetrating into even a bitter or a
horrible truth, it estimates nothing so lowly as to be
not worth testing, it is not ashamed to seek the true
psychological nucleus of even superstitious prophecies
and dreams, and learns to endure the knowledge that
in the inmost soul aggressive and sexual instincts
dwell that do not pause even at the barriers erected by
civilisation between the son and his parents.

II

*On Eye Symbolism**

Relying on psycho-analytical experience, I have tried to interpret Oedipus' self-blinding as a self-castration.[1] I wish here to relate shortly the facts on which I relied for the purpose of this interpretation.

1. A young lady suffered from a phobia of sharp objects, especially needles. Her obsessive fear ran: such an object might sometime put out her eyes. Closer investigation of the case disclosed the fact that the lady had for a number of years lived with her friend in sexual intimacy, but had anxiously guarded against permitting the intermissio penis, which would have impaired her anatomical integrity by rupturing the hymen. All sorts of accidents now kept happening to her, most of which affected the eye; most commonly unintentional self-inflicted injuries with needles. Interpretation: Substitution of the genitals by the eyes, and representation of the wishes and fears relating to the former by accidental actions and phobias relating to the latter.

2. A myopic patient with conscious fears of inferiority and compensating grandiose phantasies transferred all his hypochondriac and anxious feelings, and an exaggerated sense of shame, on to his short-sightedness; these feelings, however, relate in his unconscious to the genitals. When a small child he had sexual "omnipotent phantasies" concerning his mother

---

*Published in the Internat. Zeitschr. f. ärztl. Psychoanalyse, 1913, as a contribution to the symposium on eye symbolism.
[1] See Chapter X, Section 1.

and sister; later on painful realisation of his sexual inferiority ("small penis" complex, hypochondria, "states of weakness"), which was compensated for by excessive onanism and sadistic acts of coitus. With the help of the symbolic equating: eye = genital, he managed to represent by means of the eye a great part of his sexual wishes and fears. An incomplete analytic enlightenment reduced his hypochondria very appreciably.

3. I had the opportunity of getting to know a family whose members suffered without exception from an exaggerated fear of injuries and diseases of the eye. The mere mention of bad or injured eyes made them get pale, and the sight of such things could lead to fainting. In one member of the family the psychical disturbances of potency could be recognised to be the manifestations of masochism which had appeared as a reaction against sadistic desires; the fear of eye injuries was the reaction to the sadistic wish to injure the eye, a displacement of the sadistic coitus wish. It had been very easy for the sadistic-masochistic components of the sexual instinct to be transferred from the genital to another organ susceptible to injury.

Another member of this family extended fear and disgust for eyes on to corns as well; in this not only the external resemblance and the identity of the name,[1] but a second symbolic equating (toe = penis) played a part. This was evidently an attempt to bring the symbol (eye) once more nearer to the real thing (genital organ) with the help of a mediate idea (corn).

4. A patient who was afraid of beetles when a child

---

[1] (Corns in German are called "Hühneraugen," literally "fowls' eyes." Transl.).

developed at the time of puberty a dread of seeing himself in a mirror, especially of seeing his own eyes and eyebrows. This dread turned out to be on the one hand an auto-perception of his tendency to repression (not wanting to look himself in the eye), on the other hand a representation of the fear of onanism. With the help of the idea of movability the child succeeded in displacing his attention and affects from the spontaneously movable (erectile) organ on to the movable beetle. The beetle's vulnerability also, the way in which even a child can so easily crush it under foot, renders it a suitable object for taking the place of the original object of attack, the sexual organ. A further displacement then set the equally movable and vulnerable eye in place of the beetle. I might also mention that in Hungarian the pupil is designated by a word meaning literally, "eye-beetle."

5. In a whole series of anxiety dreams (mostly recollected from childhood) eyes figure that grow alternately larger and smaller. From the total context I have had to regard these eyes as symbols of the male sexual organ in its changing size (erection). The apparent change in size of the eyes on opening and closing the lids is obviously used by the child to represent genital processes that are accompanied by changes in size. Children's dread, often excessive, of their parents' eyes has also, in my opinion, a sexual-symbolic root.

6. In another series of dreams, eyes (as paired organs) represent the testicles. Since the face (apart from the hands) is the only uncovered part of the body, children have to satisfy all their curiosity relating to other parts of the body on the head and face of their adult friends, especially the parents. Each part of the face thus

becomes the representative of one or more genital areas. The face is specially well adapted (nose in the middle between the eyes and eyebrows, with the mouth below) for representation of the penis, testicles, pubic hair, and anus.

I have no doubt that the sense of embarrassment one experiences on being stared at, and which keeps one from staring hard at others, finds its explanation in the sexual-symbolic significance of the parts of the face. This must also go to explain the marked effect of the hypnotiser's eyes on his medium. I may refer also to the sexual symbolism in ogling, in the bashful drooping of the eyes, casting of the eyes on someone, etc., further such expressions as "to cast eyes at someone, to throw sheep's eyes,"[1] etc.

7. Finally I may relate the case of an obsessional patient who confirmed subsequently my interpretation of Oedipus' self-blinding. As a child he was unusually spoilt, fixed on his parents, but very bashful and modest. One day he learnt from other children the real course of sexual relations between the parents. At this he displayed intense anger at his father, often with the conscious phantasy that he was castrating him (the father), which was always followed, however, by remorse and self-punishment. Now one of these self-punishments was that he destroyed the eyes in his own portrait. I was able to explain to the patient that in doing so he was only expiating in a disguised way the castration he had wished to perform on his father, in accordance with the Mosiac talion threat of punishment, "an eye for an eye, and a tooth for a tooth," which, by the way, takes for example just the two

[1] (Cp. the modern slang expression, "to make a glad eye." Transl.)

castration symbols, blinding and tooth-extraction.[1]

In a work on the stages in the development of the sense of reality[2] I have attempted to explain the origin of symbolism from the impulse to represent infantile wishes as being fulfilled, by means of the child's own body. The symbolic identification of external objects with bodily organs makes it possible to find again, on the one hand, all the wished-for objects of the world in the individual's body, on the other hand, the treasured organs of the individual's body in objects conceived in an animistic manner. The tooth and eye symbolism would be examples of the fact that bodily organs (principally the genital ones) can be represented not only by objects of the outer world, but also by other organs of the body. In all probability this is even the more primary kind of symbol-creation.

I imagine that this symbolic equating of genital organs with other organs and with external objects originally happens only in a playful way, out of exuberance, so to speak. The equations thus arising, however, are secondarily made to serve repression, which seeks to weaken one member of the equation, while it symbolically over-emphasises the other, more harmless one by the amount of the repressed affect. In this way the upper half of the body, as the more harmless one, attains its sexual-symbolic significance, and so comes about what Freud calls "Displacement from below upwards." In this work of repression the eyes have proved to be specially adapted to receive the affects displaced from the genital region, on account of their shape and changeable size, their movability, their high

[1] See my remarks on tooth-symbolism in Chapter VI.
[2] Chapter VIII.

value, and their sensitiveness. It is to be supposed, however, that this displacement would not have succeeded so well, had not the eye already had from the beginning that significant libidinous value that Freud describes in his "Sexualtheorie" as a special component of the sexual instinct (the impulse of sexual visual curiosity).

III

The Ontogenesis of Symbols*

Dr. Beaurain's remarks[1] about the ways in which the child comes to form its first general concepts can be fully confirmed by whoever has had the opportunity to watch the mental development of the child, either directly, or else indirectly *via* parents whose powers of observation had been psychologically sharpened. There can be no doubt that the child (like the unconscious) identifies two things on the basis of the slightest resemblance, displaces affects with ease from one to the other, and gives the same name to both. Such a name is thus the highly condensed representative of a large number of fundamentally different individual things, which, however, are in some way or other (even if ever so distantly) similar and are for this reason identified. Advance in the knowledge of reality (intelligence) then manifests itself in the child in the progressive resolution of such condensation-products into their elements, in learning to distinguish from one another things that are

*Published in the Internat. Zeitschr. f. ärztl. Psychoanalyse, 1913.
[1]Beaurain, "Ueber das Symbol und die psychischen Bedingungen für sein Entstehen beim Kinde," in the same number of the Zeitschrift.

similar in one respect but otherwise different. Many writers have already rightly grasped and described this process; Silberer's and Beaurain's communications on the subject have brought further confirmation and have deepened our insight into the details of this developmental process in the mind.

All these authors see in the infantile inadequacy of the capacity for making distinctions the chief factor in the origination of the ontogenetic and phylogenetic preliminary stages of the knowledge processes.

I should like here to raise an objection only against designating all these preliminary stages in knowledge with the word "Symbol;" similes, allegories, metaphors, allusions, parables, emblems, and indirect representations of every sort might also in a certain sense be conceived as products of this lack of sharpness in distinction and definition, and yet they are not—in the psycho-analytical sense—symbols. Only such things (or ideas) are symbols in the sense of psycho-analysis as are invested in consciousness with a logically inexplicable and unfounded affect, and of which it may be analytically established that they owe this affective over-emphasis to *unconscious* identification with another thing (or idea), to which the surplus of affect really belongs. Not all similes, therefore, are symbols, but only those in which the one member of the equation is repressed into the unconscious.[1] Rank and Sachs conceive a symbol in the same sense[2] "We understand by this," they say, "a special kind of indirect repre-

[1] See on this matter my remarks in earlier articles, Ch. VI, Ch. VIII, Ch. X, Sect. 2, and my review on Jung's Libido essay in the Internat. Zeitschr. f. ärztl. Psychoanalyse, Jahrg. I, S. 393.

[2] Rank und Sachs. Die Bedeutung der Psychoanalyse für die Geisteswissenschaften. 1913. S. 11. et seq . .

sentation which is distinguished by certain peculiarities from other allied kinds, such as the simile, the metaphor, the allegory, the allusion, and other forms of figurative representation of thought-material (of the rebus variety)", and "it is a substitutive, illustrative replacement-expression for something hidden."

This being so, it is more prudent not to assume that the conditions under which symbols arise are identical with those for analogy-formation in general, but to presuppose for this specific kind of analogy-formation specific conditions of origin, and to search for these.

Now analytical experience shews us in fact that although the condition of intellectual insufficiency has to be fulfilled with the formation of real symbols as well, the chief conditions for their production are not of an intellectual, but of an affective nature. I will demonstrate this with individual examples from sexual symbolism.

So long as the necessities of life do not compel them to adaptation and therewith to the knowledge of reality, children concern themselves to begin with only about the satisfaction of their instincts, *i. e.* about the parts of the body where this satisfaction takes place, about the objects suited to evoke this, and about the actions that actually evoke the satisfaction. Of the sexually excitable parts of the body (erogenous zones), for instance, they are specially interested in the mouth, the anus, and the genitals. "What wonder, then, if also his attention is arrested above all by those objects and processes of the outer world that on the ground of ever so distant a resemblance remind him of his dearest experiences."[1] Thus comes about the "sexualisation

[1] Ch. VIII. P. 193.

of everything "[1] In this stage small boys are prone to apply the childish term for genitals to all long objects, they see an anus in every hole, urine in every fluid, and faeces in every softish material.

A boy, aged about one and a half, said when he was first shewn the Danube: "What a lot of spit!" A two-year-old boy called everything that could open, a door, including even his parents' legs, since these can open and shut (be abducted and adducted).

Similar analogies are formed also within the sphere of the bodily organs themselves: Penis and tooth, anus and mouth, become equated. Perhaps the child finds an equivalent in the upper part of the body (especially on the head and face) for every affectively important part of the lower half.

This equating, however, is not yet symbolism. Only from the moment when as the result of cultural education the one member of the equation (the more important one) is repressed, does the other previously less important member attain affective over-significance and become a symbol of the repressed one. Originally penis and tree, penis and church-steeple, were consciously equated; but only with the repression of the interest in the penis do the tree and church-steeple become invested with inexplicable and apparently ungrounded interest; they become penis symbols.

In this way also eyes become symbols of the genitalia, with which they had previously been identified—on the ground of extrinsic resemblance. There thus comes about a symbolic over-emphasis of the upper half of the body in general, after interest in the lower half has been repressed, and all genital symbols that play such

[1](A well-known expression of the philologist Kleinpaul. Transl.).

an extensive part in dreams (necktie, snake, tooth-drawing, box, ladder, etc.) must have originated ontogenetically in the same way. I should not be surprised if in a dream of the boy mentioned above a door re-appeared as a symbol of the parental lap, and in a dream of the other boy's the Danube as a symbol of bodily fluids.

I desired with these examples to point out the over-whelming significance of affective factors in the production of true symbols. It is they that have to be taken into consideration in the first place when one wishes to distinguish symbols from other psychical products (metaphors, similes, etc.), which are also the result of condensation. One-sided consideration of formal and rational conditions in the explanation of psychical processes can easily lead one astray.

For instance, one was formerly inclined to believe that things are confounded because they are similar; nowadays we know that a thing is confounded with another only because certain motives for this are present; similarity merely provides the opportunity for these motives to function. In the same way it must be said that apperceptive insufficiency alone, without consideration of the motives impelling towards analogy-formation, do not adequately explain the creation of symbols.

CHAPTER XI

(*Contribution to the Psychology of "System-Constructions"*)

I

THE sister of a young artist called on me one day and told me that her brother A., a very talented man, had been behaving for some time in a very peculiar manner. He had read a doctor's treatise on the serum treatment of tuberculosis,[1] since when he had been the whole time concerned only about himself, had got his urine and sputum examined for abnormal constituents, and, although there were none present, had undergone the serum treatment with the doctor in question. It was soon plain that it was not a question of a simple hypochondriac moodiness with him. Not only the treatise, but also the doctor's personality made an unusual impression on him. When on one occasion the doctor treated him in a rather off-hand way, he immersed himself in making notes (which the sister gave me to

---

*Published in the Internat. Zeitschr. f. ärztl. Psychonalyse, 1914.
[1]This treatise, which traced almost all nervous and psychical disturbances to tuberculosis, and advised a corresponding treatment, gave my psychoneurotics plenty to do.

read) of endless worryings as to how this behaviour of
the doctor could be harmonised with the fact that he
was a real *savant* (which he did not venture to doubt).
It then turned out that his hypochondriacal ideas were
interwoven in a larger philosophical system, built, so
to speak, into the structure of the latter. For a long
time the young man had been interested in Ostwald's
natural philosophy, and was an eager follower of his;
the energetic main idea and the marked emphasis laid
on the economic principle in Ostwald's proposals had
made a specially deep impression on him. The statement that one should accomplish as much as possible
with as little expenditure of energy as possible he
wanted to realise in every respect in the practical affairs
of his life, but in doing so he went to extremes that struck
even his sister (who had a specially high estimation of
her brother's intelligence) as peculiar. So long as he
only prescribed (in writing) uncommonly exact arrangements for the day, in which every bodily and every
kind of mental activity was allotted a definite time,
he might still have passed as a specially dutiful pupil
of his master, but later he began to exaggerate the
tendency to economy to such an extent as to drive it—
unconsciously, of course—to downright absurdity.
This became most evident when the amalgamation
with the hypochondriacal ideas came about. He experienced paraesthesias in the most diverse organs,
among others in the legs; he remarked that the latter
ones disappeared when he lifted his leg. In order, now,
to deflect his attention (whose energy, according to his
convictions, he felt obliged to employ for more valuable
matters than the perception of bodily states) from the
sensations in the leg, his sister had to hold his leg up in

the air so that he could engross himself in thought undisturbed, the most valuable accomplishment of which he was capable. The sister often faithfully carried out this wish. Gradually he came to see that he ought really not to perform any work at all himself except thinking; the carrying out of his ideas in detail— a subordinate task—must be left to people with feebler capacities. In this way he finally became occupied only with the statement of problems, and employed his whole time in reflecting on ultimate scientific, psychological, and philosophical questions. He directed those around him to see to it, in ways exactly prescribed by him, that he had absolute rest during his mental work. All this still would not have caused his family any serious solicitude had he not given himself up to complete inactivity, after having up till then conscientiously carried out his projects. In his endeavour to work "with the most favourable coefficients possible" he had thus brought himself to a point where he neglected the tasks that lay nearest to hand (since they could not be literally harmonised with the theory of energetic economy); the precept of creating in the most economic way possible thus served him, and quite consistently, for the purpose of giving up creating altogether. He lay inactive for hours in certain artificially arranged positions. This latter I had to regard as a variety of catatonic posture, and the purely psychical symptoms as fragments of hypochondriacal and megalomaniac ideas; I gave the patient's family to understand that I considered the case to be one of paranoid paraphrenia (dementia praecox), and that the young man needed for the time being to be certified as insane. The family at first refused to accept the diagnosis and the advice, although I left open the possibility that it might prove to be a slight and passing attack.

Soon after, the sister came again and told me that the brother had begged her to sleep in his room, on the ground that he felt better so, which was good for his mental capacity; the sister assented to his wishes. For a few nights he did nothing but get her to hold his leg up. Then he began to talk to her of erotic longings and erections, which disturbed him in his work. In between he spoke of his father, who, he said, had treated him too strictly, and towards whom he had until then felt coldly; only now had he discovered in her, as in the father, their fondness for him. Suddenly he said: It was against energetic economy for him to satisfy his erotic needs with strange women and for money; it would be simpler and less trouble, not to mention without danger or expense: in a word, more economical, if the sister, in the interest of his psychical capacity and faithfully following the "energetic imperative," gave herself to him. After this occurrence (which, by the way, the sister kept secret), and after the patient had threatened to commit suicide, he was committed to an asylum.

II

A very intelligent young man, B., who besides punctiliously fulfilling his official duties achieved quite remarkable poetic accomplishments, and whose development I had watched for over fourteen years, was always recognised by me to be one of those insane persons, with delusions of grandeur and of persecution, who know how to keep their symptoms within such bounds that they can still exist in society. Since I liked his literary works and had several times tried—in vain, however—to direct the interest of some prominent people to him, he became very fond of me. He called on me about once a month, told me his troubles as to a father-confessor, and always went away to some extent relieved. At his work his colleagues and superiors— so he told me—placed him in the most painful situations. According to him, he always did his duty, indeed, as a rule, more than was asked of him, and still (or perhaps for that very reason!) they were all hostile to him. They were evidently envious of him on account of his superior intelligence and his high connections. When asked about the annoyances under which he had to suffer, he could only give as examples some trivial jokes of his colleagues and a degree of disdain on the chief's part that did not go beyond what is common enough. He took his revenge in making a special note of all the pieces of carelessness, of slackness, and of rule-breaking, also of supposed unfair advantages, with which the other officials could be charged. From time to time, when his pent-up discontent broke out in open rebellion, he would rake up all these matters, mostly quite things of the past, and bring them to the knowledge of the director, with the result that he himself always incurred unpleasantnesses and reproofs, but sometimes his colleagues and superiors likewise. Finally he really managed to embroil himself with almost everybody, and so was spared the trouble of having to construe his colleagues' hostility out of trivial indications; he got himself thoroughly hated; every department was glad to get rid of him, and made use of every opportunity to get him transferred to another.   After such transferences there were also "transference-improvements."[1] With every new chief he expected that his virtues would at last be recognised, and with each he believed that he could remark unequivocal signs of special esteem for his capacities and of great liking for him; but soon enough it would turn out that the new chief was no better than the previous ones.   To be sure, these previous ones had without doubt denounced him to the new chief; the whole lot of them hung together, etc. It went just as badly with him in his literary activity. Those writers who were already recognised constituted themselves—so he told me—into a community of mutual interests, a "maffia," which kept back young talents.   And yet, according to him, his works were fit to stand beside the most renowned ones in the literature of the world.

As regard sexuality his wants always seemed to be slight.   He had sometimes noticed that he was inexplicably fortunate with women, he pleased them all without bothering himself much about them, he had to take great care of himself in regard to them, etc., (*i. e.* in addition to the delusions of persecution and grandeur he also produced those of erotomania).

From communications made from time to time, the deeper layers also of his mental existence became known to me.   He lived in poor circumstances, a fact that led to an early estrangement with his father, whom to begin with he had tenderly loved; he then transferred

---

[1] (*Versetzungsbesserungen:* A term used in German psychiatry to denote the improvements that often come about with insane patients merely as the result of their being transferred from one locality, or part of the asylum, to another. Transl.)

(in his phantasy) the father-part to an uncle, who had had considerable success in literary renown and in social rank, but he was soon obliged to see that he had nothing to expect from this egoist, so withdrew his love from him also and made—as we saw—on the one hand vain attempts to find again the lost father-imago in his superiors, while on the other hand he withdrew his sexual hunger in a narcissistic way on to himself, and took delight in his own distinguished attributes and achievements.

About the twelfth year of our acquaintanceship, however, there came a break. In an over-intense indignation at a supposed piece of bad treatment he attacked his highest superior at the office (physically). This led to a tedious and painful investigation, which ended relatively favourably; the patient was declared to be "ill with his nerves" and was retired with a pension. At about the same time as this—perhaps rather earlier, but especially after his dismissal from his post—he began to take an extensive interest in psycho-analytical literature.[1] He read among other things my essay on the connection between paranoia and homosexuality. He put the question directly to me, whether I considered him to be a paranoiac and homosexual, and made very merry at the idea in a patronising way. Still the idea seemed to have taken root in him, and to have flourished alongside his prevailing inactivity in other directions, for one day he came to me, very excited and enthusiastic, saying that on thinking it over he had to agree with my opinion(!); he used really to suffer from delusions of persecution; it had come over

[1]As it seemed to me to be quite without prospects I did not want him to go through an analysis.

him like an illumination that deep down inside he was a homosexual; he recollected various incidents that directly confirmed this, in his opinion. Now, so he said, he was able to explain the curious sensations—half fearful, half libidinous—that he always experienced in the presence of an older friend or patron; he also understood now why he had the tendency to come so near to me physically that he could feel my breath in his face.[1] He now knew, further, why he accused certain patrons of having homosexual intentions in regard to him; it was simply that the wish was father to the thought.

I was very pleased at this turn, not only out of consideration for the patient's welfare, but also because the case supported my secret hope that perhaps after all the outlook for the treatment of paranoia in general might not be quite so desperate as it has seemed.

A few days later the patient came back again. He was still excited, but no longer so euphoric. He was very afraid, he told me; the homosexual phantasies that swept over him were more and more intolerable; he saw large phalli in front of him, which disgusted him; he kept fancying paederastic situations with other men (also with myself). I tried—successfully—to calm him, telling him that it was only because of their unaccustomed nature that these phantasies had such an effect on him, and that later on he would certainly not have so much to suffer from the ideas.

Then for a few days I heard nothing of him, until one of the members of his family called to tell me that the patient, who for the past two or three days had been

[1]This peculiarity of his I had already noticed in fact and had interpreted in the sense of transferred erotism; naturally I had taken care not to call his attention to it nor to explain the symptom to him.

inaccessible, had hallucinations, kept talking to himself, and had broken into his uncle's house the day before, and then into a magnate's palace, where he created a disturbance. Ejected from here, he went home, and lay in bed refusing to speak a word; every now and then, however, he was quite clear and assured them that there was nothing wrong with him and that he was not to be transported to an asylum.

I visited the patient and found him in a deep catatonic state (rigid posture, negativism, inaccessibility, hallucinations). When I came in he appeared to recognise me and shook hands, but immediately after he fell back into the catatonic stupor. It took weeks before he gradually improved a little in the asylum where he was confined, and months before he could be discharged from there—improved. When I saw him again he did not have complete insight into his pathological state—he objectified some of his feelings of being aggrieved, and a part of the old paranoiac delusional formation was again active; on the other hand, he fled terrified from homosexual thoughts, denied that he was suffering from a psychosis, and no longer believed in the causal connection between his psychical experiences and homosexuality. Naturally I did not try to penetrate further into his mind, nor to restore his previous convictions. From now on the patient avoided me in a striking manner; I gathered later that he had to be confined again because of a recurrence of his excitement, this time for a somewhat shorter period.

What is common to the two cases here communicated (apart from the latent homosexuality demonstrable in every case of paranoia and paraphrenia, a matter

I do not propose to discuss in more detail at this point)[1] is that they both throw an interesting light on the part played in.paranoia by the formation of delusional systems. The patient A. became ill in adopting *en bloc* a ready-made philosophical system (Ostwald's natural philosophy), instead of taking the trouble to construct a system of his own. Philosophical systems that seek to explain rationally the whole order of the world, leaving no room over for irrationality (*i. e.* for 'what is not yet explicable), have been, as is well-known, compared with the paranoiac delusional systems. At all events such systems excellently meet the needs of paranoiacs, whose symptoms spring from the impulse to explain rationally by the external order of the world their own irrational inner strivings. It may be very clearly seen here also how the adopted system gradually gets more and more made use of to rationalise the patient's own purely egocentric, repressed wishes (doing nothing, incestuous desires in regard to the sister).

Case B. shows again how fateful it may be for the paranoiac when the system that he has laboriously built up, and which allows him to be still socially active, is suddenly torn from him. B. succeeded in projecting all his ethically incompatible longings on to the environment in his office; he became the victim of a systematic persecution. Dismissed from his post, he had, so to speak, been robbed of his system; by chance he came across the psycho-analytical literature just at this time of the loss of his system, and this—although

[1]The reader may be referred to Freud's work on the subject ("Ein autobiogr. beschr. Fall von Paranoia," Jahrb. d. Psychoanalyse, Bd. III) and to my own, Chapter V of the present book.

he had previously heard something of it—for the first time was able to appear evident to him. For a short while he seemed inclined to exchange his persecution system for what in our opinion would be correct insight into his true personality, and to make friends with his own repressed complexes. But it soon became plain that this insight was unendurable to him, so that— since he had no other suitable system at his disposal, and since this made it possible for him to anchor at a second neurotic point of fixation[1]—he had to flee from the turmoil of morbid dread into dementia. He recovered from the paraphrenic attack only in so far as it was possible for him to do away once more with the psycho-analytical insight, and to reconstruct the persecution system.

The close relations, such as these, between system-formation and paranoia perhaps also explain the fact that there is always a large crowd of psychopathic hangers-on in the train of new scientific (*e. g.* physical and philosophical) systems, discoveries, and theories. In the therapeutic respect Case B. cautions us to uphold Freud's pessimistic opinion as to the psycho-analytic treatment of paranoia.[2]

The peculiar catatonic posture of patient A. (lying with upraised leg) deserves, in my opinion, special attention. The patient made the interpretation of this symptom easy by transferring to the sister the task of holding the leg, and by soon after approaching her

[1] (Referring to the fixation-point of paranoia at the narcissistic-homosexual stage of infancy, that of paraphrenia [dementia praecox] at the still earlier one of auto-erotism. Transl.)

[2] In contrast with Bjerre, who says he has cured a case of paranoia by analysis (Jahrb. d. Psychoanalyse, Bd. II). This case of Bjerre's was in my opinion, and Freud's, not a true paranoia.

with incestuous proposals. When we take into consideration the long known symbolic identification of leg and penis, we may regard this catatonic posture as a means of expression (and at the same time a defensive measure) of repressed erection-tendencies. It is thinkable that the collection of similar observations will explain in this sense catatonic rigidity in general. In support of this idea I can bring forward a third case.

III

A paraphrenic who had an uncommonly keen capacity for self-observation spontaneously explained to me that with all his curious catatonic postures and movements he was seeking to defend himself from erotic sensations in the various parts of the body concerned. The extreme bowing forwards of the body that he kept up for minutes at a time served, for instance, "to break the erection of the intestine."

CHAPTER XII

WHAT we have learned about homo-sexuality through psycho-analysis may be put together in a few sentences. The first and most important step towards a deeper knowledge of this instinct-aim was the supposition by Fliess and Freud[1] that really every human being traverses a psychically bisexual stage in his childhood.[2] The "homosexual component" falls later a victim to repression; only a minor part of this component gets rescued in a sublimated form in the cultivated life of adults, in playing, in readiness for social help, in friendship leagues, in club life, etc, a part that is not to be underestimated. Insufficiently repressed homosexuality can later, under certain circumstances, become once more manifest, or express itself in neurotic symptoms; this is especially the case with paranoia, concerning which the more recent investigations have

*Delivered at the Third Congress of the Internat. Psycho-Analytical Association at Weimar, October 1911; Published in the Internat. Zeitschr. f. Ärztl. Psychoanalyse, 1914.

[1]Freud, Drei Abhandlungen zur Sexualtheorie.

[2]On a previous occasion I proposed the use of the expression"ambisexual" instead of that of "bisexual," it being thereby expressed that the child in certain stage of development feels amphi-erotically, *i. e.* can transfer his sexual hunger to man and woman (father and mother) at the same time. In this way the contrast between Freud's conception and Fliess' theory of biological bisexuality would be clearly brought out.

been able to establish that it is really to be conceived as a disguised manifestation of the inclination towards the person's own sex.[1]

A newer point of view, which renders more easy the understanding of homosexuality, we owe to Sadger and Freud. Sadger discovered in the psycho-analysis of several male homosexuals that intense heterosexual inclinations had been displayed in their early childhood; indeed that their "Oedipus complex" (love for the mother, attitude of hate towards the father) had come to expression in a specially pronounced manner. He considered that the homosexuality which later develops in them is really only an attempt to restore the original relation to the mother. In the homosexual pleasure-objects of his desires the homosexual is unconsciously loving himself, while he himself (also unconsciously) is representing the feminine and effeminate part of the mother.

This loving of oneself in the person of another human being Sadger called Narcissism.[2] Freud has shewn us that narcissism possesses a much greater and more general significance than had been thought, and that every human being has to pass through a narcissistic stage of development. After the stage of "polymorphous-perverse" auto-erotism, and before the real choice of an external love-object takes place, every human being adopts himself as an object of love, in that he collects the previously autistic erotisms together into a unity, the "darling ego." Homosexuals are only more strongly fixed than other people in this

[1]Freud, Jahrb. d. Psychoanalyse, Bd. III; Ferenczi, Ch. V of the present book.

[2](Or, rather, borrowed the term from Naecke. Transl.).

narcissistic stage; the genital organ similar to their own remains throughout life an essential condition for their love.

All these pieces of knowledge, however, important as they are in themselves, give no explanation of the peculiarities of the sexual constitution and the special experiences that lie at the base of manifest homosexuality.

I may say at once that, in spite of much puzzling over them, I have not succeeded in solving these questions. The aim of this communication is nothing more than to bring forward some facts of experience and points of view that have spontaneously forced themselves on me in the course of many years' psychoanalytic observation of homosexuals, and which may be capable of rendering easier the correct nosological classification of homosexual clinical pictures.

It seemed to me from the beginning that the designation "homosexuality" was nowadays applied to dissimilar and unrelated psychical abnormalities. Sexual relations with members of a person's own sex are only a symptom, and this symptom may be the form in which the most diverse psychical disorders and disturbances of development, as well as normal life, appear. It was thus *a priori* improbable that everything to which the name "homosexuality" is now applied would in a simple way yield itself as a clinical unity. The two types of homosexuality, for example, distinguished as "active" and "passive" have been up to the present conceived as obviously two forms in which the same condition may appear; in both cases one spoke of "inversion" of the sexual instinct, of "contrary" sexual sensation, of "perversion," and overlooked the possibility that in this way one might be confounding two essentially different morbid states merely because a striking symptom is common to both. Yet even superficial observation of these two kinds of homo-erotism[1] shews that they belong—in the pure cases, at all events,—to quite different syndromes, and that the "acting" and the "suffering" homo-erotics represent fundamentally different types of men. Only the passive homo-erotic deserves to be called "inverted", only in his case does one see real reversal of normal psychical—and perhaps also bodily—characteristics, only he is a true "intermediate stage." A man who in intercourse with men feels himself to be a woman is inverted in respect to his own ego (homo-erotism through subject-inversion, or, more shortly, "subject-homo-erotism"); he feels himself to be a woman, and this not only in genital intercourse, but in all relations of life.

It is quite otherwise with the true "active homosexual." He feels himself a man in every respect, is as a rule very energetic and active, and there is nothing effeminate to be discovered in his bodily or mental organisation. The object of his inclination alone is exchanged, so that one might call him a homo-erotic through exchange of the love-object, or, more shortly, an object-homo-erotic.

A further striking difference between the "subjective" and the "objective" homo-erotic consists in the fact that the former (the invert) feels himself attracted by more mature, powerful men, and is on

[1] The word comes from Karsch-Haack (Das gleichgeschlechtliche Leben der Naturvölker, 1911) and is in my opinion preferable to the ambiguous expression homosexuality, since it makes prominent the psychical aspect of the impulse in contradistinction to the biological term "sexuality."

friendly terms, as a colleague, one might almost say, with women; the second type, on the contrary, is almost exclusively interested in young, delicate boys with an effeminate appearance, but meets a woman with pronounced antipathy, and not rarely with hatred that is badly, or not at all, concealed. The true invert is hardly ever impelled to seek medical advice, he feels at complete ease in the passive role, and has no other wish than that people should put up with his peculiarity and not interfere with the kind of satisfaction that suits him. Not having to fight with any inner conflicts, he can sustain fortunate love-relationships for years, and really fears nothing except external danger and being shamed. With all this his love is feminine to the finest details. He lacks the sexual overestimation, which according to Freud characterises a man's love; he is not very passionate, and, as a true Narcissus, chiefly demands from his lover the recognition of his bodily and other merits.

The object-homo-erotic, on the other hand, is uncommonly tormented by the consciousness of his abnormality; sexual intercourse never completely satisfies him, he is tortured by qualms of conscience, and overestimates his sexual object to the uttermost. That he is plagued with conflicts and never comes to terms with his condition is shewn by his repeated attempts to obtain medical help for his trouble. It is true that he often changes his companions in love, not from superficiality, however, as the invert does, but in consequence of painful disappointments and of the insatiable and unsuccessful pursuit of the love-ideal ("formation of series," as Freud calls it).

It may happen that two homo-erotics of different

types unite to make a pair. The invert finds in the object-homo-erotic a quite suitable lover, who adores him, supports him in material affairs, and is imposing and energetic; the man of the objective type, on the other hand, may find pleasure in just the mixture of masculine and feminine traits present in the invert. (I also know active homo-erotics, by the way, who exclusively desire non-inverted youths, and only content themselves with inverts in the absence of the former).[1]

However simply these two character pictures of homo-erotism lend themselves to distinction, they signify no more than a superficial description of syndromes so long as they are not submitted to the resolving procedure of psycho-analysis, which alone can render their mode of origin psychologically comprehensible.

Now I have had the opportunity of treating psycho-analytically a number of male homo-erotics; many for only a short period (a few weeks), others for months, a whole year, and even longer. Rather than narrate any anamneses in this summary, it seems to me more instructive to condense my impressions and experiences on homo-erotism into two psycho-analytical Galton photographs.[2]

[1] I am conscious that, when I call inverts "female" and object-homo-erotics "male," I am using terms the scope of which is not sufficiently sharply defined. It may be just indicated here that by maleness I understand activity (aggressivity) of the sexual hunger, highly developed object-love with overestimation of the object, a polygamy that is in only apparent contrast with the latter trait, and, as a distant derivative of the activity, intellectual talent; by femaleness I understand passivity (tendency to repression), narcissism and intuitiveness. The psychical attributes of sex are, of course, mingled in every individual—although in unequal proportion. (Ambisexuality).

[2] A further motive for this is consideration for the patients' anonymity, which it is especially important to preserve.

I may at once forestall the final result of my investigations: Psycho-analysis shewed me that the subject- and object-homo-erotism are really essentially different conditions. The former is a true "sexual intermediate stage" (in the sense of Magnus Hirschfeld and his followers), thus a pure developmental anomaly; object-homo-erotism, however, is a neurosis, an obsessional neurosis.

In both types of amphi-erotism[1] the deepest layers of the mind and the oldest memory-traces still bear testimony to the investment of both sexes, or the relationship to both parents, with sexual hunger. In the subsequent development, however, inversion and object-homo-erotism diverge far from each other.

We can dig down very deeply into the early history of the subject-homo-erotic and find already everywhere signs of his inversion, namely, the abnormal effeminate being. When merely a quite young child he imagined himself in the situation of his mother and not in that of his father; he even brings about an inverted Oedipus complex; he wishes for his mother's death so as to take her place with the father and be able to enjoy all her rights; he longs for her clothes, her jewelry, and of course also her beauty and the tendernesses shewn to her; he dreams of begetting children, plays with dolls, and is fond of dressing up as a girl. He is jealous of his mother, claims for himself all his father's tenderness, whereas his mother he rather admires as something enviably beautiful. In many cases it is plainly to be seen that the tendency to inversion, which is probably always constitutionally conditioned, is strengthened

[1] This word renders, I believe, the psychological character of what is intended better than the term "ambisexuality," previously suggested by me.

by external influences as well. "Only children" who
are spoilt, little favourites who grow up in an exclusively feminine environment, boys who, because they made
their appearance in the place of the girl that was
longed for, are brought up in a girlish way, can sooner
become inverted, given the corresponding predisposition in their sexual character.[1]

On the other hand, the narcissistic nature of a boy
can provoke excessive indulgence on the parents' part,
and so lead to a vicious circle.   Bodily attributes also—
girlish figure and features, a wealth of hair, and so on—
may contribute to the consummation of a boy being
treated as a girl.   In this way the father's preference
and its response may have arisen altogether as a
secondary process in relation to the child's narcissism;
I know cases in which a narcissistic boy provoked the
father's latent homo-erotism in the form of excessive
tenderness, the latter then contributing not a little to
the fixation of the former's own inversion.

Nor can psycho-analysis tell us anything new concerning the subsequent fate of these boys; they stay
fixed in this early stage of development, and become
finally such personalities as we know well enough from
the autobiographies of urnings.   I can here lay stress
on only a few points.   Coprophilia and pleasure in
smell are deeply repressed with them, often to the extent

[1]Among boys who grow up without a father homo-erotics are to be found
relatively often.   I imagine that the fixation on the Imago of the father who
was lost early or never known results, at least in part, from the fact that under such circumstances the otherwise unavoidable conflict between father
a nd son is absent. ("A man always credits fate twice as highly for something that is lacking as for something that he really possesses; thus my
mother's long accounts filled me with more and more longing for my father,
whom I no longer knew."   G. Keller, "Der grüne Heinrich," Cap. II.)   In
families where the father is alive, but is inferior or insignificant, the son
longs exceedingly for a "strong" man and remains inclined to inversion.

of aestheticism; there is a fondness for perfumes, and as a sublimation an enthusiasm for art. Characteristic, further, is their idiosyncrasy against blood and all bloody things. They are mostly very suggestible and can easily be hypnotised; they are fond of imputing their first seduction to the "suggestion" of a man who stared hard at them or otherwise pursued them. Behind this suggestion there lurks, of course their own traumatophilia.

Since analysis of inverts does not really elicit any affects that might result in changing his previous attitude towards the male sex, inversion (subject-homo-erotism) is to be regarded as a condition incurable by analysis (or by any kind o psychotherapy at all). Psycho-analysis does not remain, however, without any influence on the patient's behaviour; it removes any neurotic symptoms that may accompany the inversion, especially the morbid anxiety, which is often by no means slight. The invert acknowledges his homo-erotism more frankly after the analysis than before. It must urther be remarked that many inverts are by no means quite insusceptible to the endearments of the female sex. It is through intercourse with women (*i. e.* their like) that they dispose of what may be called the homosexual component of their sexuality.

How differently does the picture of object-homo-erotism present itself even after only a superficial analysis. After the very shortest examination those suffering from it prove to be typical obsessional patients. They swarm with obsessions, and with obsessional procedures and ceremonies to guard against them. A more penetrating dissection finds behind the compulsion the torturing doubt, as well as that lack of balance in love and hate which Freud discovered to be the basis of the obsessional mechanisms. The psycho-analysis of such homo-erotics as only feel abnormally in reference to their love-object, and are otherwise of a purely masculine type, has shewn me plainly that this kind of homo-erotism in all its phenomena is itself nothing else than a series of obsessive feelings and actions. Sexuality in general is obsessive enough, but, according to my experience, object-homo-erotism is a true neurotic compulsion, with logically irreversible substitution of normal sexual aims and actions by abnormal ones.

The average (analytically investigated) early history of homo-erotics of the masculine type is somewhat as follows:

They were all very precocious sexually, and hetero-sexually aggressive (thus confirming Sadger's finding). Their Oedipus phantasies were always "normal," culminating in sexual-sadistic plans of assault on the mother (or her representative) and cruel death-wishes against the disturbing father. Further, they were all intellectually precocious, and in their impulse for knowledge created a number of infantile sexual theories; this forms also the foundation of their later obsessional thinking. Apart from aggressivity and intellectuality their constitution is characterised by unusually strong anal-erotism and coprophilia.[1] In the earliest childhood

[1]The view defended in this essay, that object-homo-erotism is an obsessional neurosis, was strengthened when Freud, in his work on 'Die Disposition zur Zwangsneurose." (This Zeitschrift, Jahrg. I, Heft 6) announced that the constitutional basis of this neurosis is the fixation on a pregenital, sadistic-anal-erotic stage in the development of the sexual hunger. It was precisely sadism and anal-erotism that I found at the basis also of object-homo-erotism, a fact that speaks decidedly in favour of the inherent connection of these morbid states. See also Ernest Jones, "Hass und Analerotik in der Zwangsneurose," (this Zeitschrift, Jahrg. I, Heft 5.).

they had been severely punished by one of the parents[1] for a hetero-erotic delinquency (touching a girl indecently, infantile attempt at coitus), and on such an occasion (which was often repeated) had to suppress an outburst of intense rage. Following on this they became especially docile in the latency period (which set in early), avoided the society of girls and women half obstinately, half anxiously, and consorted exclusively with their friends. In one of my patients there occurred several times "irruptions" of homo-erotic affection in the latency period; in another the latency was disturbed through overhearing parental intercourse, after which the previous good conduct was interrupted by a transitory period of naughtiness (revenge phantasies). When the sexual hunger increases at the time of puberty the homo-erotic's inclinations again turn at first towards the opposite sex, but the slightest reproval or warning on the part of someone they respect is enough to re-awaken the dread of women, whereupon there takes place, either immediately or shortly after, a final flight from the female to his own sex. One patient when he was fifteen fell in love with an actress about whose morality his mother passed some not quite flattering remarks; since then he has never approached a woman and feels himself impulsively drawn to young men. In the case of another patient puberty set in with an absolute frenzy of heterosexuality; he had to have sexual intercourse every day for a year, and obtained the money for it, if necessary, in dishonourable ways. When he made the house servant pregnant,

[1] It struck me how often it was the mother who administered these reprovals to later homo-erotics, but I attached no special significance to this circumstance until Professor Freud called my attention to the importance of this very factor.

however, and was called to account for it by his father
and vilified by his mother, he applied himself with the
same ardour to the cult of the male sex, from which no
effort has been able to wean him ever since.

In the transference-relation to the physician object-
homo-erotics recapitulate the genesis of their trouble.
If the transference is a positive one from the beginning
then unexpected "cures" come about even after a short
treatment; on the slightest conflict, however, the
patient relapses into his homo-erotism, and only now,
on the setting in of resistance, does the real analysis begin.
If the transference is negative from the outset, as it is
especially apt to be with patients who come to the
treatment not on their own accord, but at their
parents' bidding, then it takes a long time to reach any
real analytic work, the patient wasting the hour with
boastful and scornful narrations of his homo-erotic
adventures.

In the object-homo-erotic's unconscious phantasy
the physician can represent the place of man and
woman, father and mother, reversals[1] of the most
diverse kind playing a very important part in this. It
turns out that an object-homo-erotic knows how to
love the woman in a man; the posterior half of man's
body can signify for him the anterior half of a woman's,
the scapulae or nates assuming the significance of the
woman's breasts. It was these cases that shewed me
with especial plainness that this kind of homo-erotism

[1] The dreams of homo-erotics are very rich in reversals. Whole series of
dreams have often to be read backwards. The symptomatic action of
making a slip of the tongue or pen in the use of the gender of articles is
common. One patient even made up a bisexual number: the number 101
signified, as the context shewed, that for him "backwards and forwards
were the same."

is only a substitution product of the hetero-erotic sexual hunger. At the same time the active homo-erotic satisfies in this way also his sadistic and anal-erotic impulses; this holds good not only for the real paederasts, but also for the over-refined boy lovers, those who anxiously shun all indecent contact with boys; with the latter sadism and anal-erotism are replaced by their reaction-formations.

In the light of psycho-analysis, therefore, the active homo-erotic act appears on the one hand as subsequent (false) obedience, which—taking the parental inter-diction literally—really avoids intercourse with women, but indulges the forbidden hetero-erotic desires in unconscious phantasies; on the other hand the paederastic act serves the purpose of the original Oedipus phantasy and denotes the injuring and sullying of the man.[1]

Considered from the intellectual aspect obsessional homo-erotism proves to be in the first place an over-correction of the doubt concerning the love towards the man's own sex. The homo-erotic obsessional idea unites in a happy compromise the flight from women, and their symbolic replacement, as well as the hatred of men and the compensation of this. Woman being apparently excluded from the love-life, there no longer exists, so far as consciousness is concerned, any further bone of contention between father and son.

It is worth mentioning that most of the obsessional homo-erotics (as this type might also be called) I have

---

[1]One patient, whenever he felt himself insulted by a man, especially by a superior, had at once to seek out a male prostitute; only in this way was he able to save himself from an outburst of rage. The supposed "love" for a man was here essentially an act of violence and revenge.

analysed make use of the intermediary stage theory[1] of homosexual tendencies, which is now so popular, to represent their condition as congenital, and therefore not to be altered or influenced, or, to use the expression from Schreber's "Denkwürdigkeiten," "in harmony with the universe." They all regard themselves as inverts, and are glad to have found a scientific support for the justification of their obsessional ideas and actions.

I have naturally also to say something here as to my experience concerning the curability of this form of homo-erotism. In the first place I observe that it has not yet been possible (for me, at all events) to cure completely a severe case of obsessional homo-erotism. In a number of cases, however, I have been able to record very far-reaching improvement, especially in the following directions: abatement of the hostile attitude and feeling of repugnance towards women; better control of the previously urgent impulse for homo-erotic satisfaction, the direction of the impulse being otherwise retained; awakening of potency towards women, therefore a kind of amphi-erotism, which took the place of the previously exclusive homo-erotism, often alternating with the latter in periodic waves. These experiences encourage me, therefore, to expect that obsessional homo-erotism will be just as curable by means of the psycho-analytic method as the other forms of obsessional neurosis. In any case I imagine that the fundamental reversion of an obsessional homo-erotism that has been firmly rooted for a long time must need whole years of analytic work. (In one very

[1](About equivalent to what we call the "third sex" theory in English countries. Transl.)

hopeful case I was treating the cure had to be broken off for extrinsic reasons after almost two years). Only when we have at our disposal cured cases, *i. e.* cases analysed to the end, will it be possible to pass a final judgement on the conditions under which this neurosis arises, and on the peculiarities of its dispositional and accidental factors.

It is possible, indeed probable, that homo-erotism s to be found not only in those here described, but also in other syndromes; with the isolation of these two types I certainly do not mean to exhaust all the possibilities. In making the nosological distinction of subject- from object-homo-erotism I only wanted in the first place to direct attention to the confusion of ideas that prevails even in the scientific literature on the homosexuality problem. Psycho-analytic investigation shews further that nowadays the most heterogeneous psychical states are treated alike under the title "homosexuality;" on the one hand true constitutional anomalies (inversion, subject-homo-erotism), on the other hand psychoneurotic obsess onal states (obsessional or object-homo-erotism). The individual of the first kind feels himself to be a woman with the wish to be loved by a man, the feeling of the second is rather neurotic flight from women than sympathy towards men.

In designating object-homo-erotism as a neurotic symptom I come into opposition with Freud, who in his "Sexualtheorie" describes homosexuality as a perversion, neuroses on the contrary as the negative of perversions. The contradiction, however, is only apparent. "Perversions," *i. e.* tarrying at primitive or preparatory sexual aims, can very well be placed at the disposal of neurotic repression tendencies also, a part of true (positive) perversion, neurotically exaggerated, representing at the same time the negative of another perversion.[1] Now this is the case with "object-homo-erotism." The homo-erotic component, which is never absent even normally, gets here over-engaged with masses of affect, which in the unconscious relate to another, repressed perversion, namely, a hetero-erotism of such a strength as to be incapable of becoming conscious.

I believe that of the two kinds of homo-erotism here described the "objective" one is the more frequent and the more important socially; it makes a large number of otherwise valuable men (psychoneurotically disposed, it is true) impossible in society, and excludes them from propagation. Further, the constantly increasing number of object-homo-erotics is a social phenomenon the importance of which is not to be underestimated, and one that demands explanation. As a provisional explanation I assume that the extension of object-homo-erotism is an abnormal reaction to the disproportionately exaggerated repression of the homo-erotic instinct-component by civilised man, *i. e.* a failure of this repression.

In the mental life of primitive peoples (as in that of children) amphi-erotism plays a much greater part than in that of civilised people. But even with certain highly civilised races, *e. g.* the Greeks, it used to be not merely a tolerated, but a recognised kind of way for the satisfaction of desire; it is still so in the Orient of today.

[1](Abraham has shewn that the same is true of another perversion: exhibitionism. Jahrbuch der Psychoanalyse. 1914. Transl.)

In modern European regions of culture, however, and in those attached to them, not only is actual homo-erotism lacking, but also the sublimation of it that appeared so obvious to the people of antiquity, enthusiastic and devoted friendship between men. It is in fact astounding to what an extent present-day men have lost the capacity for mutual affection and amiability. Instead there prevails among men decided asperity, resistance, and love of disputation. Since it is unthinkable that those tender affects which were so strongly pronounced in childhood could have disappeared without leaving a trace, one has to regard these signs of resistance as reaction-formations, as defence symptoms erected against affection for the same sex. I would even go so far as to regard the barbarous duels of the German students as similarly distorted proofs of affection towards members of their own sex. (Only slight traces still exist today in a positive direction; thus, in club and party life, in "hero worship," in the preference of so many men for boy-girls and for actresses in male parts, also—in attacks of cruder erotism—in drunkenness, where the alcohol reverses the sublimations).

It looks, however, as if these rudiments of the love for their own sex would not fully compensate the men of today for losing the love of friends. A part of the unsatisfied homo-erotism remains "free floating," and demands to be appeased; since this is impossible under the conditions of present-day civilisation, this quantity of sexual hunger has to undergo a displacement, namely, on to the feeling-relationship to the opposite sex. I quite seriously believe that the men of today are one and all obsessively heterosexual as the result of this affective displacement; in order to free themselves from men, they become the slaves of women. This may be the explanation of the "chivalry" and the exaggerated, often visibly affected, adoration of woman that has dominated the male world since the middle ages; it may also possibly be the explanation of Don-Juanism, the obsessive and yet never fully satisfied pursuit of continually new heterosexual adventures. Even if Don Juan himself would find this theory ridiculous, I should have to declare him to be an obsessional invalid, who could never find satisfaction in the endless series of women (so faithfully drawn by Leporello in his book) because these women are really only substitutes for repressed love-objects.[1]

I do not wish to be misunderstood: I find it natural and founded in the psycho-physical organisation of the sexes that a man loves a woman incomparably better than his like, but it is unnatural that a man should repel other men and have to adore women with an obsessive exaggeration. What wonder that so few women succeed in meeting these exaggerated demands and in satisfying, as well as all the other ones, also the man's homo-erotic needs by being his "companion", without doubt one of the commonest causes of domestic unhappiness.

The exaggeration of hetero-erotism for the purpose of repressing love towards the same sex involuntarily reminds one of an epigram of Lessing's (Sinngedichte, Buch II, Nr 6):

"The unjust mob falsely imputed love of boys to the righteous Turan.

[1] There also exists a Don-Juanism of unsatisfied hetero-erotism.

To chastise the lies what else could he do but—sleep with his sister."

The reason why every kind of affection between men is proscribed is not clear. It is thinkable that the sense of cleanliness which has been so specially reinforced in the past few centuries, *i. e.* the repression of anal-erotism, has provided the strongest motive in this direction; for homo-erotism, even the most sublimated, stands in a more or less unconscious associative connection with paederastia, *i. e.* an anal-erotic activity.

The increasing number of obsessional homo-erotics in modern society would then be the symptom of the partial failure of repression and "return" of the repressed material.

In a brief summary, therefore, the attempt to explain the prevalence of object-homo-erotism would run somewhat as follows: The exaggerated repression of the homo-erotic instinct-component in present-day society has resulted in general in a rather obsessive reinforcement of hetero-erotism in men. If now the hetero-erotism is also inhibited or strictly restrained, as is necessarily the case during education, the consequence may easily be—in the first place with those who are predisposed to it for individual reasons—a reverse displacement of the compulsion from hetero-erotism to homo-erotism, *i. e.* the development of a homo-erotic obsessional neurosis.

CHAPTER XIII

THE ONTOGENESIS OF THE INTEREST IN MONEY*

THE deeper psycho-analysis penetrates into the knowledge of social-psychological productions (myths, fairy-tales, folk-lore) the stronger becomes the confirmation of the phylogenetic origin of symbols, which stand out in the mental life of every individual as a precipitate of the experiences of previous generations. Analysis has still to perform the task of separately investigating the phylogenesis and ontogenesis of symbolism, and then establishing their mutual relation. The classical formula of "Daimon kai Tyche" in Freud's application (the cooperation of heredity and experience in the genesis of individual strivings) will finally become applied also to the genesis of the psychical contents of these strivings, and this also brings to the front the old dispute about "congenital ideas," though now no longer in the form of empty speculations. We may already, however, anticipate to this extent, namely, that for the production of a symbol individual experiences are necessary as well as the congenital disposition, these providing the real material for the construction of the symbol, while the congenital basis preceding experience has perhaps only the value of an inherited, but not yet functioning mechanism.

*Published in the Internat. Zeitschr. f. ärztl. Psychoanalyse, 1914.

I wish here to examine the question of whether, and to what extent, individual experience favours the transformation of anal-erotic interest into interest in money.

Every psycho-analyst is familiar with the symbolic meaning of money that was discovered by Freud. "Wherever the archaic way of thinking has prevailed or still prevails, in the old civilisations, in myths, fairy-tales, superstition, in unconscious thinking, in dreams, and in neuroses, money has been brought into the closest connection with filth."

As an individual-psychological phenomenon parallel with this fact Freud asserts that an intimate association exists between the strongly marked erogenicity of the anal zone in childhood and the character trait of miserliness that develops later. In the case of persons who later on were especially tidy, economical, and obstinate, one learns from the analytic investigation of their early childhood that they were of that class of infants "who refuse to empty the bowel because they obtain an accessory pleasure from defaecation," who even in the later years of childhood "enjoyed holding back the stools," and who recall "having occupied themselves in their childhood in all sorts of unseemly ways with the evacuated material." "The most extensive connections seem to be those existing between the apparently so disparate complexes of defaecation and interest in money."[1]

Observation of the behaviour of children and analytic investigation of neurotics allow us now to establish some single points on the line along which the idea of

[1]Freud. "Charakter und Analerotik," in his Sammlung kl. Schr. z. Neurosenlehre, Bd. II, S. 132 et seq.

the most valuable thing that a man possesses (money) is developed in the individual into a symbol "of the most worthless thing, which a man casts aside as dejecta."[1]

Experience gathered from these two sources shews that children originally devote their interest without any inhibition to the process of defaecation, and that it affords them pleasure to hold back their stools. The excrementa thus held back are really the first "savings" of the growing being, and as such remain in a constant, unconscious inter-relationship with every bodily activity or mental striving that has anything to do with collecting, hoarding, and saving.

Faeces are also, however, one of the first toys of the child. The purely auto-erotic satisfaction afforded to the child by the pressing and squeezing of the faecal masses and the play of the sphincter muscles soon becomes—in part, at least—transformed into a sort of object-love, in that the interest gets displaced from the neutral sensations of certain organs on to the material itself that caused these feelings. The faeces are thus "introjected," and in this stage of development—which is essentially characterised by sharpening of the sense of smell and an increasingly adroit use of the hands, with at the same time an inability to walk upright (creeping on all fours)—they count as a valuable toy, from which the child is to be weaned only through deterrents and threats of punishment.

The child's interest for dejecta experiences its first distortion through the smell of faeces becoming disagreeable, disgusting. This is probably related to the

[1]Freud. Loc. cit.

beginning of the upright gait.[1]   The other attributes of this material—moistness, discolouration, stickiness, etc.—do not for the time being offend his sense of cleanliness.   He still enjoys, therefore, playing with and manipulating moist street-mud whenever he has the chance, liking to collect it together into larger heaps. Such a heap of mud is already in a sense a symbol, distinguished from the real thing by its absence of smell.   For the child, street-mud is, so to speak, de-odourised dejecta.

As the child's sense of cleanliness increases—with the help of paedagogic measures—street-mud also becomes objectionable to him.   Substances which on account of their stickiness, moistness, and colour are apt to leave traces on the body and clothing become despised and avoided as "dirty things."   The symbol of filth must therefore undergo a further distortion, a dehydration.   The child turns its interest to sand, a substance which, while the colour of earth, is cleaner and dry.   The instinctive joy of children in gathering up, massing together, and shaping sand is subsequently rationalised and sanctioned by the adults, whom it suits to see an otherwise unruly child playing with sand for hours,—and they declare this playing to be "healthy," *i. e.* hygienic.[2]   None the less this play-

[1] Freud conceives of the repression of anal-erotism and of the pleasure in smell altogether in the human race as a result of the upright posture, the erection from the earth.

[2] The habit of euphemistically disguising coprophilic tendencies as "hygienic" is very widespread.   The fairly harmless behaviour of stool pedants is well-known, who devote to the regulation of their bowel activities a considerable part of the interest at their disposal; such persons, however, are rather prone to fall into what has been called "stool-hypochondria."   A whole series of analyses, by the way, has convinced me that in very many case hypochondria is really a fermentation-product of anal-erotism, a displacement of unsublimated coprophilic interests from their original objects

sand also is nothing other than a copro-symbol—de-odourised and dehydrated filth.

Already in this stage of development, by the way, there occurs a "return of the repressed." It gives children endless pleasure to fill with water the holes they dig in the sand, and so to bring the material of their play nearer to the original watery stage. Boys not infrequently employ their own urine for this irrigation, as though they wanted in this way to emphasise quite clearly the relationship of the two materials. Even the interest for the specific odour of excrement does not cease at once, but is only displaced on to other odours that in any way resemble this. The children continue to shew a liking for the smell of sticky materials with a characteristic odour, especially the strongly smelling degenerated product of cast off epidermis cells which collects between the toes, nasal secretion, ear-wax, and the dirt of the nails, while many children do not content themselves with the moulding and sniffing of these substances, but also take them into the mouth. The passionate enjoyment of children in moulding putty (colour, consistency, smell), tar, and asphalt is well-known. I knew a boy who had an intense passion for the characteristic smell of rubber materials, and who could sniff for hours at a piece of indiarubber.

The smell of stables and of illuminating gas greatly pleases children at this age—indeed, at much older ages even—and it is not chance that popular belief ap-

on to other organs and products of the body with an alteration of the qualifying pleasure. The choice of the organ towards which the hypochondria is directed is determined by special factors (somatic disposition, pronounced erogenicity even in diseased organs, etc).

preciates places having these smells as being "healthy," even as being a cure for diseases. A special sublimation path of anal-erotism branches off from the smell of gas, asphalt, and turpentine: the fondness for substances with an agreeable odour, for perfumes, by means of which the development of a reaction-formation—representation through the opposite—is concluded. People with whom this kind of sublimation occurs often develop in other respects as well into aesthetes, and there can be no question that aesthetics in general has its principal root in repressed anal-erotism.[1]   The aesthetic and playful interest springing from this source not infrequently has a share in the developing pleasure in painting and sculpture.[2]

Already in the mud and sand periods of coprophilic interest it is striking how fond children are of fabricating objects out of this material—so far as their primitive artistic skill allows—or, more correctly, of imitating objects the possession of which has a special value for them. They make out of them different articles of diet, cakes, tarts, sweetmeats, etc. The reinforcement of purely egoistic instincts by coprophilia begins here.

Progress in the sense of cleanliness then gradually makes even sand unacceptable to the child, and the infantile stone age begins: the collecting of pebbles, as prettily shaped and coloured as possible, in which a higher stage in the development of replacement-formation is attained. The attributes of evil odour, moisture, and softness are represented by those of

---

[1] (See on this matter a monograph of mine in the Jahrbuch, Bd. VI. Transl.)

[2] I have already in another connection pointed out the probable part played by the childish interest in flatus in later fondness for music. See Ch. IV.

absence of odour, dryness, and now also hardness. We are reminded of the real origin of this hobby by the circumstance that stones—just as mud and sand—are gathered and collected from the *earth*. The capitalistic significance of stones is already quite considerable. (Children are "stone-rich"[1] in the narrow sense of the word).

After stones comes the turn of artificial products, and with these the detachment of the interest from the earth is complete. Glass marbles, buttons[2], fruit pips, are eagerly collected—this time no longer only for the sake of their intrinsic value, but as measures of value, so to speak as primitive coins, converting the previous barter exchange of children into an enthusiastic money exchange. The character of capitalism, however, not purely practical and utilitarian, but libidinous and irrational, is betrayed in this stage also: the child decidedly enjoys the collecting in itself.[3]

It only needs one more step for the identification of faeces with gold to be complete. Soon even stones begin to wound the child's feeling of cleanliness—he longs for something purer—and this is offered to him in the shining pieces of money, the high appreciation of which is naturally also in part due to the respect in

---

[1] (A German idiom. Transl.)

[2] Cp. Lou Andreas-Salomé: "Vom frühen Gottesdienst." Imago. II. 1913.

[3] The German word "Besitz" (=possession) shews, by the way, that man tries even in his speech to represent by the idea of "sitting on it" that which is valuable to him, which belongs to him. Rationalists evidently content themselves with the explanation of this simile to the effect that the sitting on is meant to express a concealing, protecting and guarding of the valued object. The fact, however, that it is the buttocks and not the hand—which would be more natural with men—that is used to represent protection and defence speaks rather in favour of the word "Besitz" being a copro-symbol. The final decision on the point must be reserved for a philologist who has had a psycho-analytic training.

which they are held by adults, as well as to the seductive possibilities of obtaining through them everything that the child's heart can desire.   Originally, however, it is not these purely practical considerations that are operative, enjoyment in the playful collecting, heaping up, and gazing at the shining metal pieces being the chief thing, so that they are treasured even less for their economic value than for their own sake as pleasure-giving objects.   The eye takes pleasure at the sight of their lustre and colour, the ear at their metallic clink, the sense of touch at play with the round smooth discs, only the sense of smell comes away empty, and the sense of taste also has to be satisfied with the weak, but peculiar taste of the coins.   With this the development of the money symbol is in its main outlines complete. Pleasure in the intestinal contents becomes enjoyment of money, which, however, after what has been said is seen to be nothing other than odourless, dehydrated filth that has been made to shine.   *Pecunia non olet.*

In correspondence with the development of the organ of thought that in the meanwhile has been proceeding in the direction of logicality, the adult's symbolic interest in money gets extended not only to objects with similar physical attributes, but to all sorts of things that in any way signify value or possession (paper money, shares, bankbook, etc).   But whatever form may be assumed by money, the enjoyment at possessing it has its deepest and amplest source in coprophilia.   Every sociologist and national economist who examines the facts without prejudice has to reckon with this irrational element.   Social problems can be solved   only   by   discovering   the   real   psychology   of human beings; speculations about economic conditions alone will never reach the goal.

A part of anal-erotism is not sublimated at all, but remains in its original form.[1]   Even the most cultivated normal being displays an interest in his evacuation functions which stands in a curious contradiction to the abhorrence and disgust that he manifests when he sees or hears about anything of the kind in regard to other people.   Foreign people and races as is well-known, cannot "riechen"[2] each other.   In addition to the retention of the original form, however, there also exists a "return" of what is actually concealed behind the money symbol.   The intestinal disorders, first observed by Freud, that follow on a wounding of the money complex are examples of this.[3]   A further instance is the curious fact, which I have noticed in countless cases, that people are economical as regards the changing of under-linen in a way quite out of proportion to their standard of living in other respects. Meanness finally, therefore, makes use of the anal character in order to gain once more a piece of anal-erotism (tolerance of dirt).   The following is a still

[1]The sum of anal-erotism present in the constitution is thus shared in adults among the most diverse psychical structures.   Out of it develop: 1. The anal character traits in Freud's sense. 2. Contributions to aesthetics and to cultural interests. 3. To hypochondria. 4. The rest remains unsublimated. From the different proportion of the sublimated and the original parts, from the preference for this or that form of sublimation, the most variegated character types arise, which must naturally have their special conditional factors.   Anal characteristics are specially suited for rapid characterological orientation concerning an individual, indeed concerning whole races.   The anal character, with his cleanliness, love for order, defiance, and miserliness, sharply deviates from the pronounced anal-erotic, who is tolerant on the matter of dirt, extravagant, and easy-going.

[2](A German idiom, meaning "cannot stand". "Riechen" literally means to smell. Transl.)

[3]See Chapter VII. P. 176.   "Temporary rectal troubles", etc.

more striking example: A patient could not recall any kind of coprophilic manipulations, but soon after related without being asked that he took a special pleasure in brightly shining copper coins, and had invented an original procedure for making them shine; he swallowed the piece of money, and then searched his faeces until he found the piece of money, which during its passage through the alimentary canal had become beautifully shining.[1]   Here the pleasure in the clean object became a cover for satisfaction of the most primitive anal-erotism.   The curious thing is that the patient was able to deceive himself as to the real significance of his transparent behaviour.

Apart from striking examples of this sort, the erotic enjoyment of heaping in and gathering up gold and other money pieces, the pleasurable "wallowing in money," can be observed countless times in daily life. Many people are ready enough to sign documents that bind them to pay large sums, and can easily expend large amounts in paper money, but are striking tardy in giving out gold coins or even the smallest copper coins.   The coins seem to "stick" to their fingers. (Cp. also the expression "current capital," and the reverse of this, "argent sec," which is used in the Franche-Comté).[2]

The ontogenetic path of development of interest in money, as here sketched, while shewing individual

[1] The case reminds one of the coprophilic joke in which the doctor who had had succeeded in expelling by means of a purge a piece of money that a child had swallowed was told he could keep the money as his fee. As to the indentification of money and faeces see also the fairy-tale of "Eslein streck dich." The word "Losung"(=deliverance) means proceeds of a sale (in business), but in hunting speech it means the faeces of wild animals.

[2] (To be "à sec" is French vernacular for "hard up".   Transl.)

differences dependent on the conditions of life, is nevertheless on the whole among civilised people to be regarded as a psychical process which seeks realisation under the most diverse circumstances, in one way or another. It thus seems natural to regard this developmental tendency as a racial attribute, and to suppose that the biogenetic ground principle is also valid for the formation of the money symbol. It is to be expected that phylogenetic and historical comparison of the path of individual development here described will shew a parallelism with the development of the money symbol in the human race in general. Perhaps the coloured stones of primitive men which have been found in cave excavations will then be capable of interpretation; observations concerning the anal-erotism of savages (the primitive men of today, who in many cases still live in the stage of barter exchange and of pebble or shell money) should considerably further this investigation of the history of civilisation.

After what has been communicated, however, it is already not improbable that the capitalistic interest, increasing in correlation with development, stands not only at the disposal of practical, egoistic aims—of the reality-principle, therefore—but also that the delight in gold and in the possession of money represents the symbolic replacement of, and the reaction-formation to, repressed anal-erotism, *i. e.* that it also satisfies the pleasure-principle.

The capitalistic instinct thus contains, according to our conception, an egoistic and an anal-erotic component.

INDEX

Emotion, 30, 55, 63, 93, 158, 166.

Environment, 20, 42, 56.

Erection, 11, 12, 19, 170, 230, 241, 249.

Erogenous zone, 13, 77, 92, 160, 161, 235, 270.

Erotomania, 243.

Excitation, 89, 91-93, 160-162, 165, 166, 175.

Exhibitionism, 13, 89, 90, 92, 142, 146, 150, 265.

Expression displacement,177-179.

Faeces, 270, 271, 275, 278.

Father-complex, 59, 63, 64, 66-68.

Ferenczi, 10, 29, 30, 139, 196, 198, 228, 232, 234, 235, 274, 277.

Fetishism, 13, 18.

Fixation, 21, 22, 26, 28, 49, 52, 74, 152, 174, 176, 177, 179, 184, 190, 199, 200, 218, 248, 257, 259.

Flatus, 114, 121, 177.

Fliess, 156, 162, 250.

Fore-pleasure, 160, 161.

Forgetting, 13, 61, 85, 108, 127.

Free association, 18, 84, 93, 94, 110, 164, 165, 171, 173.

Freud, 9, 10, 12-36, 38-40, 42, 44-48, 50-56, 60-62, 65, 68, 72, 73, 76-78, 82-84, 86, 87, 90-97, 105, 106, 108, 109, 111, 112, 115-120, 123, 127, 131-133, 156, 159, 162, 169, 171, 176, 179, 181-183, 185, 187-191, 195, 197-201, 210, 215-217, 219, 223, 232, 233, 247, 248, 250, 251, 254, 259, 260 264, 269-272, 277.

Functional symbolism, 220, 221, 225.

Gesture, 36, 128, 184, 191, 192, 194, 195, 198, 200, 205.

Grandiose delusions, 131, 132, 140, 185, 228, 241, 243.

Gross, Otto, 33.

Hallucination, 18, 38, 81, 116-118, 120, 123, 126, 133, 160, 173, 174, 181, 188, 189, 246.

Hate, 16, 18, 31, 33, 35, 36, 38, 41, 42, 53, 54, 66, 149, 155, 209, 210, 218-220, 242, 251, 259, 263.

Heredity, 23, 24, 269.

Hirschfeld, 256.

Homo-erotism, 253-268.

Homosexuality, 17, 37, 56, 63, 77, 114, 121, 132, 133, 137, 138, 142, 144, 145, 148-150, 152, 155, 156, 170, 177, 244-246, 248, 250-253, 258, 263, 264.

Hostility. See Hate.

Hyperaesthesia, 12, 159.

Hypnagogic, 18.

THE
DEVELOPMENT OF
PSYCHO-ANALYSIS

Sandor Ferenczi
and Otto Rank

Authorized Translation by Caroline Newton

DOVER PUBLICATIONS, INC., NEW YORK

TRANSLATOR'S PREFACE.

The translator of this slender volume had the good fortune to be studying psycho-analysis in Vienna at the time of its first appearance in German in December, 1923. Dr. Rank and Dr. Ferenczi are admittedly Professor Freud's most brilliant and original followers, but the "Entwicklungsziele der Psychoanalyse" attracted a quite special attention. Both men, in addition to their other great contributions to psycho-analysis, are particularly skilful therapeutists and this book offers an opportunity for practicing analysts to see the development of analytic technique and the special angles of two of its most successful practitioners.

The book was written in the summer of 1922, somewhat modified and altered by the events of the International Psycho-analytical Congress, held in Berlin in September of that year, and completed in 1923. The authors apologize for some of the deficiencies of structure on account of this history of its origin.

The critical part of the work was originally written by Dr. Ferenczi, the didactic chapter "The Analytical Situation" by Dr. Rank and the work then jointly revised. As will be seen from the above, the book is intended primarily for practicing analysts and will appeal only to serious students of psycho-analysis. Although the number of its readers will therefore be limited it seems important to offer an English version for those adherents of the science who are not familiar with the German language, but who nevertheless wish to keep up with the recent development of analytic technique.

CAROLINE NEWTON.

DAYLESFORD, PENNA.
  August, 1924.

CONTENTS.

CHAPTER I.

INTRODUCTION.

Psycho-analysis has developed, as is well known, in the course of almost thirty years, from a simple medical method of treatment of certain neurotic disturbances to an extensive scientific theoretic system which is slowly but steadily growing and seems to lead to a new interpretation of life.

To follow the development of this process step by step, and to study, on the one hand the reciprocal relation of the therapeutic method and the medical technique, and on the other the scientific development in detail, would mean nothing less than writing a continuation of "The History of the Psycho-Analytic Movement." [1] By attacking this problem which cannot as yet be solved, it would be unavoidable to touch upon questions which extend greatly beyond the subject of psycho-analysis as such. One would have to consider the relationship between the facts dealt with by a science and this science itself. Such a task is in itself extremely difficult, because it leads to a discussion of the fundamental principles of our whole scientific method, but it becomes almost impossible in the case of psycho-analysis, which is still in a stage of development. And we who are active participants in the process, who are representatives of both the medical-therapeutic, as well as the scientific-theoretic group find it very difficult to make an objective estimate of the facts about these inter-relations.

[1] See Freud "Zur Geschichte der psychoanalytischen Bewegung (Sammlung kleiner Schriften zur Neurosenlehre 4. Folge). English Translation this Series No. 25.

On the other hand one cannot deny that in the last ten
years, a state of increasing confusion, particularly in
respect to the practical problems, has been gaining ground
among psycho-analysts. In contrast to the rapid growth
of the psycho-analytical theory, the technical and therapeutic factor which was originally the heart of the matter
and the actual stimulus to every important advance in the
theory has been strikingly neglected, in the literature, as
well as in practice. This could give the false impression [1a]
that the development of the technique had stood still in
the meantime, particularly since Freud himself has always
been, as is well known, extremely reserved on this point,
to such an extent, indeed, that it is almost ten years since
he has published any work on the subject. His few
technical articles, which are collected in the "Sammlung
kleiner Schriften zur Neurosenlehre" IV. Serie—were, for
analysts who had not themselves undergone an analysis,
the only correct indication for their technical activity
although they, according to Freud's point of view, are
certainly incomplete and in certain points, on account of
the present development, antiquated and seem to need
modification. One can therefore understand why the
majority of those analysts, who were dependent upon the
study of the literature, adhered too rigidly to these technical rules, and could not find the connection to the stages
of progress which the science of analysis had made in the
meantime.

We were dissatisfied with this state of affairs and found

[1a] The work of Ferenczi to establish active intervention in the technique
constitutes an exception. These attempts were either ignored or incorrectly
interpreted by the majority of analysts, perhaps because the author, at that
time in emphasizing the new interpretation, did not sufficiently make clear to
the reader how this point of view fits into the hitherto prevailing theory and
technique. (See "Weiterer Ausbau der aktiven Technik in der Psychoanalyse"
Zeitschrift VII, 1922.)

ourselves repeatedly forced to pause in our practical work in order to take account of these difficulties and problems. In doing this we found that our technical ability had made important strides in the meantime, the completely conscious comprehension and value of which placed us in a position to perceptibly increase our knowledge. We finally found it necessary, in the face of an evident and general need for a clarification of the situation, to inform others of our experiences, and we think that we shall do this best, by first attempting to describe in what way we practice psycho-analysis to-day, and what we now mean by it. Only then will it be possible for us to understand the difficulties which appear on all sides and how we hope to remedy them.

In order to do this we must connect directly with Freud's last technical work ("Remembering, Repeating and Working through," 1914) in which a different degree of importance is attached to the three factors mentioned in the title, inasmuch as remembering is treated as the actual aim of psycho-analytic work, whereas the desire to repeat instead of remembering, is regarded as a symptom of resistance and is therefore recommended to be avoided. From the standpoint of the compulsion to repeat, it is, however, not only absolutely unavoidable, that the patient should, during the cure, repeat a large part of his process of development, but also as experience has shown, it is a matter of just those portions which cannot be really experienced from memory, so that there is no other way open to the patient than that of repeating, as well as no other means for the analyst to seize the essential unconscious material. It is now a question of understanding also this form of communication, the so-called language of gesture, as Ferenczi has called it, and of explaining it to the patient. The neurotic symptoms, indeed, as Freud has taught us, are themselves simply distorted forms of expression of the unconscious which at first are not understood.

The first practical necessity resulting from this insight was not only not to suppress the tendency to repetition in the analysis,[2] but even to require it, provided, of course, that one knows how to master it, for otherwise the most important material cannot be expressed and dealt with. On the other hand, certain resistances—perhaps even biologically founded ones—oppose themselves to the repetition compulsion, particularly the feeling of anxiety and of guilt which we can only overcome by active intervention, that is by requiring the repetition. Thus we finally come to the point of attributing *the chief rôle in analytic technique to repetition instead of to remembering*. This however, must not be understood as simply permitting effects to vanish away into "events," but consists rather, as is described in detail further on, in a gradual *transformation of the reproduced material into actual remembering* (first permitting the reproduction and then explaining it).

The progress which we could establish, by thus taking stock of our knowledge, can be observed and formulated into two headings. From the technical point of view we undoubtedly emphasize greater "activity," by which we mean absolutely requiring the tendency to reproduce, which has up to now been neglected, indeed regarded as a disturbing secondary phenomena in the cure. From the theoretic side, we lay stress on the adequate recognition in the neurosis also of the overwhelming importance of the

[2] In which case, this tendency frequently enough expresses itself in reality; this applies particularly to the love life, to marriage, divorce and love affairs, which are subjected to the greatest privation in the analysis.

repetition compulsion, which Freud has meantime established.[3] It is really the insight gained from understanding the repetition compulsion which first makes the results of "active therapy" comprehensible and gives the theoretic reason for its necessity. We therefore believe that we are in no way differing from Freud if from now on we attribute to repetition the same rôle in our therapy which it biologically occupies in our mental life.

[3] Beyond the Pleasure Principle. 1921.

CHAPTER II.

THE ANALYTIC SITUATION.

I. *The Unwinding of the Libido and its Phases.**

If we now attempt to sketch, in broad outlines, the present stand of the therapy which is used in analysis, we would like, from the start, to have understood that we are not giving a detailed presentation of technique. In so far as this is at all possible in literary form, the task must be left for some work of quite a different character.[4] On the basis of the Freudian definition of psycho-analytic technique, which characterizes it as a method taking the mental facts of transference and resistance as the fundamental condition for the influencing of the patient, we can reach a very general definition of psycho-analysis which presents itself, at times, to the analyst conducting the treatment, *as an individually determined process of definite duration in the libido development of the patient.* The task of the analyst consists in watching the process of the automatic unwinding of the libido—which, like the organic process of healing, takes place within a definite time and contains crises. At those points where he notices a disturbance in the process in the form of a neurotic resistance he must intervene and correct it. This artificial libido process is inaugurated and determined in its course

---

* *Libido-ablauf* is here translated as *unwinding*—in the sense that as thread is unwound from a spool, so the libido is released or flows from the initial fixation stages by reason of the transference.

[4] Moreover, instead of a written presentation of analytic technique, the aim should be a well and minutely worked out plan of instruction in psycho-analytic polyclinics. This would offer the only way of properly learning correct technique.

by the transference, which Ferenczi[5] described as a special instinct of the common human desire for transference, which expresses itself unusually strongly in the neurotic and merely occurs in the analysis under particularly favorable conditions. Whereas in real life this expansion of the libido is subject to inhibition and disturbance, the analysis permits this unwinding under certain conditions, indeed, at times, it even demands it. From this interpretation, the rôle of the analyst came to be generally understood as that of a passive agent who only occasionally intervened at a few points. He had in regard to the suffering of his patient to do nothing else than to permit him to express it, not only in order to see wherein it consisted, i.e., "analytic diagnosis," but on account of certain peculiarities of the neurosis itself which presumes a revival of the old repressed material of the illness before a cure can be effected. Indeed the general practitioner can only interfere to correct an organic illness by concentrating and localizing the process of the disease. The analyst can learn from the general practitioner quiet, trained observation of the course of the illness, patience and an attitude of trusting somewhat to "nature." All the other virtues, often very valuable in a physician, may even interfere with the analytic work. The essential difference between the physician and the analyst, we can, according to Freud, formulate thus: the analyst not only uses the transference, which exists everywhere in a latent form, for the purpose of making the process of unwinding the libido easier, but also points out to the patient the transference at every step in order finally to free him from it. The last point seems to be one particularly contrary to the medical ideal,

[5] Introjektion und Uebertragung, Jahrbuch, 1909. See Sex in Psychoanalysis (Richard Badger, Boston, 1916).

since a large part of all medical art rests on the confidence of the patient, which the physician must maintain in the interest of the latter, *i.e.*, on the unconscious transference. From this point of view many more cures in internal medicine, which must use the unconscious transference as one of its most helpful weapons, are "the results of suggestion" than in psycho-analysis, for although psycho-analysis works with transference, it uses the resolution of this relationship as a therapeutic means to release the infantile libido fixation at the end of the treatment. Therefore the "ideal case," in analytic in contrast to medical practice, is that of the patient who having once been treated is never seen again, best cured when one never hears from him again. This result, however, presupposes a power of sublimation and renunciation on the part of the patient such as is not given to all people.

This interpretation of psycho-analysis, as an artificially induced process of the unwinding of the libido, for the purpose of correcting neurotic forms of discharge, answers automatically the frequent question as to the attitude of the analyst; his task is to remain rather passive in the face of the repetition of the libido overflow and to act as it were as the object or rather the phantom of the process. On the other hand, where a correction of the neurotic process is necessary he must certainly intervene "actively," behaving, so to speak, as a sort of catalyzer.

Before we answer the question how the analysis of the libidinal resistance is actually carried out, and what in general the points are at which the neurotic material presents itself for correction, we wish to emphasize that the phases of an analysis as given in the following description naturally do not occur thus schematically in actual practice. The principal question is how one deals with the phases of resistance and transference, the mastery of which takes place in the main work of the analysis which we might briefly call a libido privation cure.

In the phase of resistance in which the ego defends itself on the one hand against the unconscious itself, on the other hand, even more against the analysis of the unconscious, the material which appears is principally the preconscious memory material of the patient, or the manifest character-istics and ideals which his ego represents. All these "resistances," varying greatly in importance, which affect the course of the libido transference in the way we have described, are analyzed step by step during the analysis. Mostly the narcissistic resistances, proceeding from the ego, and the ideal formation appear at first; these are partic-ularly difficult to overcome, because the patient, with the full weight of his whole actual personality, opposes the automatic unwinding of the libido attempted by his uncon-scious. Frequently the overcoming of these ego resistances only succeed after wounding the narcissism of the patient, or by means of a temporary suspension of his old ego ideal, after which the unwinding of the libido, or more correctly put, the affective expression of the libidinal instincts and desires proceeds more freely than before. From the phenomena of the transference, which represents, as it were, a replica of the infantile libido situation of the patient, we succeed in reproducing the disturbed infantile development of the individual by means of transforming the well known expressions of the unconscious into the language of consciousness, and also by means of the tend-ency to repeat old situations of the libido.

In the phase of resistance we have to deal with the preconscious memory material which the patient, under the influence of the analytic situation, so to speak, collects

out of his varied spheres of interest and centers of cathexis.[5a] In the phase of transference—in contrast to that of
resistance—it is always a question of making conscious the
tendency of the libido, operating in the transference, to
reproduce situations which mostly were never conscious at
all, but resulted from those tendencies and impulses which
were partly experienced in the infantile development, but
were at once repressed. By analyzing in the transference
these, as it were abortive wishes, which continue to struggle
for fulfillment in the unconscious but which the ego has
long since discarded (neurotic conflict) we give the patient
the opportunity to "experience" these wishes intensely
for the first time, in order, with the help of the conviction
which he thus acquires, and avoiding the formation of
pathological reactions, to place him in the position of
attaining an adjustment to reality. The chief resistance,
which has to be overcome in this process, is infantile
anxiety, or the uniting of this anxiety with the libidinal
parental conflict as an unconscious sense of guilt. The
latter in itself already contains sources of conflict, since it
results from the struggle of the ego ideal with the libidinal
tendencies and the wishes which correspond to them. The
neurotic indeed suffers, as the classical example of the
obsessional neurosis demonstrates, but as can clearly be
recognized in every other form of pathological mentality,
such as the perversions or the psychoses, etc., from an
overmeasure of this unconscious sense of guilt. If one
can succeed in reducing this sense of guilt, which operates
out of the repressed material, to a normal amount by in
part solving and abreacting it in fear, the libidinal

[5a] Cathexis-Besetzung, of original, is the technical term for libido "investment," or "charge" of libido. In electrical terms this is analogous to
"voltage" or "amperage" or a combination of both.

tendencies, which this sense of guilt have kept in check and suppressed since childhood, venture forth in the form of the transference. They can then be made conscious, and can, as the result of the analytic insight, be elaborated by the actual ego in a new and more useful way. It is well known that this new elaboration can result partly by means of repudiation, the erection of a new ego ideal, partly it can take the form of sublimation, a part can be allowed to express itself.[6]

The fact of creating the analytic situation in itself means giving full play for a time, if only in the phantasy of the transference libido, to those satisfactions which had up to then been rejected by the ego. Having done this, the analysis must now, by deciphering the reproduction presented in the transference, not only recognize the fixation of the infantile libido of the patient, but also by simultaneously freeing the libido from the predominance of the sense of guilt and anxiety for the first time provide a discharge. Since, in every case, it is also a question of reëxperiencing, of reproducing in contrast to remembering the preconscious material, the patient will naturally attempt to withdraw certain, for him, highly valuable libidinal situations from analytic reproduction by means of actual repetition. This must, of course, be recognized and prevented as far as possible, in extreme cases even by active intervention such as forbidding. It is different with analytic repetition which offers the opportunity, not only to reproduce certain situations in the analysis, but also to understand them analytically and to learn to control them. The conscious enlightenment of the patient during the

[6] This living out, or expressing itself of the libido, must not be understood to have any particular purpose. It is merely natural that a part of the freed libido of the neurotic should be accessible for direct satisfaction and need not be given up, since it belongs to normal life.

process often shows itself to be only a means of helping to reproduce repressed situations which cannot be "remembered" as such because, as we have said, they never had been conscious. In addition to giving the patient the idea of what he must expect in connection with his associations and resistances, the privation of libido is of essential assistance in attaining the reproduction. The patient must be subjected to this privation during the analysis, since the neurosis developed under the withdrawal of a libidinal satisfaction which he had previously enjoyed. By means of this libido privation one prevents a premature evaporation of the affects in the transference situation, and forces the libido back, at the same time analyzing and demonstrating these attempts, to the point from which the wrong development began, i.e., where the fixation occurred.

When the patient has in this way been freed from the repression, from anxiety and the feeling of guilt, and has with our "active" help found the courage to recognize his libidinal tendencies, the next step is to free the whole infantile libido, which has been reproduced in the transference, from the analytic situation, and to enable the patient to put it to a new and more normal use. This task occupies a particular phase of the analysis which we have called the weaning from the libido, and which analytically means the correct resolution of the transference. That the patient is ready for this is shown by decisive signs of various sorts which cannot be misunderstood. The chief characteristic of this situation, which has already been pointed out by Freud, is that the analysis has taken the place of the old neurosis in the form of an artificial neurosis—the actual libido fixation has taken the place of the infantile one—the analysis itself has, so to speak, become a compulsion. It is then merely a question, after adequately

working through this artificial transference neurosis, of resolving it and its new, actual tendency to fixation, a process
which takes place by diminishing the transference and
which must proceed just as slowly as the automatic unwinding of the libido under the suppression of the ego
resistances of the first phase. In this gradual development
and resolution of the analytic situation, the nature of the
analysis as a displacement, or demarcation of the libido
requiring a certain time to run its course can be seen
clearly.

At this point in the analysis when the libido development of the patient splits, so to speak, and is transferred
from the spool of the infantile fixation to that of the analytic
fixation, in the course of this unwinding at least all of the
pathologic fixations having been reproduced as it were on
a film, the intervention of the analyst in the matter of duration of the analysis takes place. He sets a definite period
of time for completing the last part of the treatment in
which the libido of the patient, following an automatic
course, now shows the tendency to fix itself in the analysis
as a substitute for the neurosis.

In this last phase of the analysis, in which the patient
must show that he is able to stand the withdrawal of the
libido, new resistances proceeding from the ego naturally
appear, which take the form of a depreciation of the whole
analytic work, and an unwillingness to accept its results,
since the unconscious of the patient had become adjusted to
accepting the analysis only if it received libidinal satisfaction in the transference. This must now be given up and
the results of the analysis and the attendant changes in the
attitude must nevertheless be accepted. This constitutes a
test of patience for the patient, who, from the very nature
of the neurotic privation, attempts to show that the with-

drawal of the libido places the cure in jeopardy, whereas it is in fact the only way in which the analytic task can be successfully completed. The period fixed for terminating the analysis after the transference neurosis has been established must be adhered to exactly, and one should not be misled by the "progress" which the patient, under the pressure of this inflexibility, may appear to make, into dismissing him earlier, for it is only in this very last phase that all those things which are decisive for the therapeutic result, and to which the earlier phases were only preparatory can be accomplished.

We can now, after glancing back, summarize the actual meaning of the analytic treatment as follows: the essential of the analysis consists, as we have said, in an unwinding process of the libido within a definite space of time, in the course of which all the demands of the infantile libido find a partial fulfillment in the transference; in reality, however, these demands, simultaneously with their being granted a sort of phantasy satisfaction, experience a gradual resolution culminating in their conscious adjustment. This interpretation of analysis, taking into consideration the contents and relations of the libido reactions which Freud has clearly worked out, of the procedure in analytic treatment and the analytic situations in which it culminates, suggests the following fundamental conception.

By placing the libido of the patient in the infantile parental relationship we make it possible for his actual personality, so to speak, to gradually change back to its first infantile condition. Accordingly the first phase of the analysis is taken up with this new attitude, or more correctly expressed, this revived attitude of the patient in which he catches up, so to speak, with the cathexes of all the highly developed ramifications of his ego system, of his personality, or of his neurosis, in order to lead them back into the track of the old Oedipus libido and its preliminary stages. This is the unconscious goal which guides the patient, and which we see, as if from a great distance, through all his associations, as well as in the inhibitory utterances of his resistances. The whole process takes place under tremendous pressure from the infantile libido, which has finally caught sight of the possibility of some sort of satisfaction, and proceeds under the protest of the whole actual personality which, with its ego ideal and pseudo-narcissistic tendencies, resists this reduction to the infantile. The more intensive the pressure of the libidinal tendencies to express themselves in the transference the greater are the inhibitive resistances of the ego. Here what we mean, when we say that actually we need only eliminate the resistances which stand in the way of the development of the libido transference, becomes clear. One must say fortunately, for otherwise the analytic efforts would be simply destroyed by the force and directness of the libidinal current. But the *real resistance, far from disturbing the analytic work* is actually a requisite and acts as a mainspring in regulating its course. On the other hand one must not think that the function of the resistance is solely to regulate the course of the libido and thus make the analysis possible at all; the content of the resistance is also of importance for it almost always is a sign that the patient here, too, reproduces instead of remembers and in the material betrays also that which he would like by means of reproduction to withdraw from analytic elaboration. From this point of view the resolution of the libidinal resistances by means of the analytic situation is one of the chief accomplishments of psychoanalytic technique.

When the first adjustment to the analytic situation has

succeeded, that is when the analyst has taken the place of the libidinal ego ideal—the father or the mother—then the original neurosis which proceeded from the Oedipus situation and which was displaced from this basis by the constantly increasing repression must artificially be led back to its original source. In doing this the transference becomes fully established in the sense of the unconscious, and is now used for the purpose of transforming the old Oedipus neurosis, which, under the influence of the ego development, had taken on the aspect of one of the familiar clinical forms, into a new analytical transference neurosis. *The resolution of this then takes place by means of consistently translating the unconscious material in all of its expressions, and their interpretations not only according to the meaning of the analytic situation, but also according to the infantile,* which runs parallel with it. In this way, by experiencing and living through to the end for the first time the infantile libidinal wishes, and continual settlement in the sense of making them conscious under privation, the patient finally learns to give up for good the unadjusted realization, and the pathologic satisfaction, of his infantile libido which is now critically cast aside by his new ego ideal. This is the reëducation to which the neurotic must subject his libido in the analysis. It takes place by permitting the patient gradually, by way of the transference, to regress to the period of the development of the "Oedipus complex" (not into the situation itself) and by enlightening him about this while removing the resistances, making the channels and ways of discharge which had been shut off open and accessible.

The correct and consistent execution of this task contains the most important technical problems of the psychoanalysis. For the particular way in which the normal

Oedipus libido is elaborated (mostly repressed) by the ego expresses itself in every individual case in the phenomena of transference and resistance, which must be understood, correctly reëstablished and then resolved. In the process certain typical forms of expression have naturally come to be recognized by repeated analytic experience, and have left their precipitate upon the theory, just as there are typical ways in which the ego attempts to master the libido, creating neurotic types or character types.

One reaction to the reproduction of the Oedipus situation in the analysis which seems to occur quite regularly is the manifestation of the castration complex. This, in the case of the man, means the turning away of the libido from the mother as object, and the identification with her, from which, according to the fate of the repression of the sense of guilt, operating as a motive power, the most various pathologic forms [7] can develop. In the case of the woman we see the turning away from the father, and the identification with him, in the sense of keeping the infantile wish for a penis. Just as in the infantile development this mechanism is intended to serve the purpose of avoiding the Oedipus rôle so in the analysis, which again calls forth this situation, the castration complex appears, so to speak, as a "negative Oedipus complex". Thus what we find in the analysis as the "castration complex" corresponds to a neurotic application (defense sympton) of the normal infantile bisexuality, that is a stage of development in which there was as yet no differentiation of the sexes. Naturally this symptom points back to the deeper infantile stages of development common to both sexes, which cannot here be further discussed.[8]

[7] See Rank "Perversion and Neurosis".
[8] See now Rank "Das Trauma der Geburt". 1924.

Taking as our point of departure the already greatly distorted neurosis, as it becomes manifest in the clinical symptoms, we place the patient in the transference neurosis and thus enable him to experience in the analysis the never actually active "original neurosis" of the Oedipus complex with all its preliminary stages. This makes his illness, which was intended to replace these inaccessible repressed original expressions, useless. The two periods of the analytic intervention, the activation of the original neurosis and its resolution appear to correspond to the two periods of the development of the neurosis, the infantile neurosis and the clinical neurosis, which themselves again follow, according to Freud's elucidation, the biological facts of the two periods of sexual development characteristic of man.[9]

The neurosis is characterized by the projection into the phase of maturity, of the first, from its very nature incomplete and also incompletely overcome, phase of sexual development and repression. In his unconscious the neurotic remains therefore at a primitive biologic stage of conflict, which explains the infantile character of the neuroses as well as the necessity for analytic reëducation. Therefore not only is there a childhood neurosis back of every neurosis, but it is the direct· task of the analysis to uncover the infantile neurosis back of the clinical neurosis, that is, to reduce the clinical neurosis to its conflicting preliminary stages, even if these have never been manifest. This original neurosis can only be repeated by means of reproduction in the analysis, principally experienced in the transference and thus psychically eliminated.

[9] We here see the rare occurrence that a point of view which developed from practical (theoretical) necessity can later be used as the confirmation of an earlier theoretic assumption and not merely as a mechanical application of the same.

Psychoanalysis thus allows the patient to relive, partly even for the first time to live through to the end, the original infantile libidinal situation with a partial satisfaction under the condition of consciously giving up its unadjusted realization. This task can, under the pressure of the analysis, be executed by the adult ego of the patient so that he is able consciously to stand the unrequited Oedipus love. Indeed it is this ability to stand a partial giving up, at the same time avoiding an en bloc repression, which on the whole enables a person to seize the possibilities of substitute satisfactions which reality offers. In the analysis the infantile love impulses, which live on in the unconscious, suppressed in their development, struggle to repeat themselves, or they are brought to the surface with the help of our technique. *Thus in the correctly executed analysis the whole development of the individual is not repeated, but only those phases of development of the infantile libido on which the ego, in spite of their uselessness, has remained fixed.*

The theoretic question whether the analysis is an education of the ego, or an education of the libidinal instincts, can in practice be answered somewhat in this way. The first phase of every analysis represents an education of the ego, in so much as it accustoms the ego of the patient to recognize expressions of the libido contrary to the ego, and prevents the repetition of the old process of repression. In a later phase, after the transference has developed, the libido, the development of which was arrested in childhood, fully unfolds; in the weaning, or phase of deprivation, the ego energy or forces proceeding from the new ego ideal again see to it that the newly awakened desires adjust themselves to reality. Naturally these ego forces do not need to be thrust upon the patient by any sort of moral

talk or by giving him anagogic goals, for they exist from
the first in every patient who is not insane just as much as
the desire for transference. Indeed it is these ego forces
which finally bring about the process of cure, the further
transference of the libido from the analyst to "more real
objects" in life or which makes it possible to stand unsatisfied, free floating libido. Without the help of these ego
forces, and without some natural egoism, the final task of
psycho-analysis, the weaning from the cure, would be impossible. For in this phase the problem is to get the
patient, with the help of the love for the analyst, to give up
this love. This would be a contradiction in terms and quite
an impossibility if the intelligence of the patient did not
assist. After the patient has become convinced that he
cannot obtain the love of the analyst in reality—and that
such is the case he only admits in the very last phase of the
cure—he recognizes, consciously as well as emotionally, the
impossibility of fulfilling the demands of his infantile
libido and contents himself with the other things which life
offers. It is remarkable with what haste the libido, as it
frees itself from the cure, seeks out new interests in life.
We see the process of sublimation which in ordinary life
requires years of education, take place before our eyes
towards the end of the cure in the shortest space of time,
without any particular guidance being necessary. The
libido which has become available spontaneously seizes
every opportunity, every possibility of discharge for expressing itself in a way compatible with its ego.

II. The Freeing of the Libido Fixation in the Factor
of Experience.

The creation of the analytic situation really exposes the
patient a second time to his infantile trauma by offering

his unsatisfied Oedipus libido, which had displaced itself neurotically upon inadequate objects, the actual old object. The discharge of libidinal excitation thus inaugurated, represents for the unconscious of the patient a satisfaction which he is not able to find anywhere else in life, and which binds him to the situation. We give the patient the parental imago which he has sought from earliest childhood and on which he can emotionally live out his libido. The patient, by identifying us with his father or mother, shows clearly that it is this ideal parental imago which he seeks, which we, however, cannot offer him permanently in the form in which he wishes it. However, if we did so, we would, as frequently enough happens, apparently "cure" the patient by making him happily in love, whereas the analysis must aim to get him to give up a part of this infantile libido by realizing that its satisfaction is unattainable. We have finally to show him by a painful experience, so to speak, that the fulfillment of his wishes would be contrary to his adult ego ideal and in what manner.

During and by means of the transference the erection of a new temporary ideal takes place; the ego ideal, which the patient has brought with him, defends itself against the provisional ideal in the form of resistances, whereas his old repressed infantile nature struggles for it. By acting at first, as Freud expressed it, as the champion of the repressed material one is able to clear away the resistances proceeding from the ego. One of the most frequent manifestations of the resistance, in the beginning of the analysis, is the identification with the father, with the obstinate wish to surpass him in everything which opposes the acceptance of the infantile situation presented by the analysis. This first phase of the analysis of the ego resist-

ances sometimes already requires the active intervention
of the analyst which, however, need not go beyond the rôle
of the analytical parental authority which is given by the
transference. When the ego resistances have been cleared
away and the transference fully and adequately established, it is used for the reproduction in the analysis, until
finally the libido resistance, which is the second big resistance after the ego resistance, develops out of the transference, which means the natural striving against the necessarily enforced privation. It is only at this point that the
transference which up to now has been a means of promoting the analysis becomes its object and must be explained to the patient as such.

In general one must not estimate too highly the direct
therapeutic value of explanations which do not directly
serve to clear away resistance. One need not even think of
the well known type of the obsessional neurotic who, after
a lengthy analysis, has the whole analytic knowledge of his
analyst in his little finger, and can even surpass him in
analyzing his own symptoms without having been in the
least helped in regard to his suffering. No matter how
much such a patient has learned from his analyst, and even
understood, he has not yet experienced anything which has
brought this "knowledge" home to him. But one does not
have to go so far to see an example of the therapeutic uselessness of this "mere knowledge". It is sufficient to
think of those people who somehow—mostly out of neurotic motives—have come to practice psycho-analysis only
to realize after a few failures that they need analysis themselves. Such persons generally come to the treatment with
more or less ready knowledge—even of their own symptoms—which as they themselves demonstrate could not
prevent them from becoming the victim of a neurosis and

was not able to free them from it. On the contrary for such analysts the practice of psycho-analysis seems to have been a symptom of their own neuroses, in so far as the analysis reactivated the old Oedipus situation for themselves, which they are therefore never in a position to fully resolve in their patients.[10] The analysis of such persons would be an instructive object lesson for beginning analysts and would probably save them from certain technical mistakes. For they would then find themselves confronted by a patient whose theoretical knowledge of analysis was somewhat commensurate with their own, and would therefore be placed before the task of discovering that the therapeutic influencing of a patient is something in its very nature entirely different from the mere imparting of theoretical knowledge. By comparing such analyses with those of more naïve patients one can best recognize that *all enlightenment and explanation alone is only a first help in making* clear to the patient the meaning of the reproduction that he is to expect in the analytical experience. One need in no way fear that the patient will be "frightened" by a premature explanation and fall into a state of resistance. Of course there are situations in the analysis in which not interpreting is the proper reaction in order to get from the patient all the material belonging to a certain situation, whereas by a premature interpretation in such a case the last unconscious motive of the often very important connecting links may get lost.[11] If the analyst does not understand and control the analytical situation he cannot

10 We have indeed found from experience that some supporters, while consciously recognizing analysis, simply reacted with their latent neurosis out of which they then created their resistances in the form of scientific objections.

11 It would be somewhat as if one were to interpret the loosing of an object symbolically as "castration" without paying any attention to the finer mechanics of the slip (such as sacrifice or sense of guilt).

do anything except let the patient "associate" and "interpret" to him the single associations. The protraction of this method reduces the analysis to the level of an association experiment as if the point were to prove to the patient that he has complexes and which ones.

It is the fundamental rule of analytic technique, that the analyst should only come out from his shell of observational reserve, from the rôle of merely existing, when it is absolutely necessary, that is in general when the resistances require him to intervene in the unwinding of the libido in the way which we have above indicated. As much as possible this should occur only in the few big and really decisive situations of the analysis, whereas one should carefully avoid trying to be overconscientious about interpreting details, or wishing to understand at once everything that the patient says or does and to explain it to him. Such excess of zeal means disregarding the fact, which is also of theoretic importance, that the associations are often only brought forward by the patient for some purpose and this must then be made conscious to the patient instead of losing oneself in the details of interpreting single associations. The same considerations must be observed to an even greater degree in the interpretation of dreams which, in the practical analysis, need not be carried out as though the point were to prove the correctness of theory,[12] but so as to take out of the dream what corresponds in importance to the analytic situation. Otherwise one falls into the disastrous mistake of neglect-

[12] Meantime Freud's work *Zur Theorie und Praxis der Traumdeutung* (Zeitschrift IX, 1, 1913) which belongs here has appeared.

"Analyses of dreams" occasionally published with pride which have been "worked" upon many hours are not very good evidence for the analyst, no matter what interesting material such studies may give for the psychology of dreams or the technique of the interpretation.

ing the actual task for the sake of the psychological interest. This consists in understanding and interpreting every expression of the patient above all as a reaction to the present analytical situation (defense against, or recognition of the exposition of the analyst, emotional reactions to these, etc.), in doing which it is important to differentiate between what is actually provoked and infantile repetition, or at times to understand and get the patient to recognize what is common to both.

This holds for every separate symptom, for every dream, even for the understanding of the separate associations, but above all for the whole analytical situation. Thus it becomes particularly important to analyze the unconscious conditions which have brought the patient to the analysis, as well as the conditions and requirements which he associates with the end of the analysis, among these particularly conditions as to the length of time (for example when the patient from the first wishes to set a definite date for finishing). Such an attitude, if it is not disposed of from the first, can defeat the final result of an analysis, no matter how well it has been carried out in the details. The previous exposition shows clearly how the original abreacting of the affects—in spite of all the increase in our knowledge—has actually still remained the essential therapeutic agent, with, however, the important advance that we no longer leave the course to be determined by the compulsion to repeat and also no longer restrict it to one single "jammed in" affect. The tremendous difference between the abreaction in catharsis and that in the "psycho-analytical experience," according to our meaning, is that in catharsis one tried to provoke the discharge of the affects in direct connection with the reawakening of the pathological memory traces, whereas our present day analytic technique allows the affects which are pathological in their working to run off, or to be provoked in the relation to the analyst, or the analysis, that is in the analytic situation, first using these affective expressions in order spontaneously to bring to memory or to reproduce[13] the traumatic factors of the past.

In the difference here given, between seeking memories for the purpose of reaching the affects and provoking the affects for the sake of uncovering the unconscious, we can see the deepest causes why psycho-analysis as a science had first to go through a phase of understanding before it could come to a full appreciation of the factor of experience.

Only at this point can we understand and solve the apparent contradiction between Freud's interpretation of the predominating importance of remembering and our emphasis on experience and on its reproduction. The tendency, which we also pursue, of provoking the repetition in the analytical situation finally ends by creating for the patient, so to speak, new actual memories in place of the pathological complexes shut off from the rest of the mental content. These pathologic complexes are reawakened and translated into "remembering" by being made conscious during the experience without permitting the time and possibility for "repression." Thus in the end remembering still remains the final factor of healing and the actual problem is constantly to transform one—as it were organic —kind of repeating, the reproducing, into another mental form of repeating, the remembering, which itself is only a form of the mnemonic repetition-compulsion. In this proc-

[13] See Ferenczi: Weitere Beiträge zur aktiven Technik in der Psychoanalyse (Zeitschrift, 1921). Now and again a spontaneous "cathartic" discharge takes place generally in connection with not very deeply repressed memory material.

ess it becomes clear why just the analytic privation, which represents as it were a repetition of the trauma for the patient, is indispensable in obtaining the conviction necessary to the cure. Indeed to consciously become aware of anything is, in general, a mental phenomenon which human beings never produce except under the pressure of a privation-situation, that is in order to avoid pain. The note of conviction is missing about knowledge[14] acquired in any other way, no matter how compelling it may be in point of logic.

Therefore we must force the individual in the analysis to reproduce the essentially unconscious part of his faulty development, allowing him to live out a part of the libido which had been deprived of satisfaction, under the condition that he, by discharging it, and at the same time by insight into its mechanisms, gives up the false adjustment, and on the basis of a new advance in development, substitutes a more real adjustment. This takes place by leading the course of excitation from the unconscious phantasies to the higher preconscious thinking in the analytical situation. This for the first time paves the way for a discharge of the affects and thus raises the whole mental existence to a different level, that of adjustment to reality. A correctly executed psycho-analysis is from this point of view a social process, a "mass structure of two," according to an utterance of Freud, in which the analyst must take the place of the whole heterogeneous environment, particularly of the most important persons in the surroundings of the patient.

[14] See Ferenczi: *Introjektion und Übertragung*, Jahrbuch I, 1909.

CHAPTER III.

Now that we have in a brief outline described what we mean by the psycho-analytic method, we are able to look back and to recognize that a series of mistakes in the technique correspond to remaining stationary at certain stages of development in analytic perception. It is only natural that such inhibitions in development not only were possible and occurred in all the phases of the analytic progress, but also that they still exist, or repeat themselves to-day.

We wish not only to show in individual points how this is to be interpreted, and thus to throw a side light on the historic development of psycho-analysis, but also principally to help to avoid such faulty developments in the future. What now follows is actually the presentation of a series of incorrect methods, that is of such as no longer correspond to an up-to-date conception of the psychoanalytic technique.

In view of the general clinical, phenomenalistic point of view in medicine, it is not to be wondered at that in the medical practice of psycho-analysis a kind of descriptive analysis, actually a contradiction in terms, was reached. Such an analysis, as a rule, limited itself to listening, or to an expansive description of the symptoms, or the perverse wishes of the patient, without any essential therapeutic effect resulting from this mere "talking out," because the dynamic factor of experience was neglected.

A similarly misunderstood kind of analysis consisted in the collecting of associations, as if these were in themselves the essential thing, and not merely rising bubbles of consciousness showing us where, or perhaps at what depth under the surface, the active affects were concealed, and particularly what motives drove the patient in a given case to use the ways of association which he seemed to prefer.

Less harmless was the fanaticism for interpreting, which resulted in overlooking, in a cut and dried translation according to the dictionary, the fact that the technique of interpretation is but one of the means of help in understanding the unconscious mental condition of the patient, and not the aim, or certainly not the chief aim, of the analysis. This translation of the associations of the patient is of the same value as in the realm of language from which the comparison is taken. The unavoidable preliminary work to the understanding of the whole text, is the looking up of unknown words, but it is not an aim in itself. This "translation" must be followed by the "interpretation", so as to give a comprehensible connection. Viewed from this angle, the frequent disputes over the correctness of an interpretation, *i.e.*, translation, disappear. Questions from analysts whether this or that "interpretation"—in our sense of the word translation is meant—be correct or the query what this or that, perhaps in a dream, "means", show an incomplete understanding of the whole analytic situation and an overestimation, such as we have just pointed out, of isolated details. These can mean sometimes one thing, sometimes another. The same symbol in the same patient can have, or take on, a different meaning under the pressure or the loosening of a resistance. In an analysis fine details, apparent incidentals such as voice, gesture, expression, are so important. So much depends upon the successful interpolation, upon the comprehensible relationship, upon the meaning which the expressions of the patient acquire by his own unconscious commentary with the help of our interpretation. Thus the technique of translation forgot in the interest of the "correct" translation of details, that the whole, that is the analytic situation of the patient as such, also has a meaning, and indeed the chief meaning. Only from an understanding of the whole can the correct interpretation of the translated parts follow; this is then free and certain, whereas the fanaticism of translation leads to mere routine work and is therapeutically fruitless.

Another faulty method was holding fast to the already overcome phase of the analysis of the symptoms. It is well known that there was an early period of psychoanalysis in which, by proceeding from the separate symptoms, and by suggestive pressure those memories were called forth, which, working in the unconscious, produced the symptoms. On account of the later development in the psychoanalytic technique this method has long been given up. It is, indeed, not even a question of getting the symptoms to disappear, which every suggestive method can easily accomplish, but rather preventing their return, which means making the ego of the patient more capable of resistance. For this purpose an analysis of the whole personality is necessary. The analyst should, according to Freud's direction, always proceed from what is at the time the mental surface and must not pursue the associative connections with the symptoms. Evidently it was too tempting and easy to obtain information about the neurotic, or perverse behavior of the patient by directly asking him and thus let him directly remember the history of the development of his abnormality.[15]   Only a series of converg-

---

[15] This rejection of the principle of the "analysis of symptoms" naturally does not preclude at times asking the patient the reason for the particular obtrusiveness of some symptomatic expression (for example the so-called temporary symptoms).

ing experiences can place us in the position of understanding the many "interpretations" which one symptom can have in a particular case. Direct questions merely succeeded in turning the attention of the patient towards this factor at the wrong time, thus establishing his resistances at this point, for the patient was able to misuse this, in itself, not entirely unjustified direction of his attention. Thus it could happen that the "analysis" was unduly protracted, but the original infantile story, without the reconstruction of which no treatment can be called a real analysis, was never reached.

We must deal, somewhat more in detail, with one phase of analysis which can be called the "analysis of complexes" and which preserves an important stage of the amalgation with academic psychology. The word "complex" was first used by Jung as the simplification of a complicated psychological fact, to designate certain tendencies, characteristic for the person in question, or a related group of affect-colored conceptions. This interpretation of the word which was constantly becoming more comprehensive, and had thus come to have almost no meaning, was then limited by Freud who described the *unconscious repressed parts* of those group conceptions with the name "complex." As the more subtle, labile, fluctuating processes of cathexis in the psyche became accessible to research, the acceptance of such inflexible, separate mental components became more and more superfluous. They were too coherent, they could only be excited and displaced in toto, they were much too "complex," as more exact analysis showed, to be treated as elements which could not be further reduced. Indeed in the newer works of Freud, this conception merely figures as the survival of a period of psycho-analysis, for which we have actually no more use, especially since the creation of our meta-psychology.

The most consistent thing would have been to have done away entirely with this now useless rudiment of an earlier time, and to have given up the terminology, which had become dear to most analysts, in favor of a better understanding. Instead of doing this, the whole of mental life was often regarded as a mosaic of such complexes, and the analysis then carried out with the object of "analyzing out" one complex after the other, or the attempt was made of treating the whole personality as a sum total of father-mother-, brother-, and sister-complexes. It was naturally easy to collect material for these, since every one has, of course, all the complexes, that is, every one must, in the course of his development, somehow get on with the persons and objects which surround him. The connected recounting of complexes, or the attributes of these, may have its place in descriptive psychology, but not in the practical analysis of the neurotic, nor does it even belong in the psycho-analytic study of literary, or ethno-psychological products where it must undoubtedly lead to a monotony in no way justified by the many sidedness of the material, and which was scarcely tempered by giving preference, first to one and then to the other complex.

Although such a flattening out may have to be put up with at times, as unavoidable in a scientific presentation, one should not therefore transfer such a cramped interest into the technique. The analysis of complexes easily misleads the patient into being pleasing to his analyst, by bringing him "complex material" as long as he likes, without giving up any of his really unconscious secrets. Thus there came to be histories of illnesses in which the patients recounted memories, evidently fabricating them, in a way that never happens in unprejudiced analyses, and can only be looked upon as the product of such a "breeding of complexes." Such results should naturally not be used subjectively either to show the correctness of one's own method of interpreting, or as theoretic conclusions, nor yet as leading to any sort of evidence.[16]

It happened particularly frequently that the associations of the patient were directed to the sexual factor at the wrong time, or that they remained stuck at this point if—as so often happens—he came to the analysis with the expectation that he must constantly talk exclusively of his actual or infantile sexual life. Aside from the fact that this is not so exclusively the case as our opponents think, permitting such an indulgence in the sexual often gives the patient the opportunity to paralyze the therapeutic effect of the privation he must undergo.

An understanding of the many sided and important mental contents which underlie the collective name "castration complex" was also not exactly furthered by bringing the theory of the complexes into the dynamics of the analysis. On the contrary, we are of the opinion that the premature theoretic condensation of the facts under the conception of the complex interfered with the insight into deeper layers of mental life. We believe that the full appreciation of that which the analytic practitioner has accustomed himself to finish off with the label "castration complex" is still lacking, so that this attempt at an explanation should not lightly be regarded as the ultimate explanation of such varied mental phenomena and

[16] Stekel, who attributed the same neurotic symptom first to sexuality, then to crime and finally to religion, may be taken as an extreme example of the subjectivity of such a passion for complexes. He may in this way, since he asserted everything, possibly have been right in some one of his single utterances.

processes of the patient. We can, from the dynamic stand-point, which is the only justifiable one in practice, often recognize in the forms of expression of the castration complex, as they manifest themselves in the course of the analysis, only one of the kinds of resistance which the patient erects against his deeper libidinal wishes. In the early stages of some analyses the castration anxiety can often be uncovered as an expression of the dread, trans-ferred onto the analyst, as a protection against further analysis.

As we have already intimated, technical difficulties arose also from the analyst having too much knowledge. Thus the importance of the theory of sexual development con-structed by Freud, misled some analysts to apply in a mistaken and over-dogmatic fashion in the therapy of the neuroses, certain systems of organization and auto-eroticisms which first gave us an understanding of normal sexual development. In thus searching for the construc-tive elements of the theory of sex, in some cases, the actual analytic task was neglected. These analyses might be compared to psychochemical "element analyses." Here again one could see that the theoretical importance did not always correspond to the value in the practical analysis. The technique need not methodically lay bare all the, as it were, prescribed historic phases of the development of the libido, still less should the uncovering of all theoretically established details and gradations be used as a principle of healing in the neuroses. It is also practically superfluous to demonstrate all the original elements of a highly complicated "connection," while missing the intellectual thread, which combines the few fundamental elements into new and varying phenomena. The same thing holds for the erotogenic zones as for the complexes, for example the urethral or the anal erotic, and for the stages of organization the oral, anal-sadistic and other pregenital phases; there can be no human development without all of these, but one must not in the analysis attribute to them the importance, for the history of the illness, of which the resistance under the pressure of the analytic situation gives the illusion.

On closer observation a certain inner connection between "element analyses" and "complex-analyses" could be recognized, insofar as the latter, in their attempts to plumb the psychic depths, struck upon the granite of the complexes and thus the work was spread out over the surface instead of going to the bottom. Such analyses then usually tried to make up for the lack of depth in the dynamics of the libido by an excursion into the theory of sex, and united rigid attributes of complexes with equally schematically treated principles of the theory of sex, whereas they missed just the play of forces which takes place between the two.

Such an attitude naturally led to a theoretic overestimation of the factor of quantity, to ascribing everything to a stronger organ—eroticism, a point of view— which resembled that of the pre-analytical school of neurologists—who blinded themselves to any insight into actual play of forces of the pathological causes by the catch words "inheritance," "degeneration," "disposition."

Since the theory of the instincts and also the sciences of biology and physiology have been called upon partly as a help in understanding mental phenomena, in particular since the so-called "pathoneurosen," that is the neuroses on the organic level, the organ-neuroses, and even organic illnesses are treated psycho-analytically, disputes about border-line cases have taken place between psycho-analysis and physiology. The stereotyped translation of physiological processes into the language of psycho-analysis is incorrect. Insofar as one attempts to approach organic processes analytically the rules of psycho-analysis must be strictly adhered to here also. One must try to forget, so to speak, one's organic, medical and physiological knowledge and to bear in mind only the mental personality and its reactions.

It was also confusing when simple clinical facts were at once combined with speculations about becoming, being and duration and such deliberations treated like established rules in practical analysis, whereas Freud himself constantly emphasizes the hypothetical character of his last synthetic works. Often enough such a wandering into speculation seems to have been a dodging of uncomfortable technical difficulties. We know how a desire to prematurely condense everything under a speculative principle can wreak vengeance from the point of view of technique.[17] (The Jungian theory).

It was also a mistake, while neglecting the individual, in the explanation of the symptoms, to make cultural and phylogenetic analogies at once, no matter how fruitful the latter might be in themselves. On the other hand, the overestimate of the actual factors led to an anagogic prospective interpretation, which was useless so far as the pathologic fixations were concerned. The adherents of the "anagogic," as well as some of those of the "genetic" school, in their interest in the future and in the past,

---

[17] It is well known that Jung went so far as to neglect the mnemonic importance of the infantile experiences brought to light in the analysis and of the personalities playing an important part in them in favor of an analysis on the "subjective-level". It shows a high degree of flight from reality to be willing to acknowledge the existence and force of only the idealized, or much too impersonal conception, of the obscure derivations of the original memories of objects and of people.

neglected the present condition of the patient. And yet almost all of the past, and everything that the unconscious attempts, insofar as it is not directly conscious or remembered (and this occurs extremely seldom), expresses itself in actual reactions in relation to the analyst or to the analysis, in other words in the transference to the analytic situation.

The requirements of the Breuer-Freud catharsis that the affects, displaced upon symptoms, should be led back directly to the pathologic memory-traces, and at the same time brought to a discharge and bound again proved to be unrealizable, that is, it succeeds only in the case of incompletely repressed, mostly preconscious memory-material as in the case of certain derivatives of the actual unconscious. This itself, the uncovering of which is the chief task of the analysis, since it was never "experienced" can never be "remembered," one must let it be produced on the ground of certain indications. The mere communication, something like "reconstruction," is in itself not suited to call forth affect reactions; such information glides off from the patients without any effect. They can only convince themselves of the reality of the unconscious when they have experienced—mostly indeed only after they have frequently experienced—something analogous to it in the actual analytic situation, that is, in the present. Our new insight into the topography of mental life and the functions of the separate depth levels gives us the explanation for this state of affairs. The unconscious repressed material has no approach to motility, nor to those motor innervations in the sum total of which the affect discharge consists; the past and the repressed must find their representative factors in the present and the conscious (preconscious) in order that they may be affectively experienced and develop further. In contrast to the stormy abreaction one could designate the unwinding bit by bit of the affects in analysis as a fractional catharsis.

We believe, moreover, in general that affects in order to work convincingly must first be revived, that is made actually present and that what has not affected us directly and actually must remain mentally ineffective.

The analyst must always take into account that almost every expression of his patient springs from several periods, but he must give his chief attention to the present reaction. Only from this point of view can he succeed in uncovering the roots of the actual reaction in the past, which means changing the attempts of the patient to repeat into remembering. In this process he need pay little attention to the future. One may quietly leave this care to the person himself who has been sufficiently enlightened about his past and present mental strivings. The historic, cultural and phylogenetic analogies also need, for the most part, not be discussed in the analysis. The patient need hardly ever, and the analyst extremely seldom, occupy himself with this early period.

At this place we must consider certain misunderstandings about the enlightenment of people who are being analyzed. There was a phase, in the development of psycho-analysis, in which the goal of the analytic treatment consisted in filling the gaps in the memory of the patient with knowledge. Later one recognized that the neurotic ignorance proceeded from the resistance, that is from not wishing to know, and that it was this resistance which had to be constantly uncovered and made harmless. If one proceeds thus the amnesic gaps in the chain of memories fill themselves in, for the most part automatically, the other part with the help of sparse interpretations and explanations. The patient therefore learns nothing more and nothing other than what he needs, and in the quantity requisite to allay the predominating disturbances. It was a fatal mistake to believe that no one was completely analyzed who had not also been theoretically familiarized with all the separate details of his own abnormality. Naturally it is not easy to set a boundary line up to which the instruction of the patient should be carried. Interruption of the correct analysis by formal courses of instruction may satisfy both the analyst and the patient, but cannot effect any change in the libido-attitude of the sick person. A further result of such instruction was that, without noticing it, one pushed the patient into withdrawing himself from the analytical work by means of identifying himself with the analyst. The fact that the desire to learn and to teach creates an unfavorable mental attitude for the analysis is well known but should receive much more serious attention.[18]

At times one heard from analysts the complaint that this or that analysis failed on account of "too great resistances" or a too "violent transference." The possibility in principle of such extreme cases is admitted; we do find ourselves at times confronted with quantitative factors, which we must in no way practically underestimate, since they play an important part in the final outcome of the analysis, as well as in its causes. But the factor of quantity, so important in itself, can be used as a screen for incomplete insight into the play of forces which finally decide the kind of application and the distribution of

[18] This holds also for persons who come to be analyzed only for the sake of learning (the so-called "didactic analyses"). In such cases it occurs only too easily that the resistances get displaced onto the intellectual field (science) and so remain unexplained.

those very quantities. Because Freud once uttered the sentence, "Everything which impedes the analytic work is resistance," one should not, every time the analysis comes to a standstill, simply say, "this is a resistance." This resulted, particularly in patients with an easily aroused sense of guilt, in creating an analytic atmosphere in which they, so to speak, were fearful of making the "faux pas" of having a resistance, and the analyst found himself in a helpless situation. One evidently forgot another utterance of Freud, namely, that in the analysis we must be prepared to meet the same forces, which formerly caused the repression as "resistances," as soon as one sets to work to release these repressions.

Another analytical situation which one was also in the habit of labelling incorrectly as "resistance" is the negative transference, which, from its very nature, cannot express itself otherwise than as "resistance" and the analysis of which is the most important task of the therapeutic activity. One need, of course, not be afraid of the negative reactions of the patient for they constitute, with iron necessity, a part of every analysis. Also the strong positive transference, particularly when it expresses itself in the beginning of the cure, is only a symptom of resistance which requires to be unmasked. In other cases, and particularly in the later stages of an analysis, it is an actual vehicle for bringing to light desires which have remained unconscious.

In this connection an important rule of psycho-analytic technique must be mentioned in regard to the personal relation between the analyst and the patient. The theoretic requirement of avoiding all personal contact outside of the analysis mostly led to an unnatural elimination of all human factors in the analysis, and thus again to a theorizing of the analytic experience.

From this point of view some practitioners all too readily failed to attribute that importance to a change in the person of the analyst, which results from the interpretation of the analysis as a mental process, the unity of which is determined by the person of the analyst. A change of analysts may be unavoidable for outer reasons in rare, exceptional cases, but we believe that technical difficulties—in homosexuals, for example—are not simply to be avoided by the choice of an analyst of the opposite sex. For in every correct analysis the analyst plays all possible rôles for the unconscious of the patient; it only depends upon him always to recognize this at the proper time and under certain circumstances to consciously make use of it. Particularly important is the rôle of the two parental images—father and mother—in which the analyst actually constantly alternates (transference and resistance).

It is not an accident that technical mistakes occurred so frequently just in the expression of transference and resistance. One was easily inclined to let oneself be surprised at these elementary experiences in the analysis and strangely enough forgot just here the theory which had been incorrectly pushed into the foreground in the wrong place. This may also be due to subjective factors in the analyst. The narcissism of the analyst seems suited to create a particularly fruitful source of mistakes; among others the development of a kind of narcissistic counter transference which provokes the person being analyzed into pushing into the foreground certain things which flatter the analyst and, on the other hand, into suppressing remarks and associations of an unpleasant nature in relation to him. Both are technically incorrect: the **first** because it can lead to an apparent improvement of the patient which is only intended to bribe the analyst and in this way to win a libidinal counter interest from him; the second because it keeps the analyst from the necessity of noticing the delicate indications of criticism, which mostly only venture forth hesitatingly, and helping the patient to express them plainly or to abreact them. The anxiety and the sense of guilt of the patient can never be overcome without this self-criticism, requiring indeed a certain overcoming of himself on the part of the analyst; and yet these two emotional factors are the most essential for bringing about and maintaining the repression.

Another form under which technical inaccessibility hid itself was an incidental remark of Freud to the effect that the narcissism of the patient could set limits to the degree to which he could be influenced by the analysis. If the analysis did not progress well, one consoled oneself with the thought that the patient was "too narcissistic." And since narcissism forms a connecting link between ego and libidinal strivings in all normal, as well as abnormal mental processes, it is not difficult to find proofs in his behavior and thoughts for the narcissism of the patient. Particularly one should not handle the narcissistically determined "castration" or "masculinity" complexes as if they set the limits for analytic solution.[19]

When the analysis struck upon a resistance of the patient one often overlooked to what extent a pseudo-narcissistic tendency was brought into the question. The analyses of people who bring a certain theoretic knowledge with them into their analyses are particularly

[19] We know that Adler, who evidently did not succeed in the analysis of the libido, remained stuck at this point.

calculated to convince one that a great deal of what one was theoretically inclined to ascribe to narcissism, is actually secondary, pseudo-narcissistic and can by continued analysis be completely solved in the parental relationship. Naturally it is necessary in doing this to take up analytically the ego-development of the patient, as indeed it is in general necessary in the analysis of the resistances to consider the up-to-now much too neglected analysis of the ego, for which Freud has recently given valuable hints.

The newness of a technical point of view introduced by Ferenczi under the name of "activity" resulted in some analysts, in order to avoid technical difficulties, overwhelming the patient with commands and prohibitions, which one might characterize as a kind of "wild activity." This, however, must be looked upon as a reaction to the other extreme, to holding too fast to an over-rigid "passivity" in the matter of technique. The latter is certainly sufficiently justified by the theoretic attitude of the analyst who must at the same time be an investigator. In practice, however, this easily leads to sparing the patient the pain of necessary intervention, and to allowing him too much initiative in his associations as well as in the interpretation of his ideas.[20]

The moderate, but, when necessary, energetic activity in the analysis consists in the analyst taking on, and, to a certain extent, really carrying out those rôles which the

[20] Patients with a strongly "masochistic" attitude are particularly fond of making use of an over "passive technique" on the part of the analysts by themselves undertaking interpretations on the "subjective level" by doing which they satisfy their tendency to torment themselves, at the same time opposing the deeper interpretation with a skeptical resistance. In the same way, one can, moreover, get any "anagogic" interpretation of dreams that one likes by letting somewhat instructed patients interpret the dream elements, without getting behind the dynamics of the resistance overcompensated by morality.

unconscious of the patient and his tendency to flight prescribe. By doing this the tendency to the repetition of earlier traumatic experiences is given an impetus, naturally with the goal of finally overcoming this tendency by revealing its content. When this repetition takes place spontaneously it is superfluous to provoke it and the analyst can simply call forth the transformation of the resistance into remembering (or plausible reconstruction).

These last purely technical remarks lead back to the often mentioned subject of the reciprocal effect of theory and practice about which we must now make some general methodological remarks.

CHAPTER IV

THE RECIPROCAL EFFECT OF THEORY AND PRACTICE.

A particular difficulty in the nature of psycho-analysis itself makes the problem of the reciprocal effect of theory and practice even more complicated in this case than it is, perhaps, in other spheres of knowledge. The psycho-analytic technique was originally, and is still to-day, a means to a causal therapy of the neuroses and aims to allay symptoms by making their unconscious roots conscious. The therapy itself, therefore, seems to rest on a kind of "knowledge" which would thus itself be closely related to theoretic knowledge. But just psycho-analysis could for the first time clearly show that there are, so to speak, two kinds of knowledge, one intellectual, the other based on a deeper "conviction"; the clear cut distinction between these two, particularly in the sphere of psycho-analysis, must be considered among the first and strictest requirements.[21] This appears to be one of the reasons why psycho-analysis lays claim to a peculiar position, for here "plausibility" and "logical necessity" do not suffice as criteria of truth, but rather a direct perception or the experience of the problems in question is necessary in order to be convincing. This "experience," however, contains at the same time certain sources of error if one is not able, to a very great extent, in crystallizing the theoretic results out of the mental experience, to eliminate again the subjective factor of one's own impressions.

With the development of psycho-analysis the thera-

[21] See also *Glaube, Unglaube und Ueberzeugung.* Ferenczi, Populäre Vorträge über Psychoanalyse.

peutic technique became increasingly more complete and detailed and this indeed with the help of this technique itself, which was thus at the same time a practical instrument for healing, as well as one of perception, since the patient was cured by his "knowledge." This fact, that the scientific instrument is at the same time the curative one, is one of the peculiarities of psycho-analysis, whereas other sciences use methods to increase their knowledge which, in relation to the object, must be designated as destructive (anatomy, vivisection, etc.).[22] Analysis has, therefore, from the very beginning two quite different aspects which constantly touch, intersect and cross one another, and the only question is from what angle one views it. If one sees the analytic technique as a means for finding out new psychological facts and connections, that is, for the investigation of mental life, one will be able to say that its therapeutic value is purely accidental; or, on the contrary, looked at from the standpoint of therapy, the scientific results would be a welcome by-product.

In "The Future Chances of Psycho-analytic Therapy"[23] Freud has already stated in anticipation the essentials of what can, in general, be said about the reciprocal relation between psycho-analytic technique and therapy. He says there, among other things, that the therapy will show much better, and probably quicker, results when we have more knowledge. Technical difficulties and the necessity for struggling with them were

---

[22] This difference seems to rest, according to Freud, on a peculiar and unique quality of mental life whereby the same psychic contents are given in various versions and can be topically separated from one another (see the topography in Freud's metapsychology). This makes it possible to make the patient live through the past mnemonically (and also in hallucination), and at the same time be the object of observations in the present without being obliged to "disturb" his present personality.

[23] Paper at the second Psycho-analytic Congress in Nürnberg, 1910.

the actual motives which led Freud to all those researches which resulted in the discovery of the unconscious mental life, its mechanisms, dynamics and economics, the knowledge of which then reapplied could increase our technical ability in the sense discussed above. One can here speak not of a vicious circle constantly creating new difficulties, but rather of a benign circle, of a mutual beneficial influence of the practice upon the theory and the theory upon the practice.

It is perhaps not an exaggeration to state that this kind of mutual control, of perception by experience (empiricism, induction) and in turn of experience by the preceding perception (systematization, deduction) is the only way of keeping a science from falling into error. A discipline which satisfies itself with one or the other methods of research alone, or too soon gives up the control offered by a counter experiment, would be doomed to sterility, pure empiricism because the productive thought would fail, pure theory because in premature omniscience the motives to further investigation would be silenced.

Freud's psycho-analysis deserves, in the theory of science, to be regarded as an example of correct ''utraquistic'' [24] research. It takes its roots in the necessity for favorably influencing certain mental functions which have fallen into the wrong grooves; i.e., it is based on reality. And psycho-analysis always turned back to this source if it wished to test the soundness of the theories which experience forced upon one, or logical necessity demanded. To illustrate the advantages of this interaction of theory and practice we would like here to point

[24] Utraquists were a religious sect who believed in partaking of both the bread and wine of communion; hence ''utraquistic'' or two sided.

to certain important stages of development in the Freudian investigations.

The first theory of Breuer and Freud, that of the abreaction of the strangulated affects, that the psyche possessed the ability to loosen affects from their original objects and to displace them upon others, apart from the fact that it made certain phenomena of mental life more plausible and comprehensible, rested entirely upon the therapeutic result of the cathartic probing into the memories in hysteria. Of course this knowledge then made the cathartic method itself, that is the search for the pathologic memories, very much easier.

The practical difficulty that one can hypnotize very few people correctly caused Freud to give up hypnosis, and then other methods of suggestion, and to allow his patients to associate freely. Thus one obtained surprising insight into unconscious material which had up to then been covered up by the hypnotic binding of the affect. The technique of free association led chiefly to the discovery of the content and forms of expression of unconscious thinking. The "fundamental rule" of the psycho-analytic technique of free association then produced the material which enabled Freud to establish the topical-dynamic point of view, later increased by the economic to the metapsychological attitude. Naturally, the theory then made an orientation in the material, obtained by free association, which could not be clearly understood, easier and set the practical task of understanding the individual case.

Since in every case of neurosis, without exception, sexual traumata in childhood had shown themselves to be the focus of the symptoms, one first set up the "traumatic theory" of hysteria. But, when it became evident that such traumata as could not possibly have occurred in reality, also came up for discussion in the free associations, Freud had to decide upon a modification of the theory which took into consideration the psychic as well as the outer reality, and particularly phantasies, as a factor in creating symptoms. What great progress this knowledge meant for analytic psychology, and how it advanced the practice and the technique of analysis need hardly be discussed here in detail.

The practical necessity, in certain cases of anxiety-hysteria, of forcing the patient, besides the free associations, to a certain overcoming of pain, as Freud described,[25] led to a consideration of all the work which the patient accomplished in the cure besides frank speaking. The theoretic observation of such mental phenomena, as occur as the result of "active" intervention, then gave us a deep insight into the dynamics of mental life in general, and we have in the course of our discussion, been able to point out to what an unexpected degree the use of "activity" in its broader sense furthers the practical work of the therapy.

The recent works of Freud, which attempt to construct the psychology of the Ego, which has up to now been neglected in favor of the study of the Libido, show plainly that our therapeutic and technical ability had also in this point gone very much ahead of our scientific knowledge. Particularly Freud's last work, the overture of which,—so to speak—we heard at the seventh congress in Berlin,[26] attempts to bring up to date and to harmonize some of the simple facts of experience, resulting from practice, with

[25] *Wege der psychoanalytischen Therapie.* Vortrag auf dem V Psycho-analytischen Kongress, Budapest, 1918.

[26] *Das Ich und das Es*—which has since appeared *in toto.*

our theoretic knowledge, or rather to enlarge and modify the latter insofar as it has proved insufficient for the explanation of these facts.

One could perhaps sum up the impression produced by these examples thus: Just as the first fundamental theoretic conceptions of Freud, worked out with exacting detail from countless impressions of experience, were the most effective stimulus to the development of the actual analytical technique—in contrast to the former method of practice,—so in increasing measure, as we have learned to understand and control the unconscious, a new piece of theory has been necessary which has again increased our technical ability.

Psycho-analysis seems now to have reached a point of development where our knowledge, of the previously neglected, but larger part of mental life, is sufficient to obtain important therapeutic results, *provided that one clearly understands how this knowledge can be effectively put into practice.* We have evidently taken this cardinal point much too little into account. It seems rather, that in the analyses, frequently that which was theoretically significant, rather than what was analytically important was sought for, whereas, on the other hand, what was practically important was often easily overestimated in the theory.

To put it extremely the problem could be formulated somewhat as follows: Psycho-analysis, which has developed from a therapy into a science, even into an attitude towards life, must carefully differentiate what part of this great theoretic structure has remained essential therapy, in the narrower sense of the word. Instead of mistakenly applying the theory "therapeutically" in a lump, one should rather ask oneself what part of the whole of psycho-analysis has proven suitable for application in medicine, and what remains as general psychological knowledge, as theory, or at the utmost as "therapy of the normal" (pedagogy). Thus, for example, the "complexes" are results of the theory which retain their value for normal psychology, their establishment must be a preliminary assumption and can never be the outcome of therapeutic endeavor (to analyze out a complex). It was a comprehensible, but fatal, mistake of some of our adherents to think that in the analysis the mere finding of the mistake in development should at once have a therapeutic effect; in contrast to this one-sided "socratic" interpretation the actual effective remedy must be sought in properly connecting the affects with the intellectual sphere.

Just as there are naturally and necessarily, advantageous mutual reactions between theory and practice, so necessarily the difference between the two resulted in disturbing and suppressing influences on both sides. We have already shown, in the critical chapter, what we chiefly mean by the disturbing influence of the theory on the practice. In general one may say that the advantages which accrued for normal psychology out of the magnificent increase of our knowledge of the unconscious were not always sufficiently used to further therapeutic interests. On the other hand, too much theoretic knowledge was often a hindrance to practical accomplishment. The analyst with too much knowledge has, so to speak, "the faults of his advantages." In a young science, in a state of development such as psycho-analysis was, one could find it justifiable that the analytic practitioner was able to combine the two tasks of healing and research, as Freud himself did in such an exemplary way. One can readily understand, however, that the attempt to follow this example frequently led more to a mixing up of these tasks than to their combination.

The theoretic analyst always runs the danger of looking, for example, for arguments to prove the correctness of a new statement, while he thinks that he is promoting the process of curing a neurosis. Important proofs for certain theories could be found in this way, but the process of healing the abnormal dynamics of mental life was scarcely promoted.

The first communications of Breuer and Freud, which still dealt exclusively with a few simple conceptions, told of splendid cures which were effected, sometimes in a few days or weeks. All of us have experinced similar good results, at the beginning of our psycho-analytic careers, some of us, perhaps, before we began to use analysis, for cures can be made with all psycho-therapeutic measures, but on account of the lack of knowledge of the processes used cannot be any evidence for or against the methods. To what extent this is true also of psycho-analysis, which, in fact, has never overestimated its therapeutic results, which are to-day unquestioned, we shall briefly discuss in our last chapter. When, with the increase of our knowledge on the whole, and with the experience of the individual analyst, such "wonder" cures became constantly more infrequent, and the analyses themselves longer, we should like to have these facts used as little against the psycho-analytic theory as in the beginning the quick results were used in favor of it. The cures, which one succeeded in making with less knowledge, are certainly not to be compared in value to those based on a deeper insight, even though these require more time. The length of the time required can never be an argument against the correctness of a method if only one can later prove that this prolongation was necessary and unavoidable in obtaining a better result, *i.e.,* a causal operating therapy.[27]

One must recommend practitioners to fill out the gaps in their theoretic knowledge by necessary study, and analyses of themselves, and one should recommend those given to too much theory to push their academic interests aside as much as possible in their practical applications. This requiring as theoretically unbiased an attitude as possible must not be counted against us as an unscientific tendency. We fully appreciate the value for the promotion of science of the requisite scientific attitude which is connected with working with one's interests concentrated on a subject to be theoretically studied. Our criticism is directed against overestimating, or remaining fixed, in this or that phase of the development of psycho-analysis, particularly at those points at which the proper relation between theory and practice had not been sufficiently recognized, or taken into account, in that much which was correct only in a certain connection, and at a certain stage of our knowledge, was taken either too literally or too generally. We think, therefore, that most of the deficiencies in technique and certain consequent therapeutic difficulties are to be regarded as the results of an insufficient orientation as to the real nature of the psycho-analytic method and the actual meaning and goal of psycho-analytic treatment.

[27] The patients who complained of the length of the psychoanalytic treatment were in a certain sense right. We could, however, say to ourselves with a free conscience that this increase in the duration of the treatment meant a better result in the end.

CHAPTER V.

The beginnings of psycho-analysis were purely practical. Very soon, however, as a by-product of the therapeutic influencing of neurotics, there resulted a scientific insight into the construction and function of the mental apparatus, into the history of the individual and the species and, finally, into the biological foundations (the theory of the instincts).

The chief result of the favorable reaction of this knowledge on psycho-analytic practice was the discovery of the Oedipus complex as the nuclear complex of the neuroses, and the significance of the repetition of the Oedipus relation in the analytic situation (transference).

The essential thing in the analytical intervention, however, does not consist either in the verification of the "Oedipus Complex", or in the simple repetition of the Oedipus situation in the relation to the analyst, but rather in the setting free and detachment of the infantile libido from its fixation on its first objects.

Thus the psycho-analytic method of treatment, as we understand it to-day, developed into a method which has as its purpose the full re-living of the Oedipus situation in the relation of the patient to the analyst, in order to bring it, with the help of the patient's insight, to a new and more fortunate conclusion.

This relation develops of its own accord under the conditions of the analysis; the analyst then has the task of noticing its development from slight indications and of bringing the patient to a complete reproduction of the relation in the analytic experience. At times he must bring mere traces of the relationship to development by appropriate measures (activity).

The theoretic knowledge, in itself indispensable, of the development of the normal mental life, the theory of dreams, the sexual theory and so forth, must be used in practice, only insofar as they help to make possible the desired reproduction of the Oedipus relation in the analytic situation, or to make it easier. To lose oneself in the details of the history of the development of the individual, without continually reconstructing these connections, is not only practically incorrect and futile, but yields theoretically fewer reliable results than those which have been confirmed by practice in accordance with the above presentation.

The scientific importance of correctly practiced technique which has hitherto been neglected must be properly estimated. Theoretic results must be applied mechanically to the theory much less frequently than heretofore, but a constant correction of the theory should result from the new insight gained in practice.

Psycho-analysis, starting from a purely practical point of departure, under the impression of the first surprising insight, reached a phase of understanding. The cures so startling in the beginning became, with the rapidly increasing knowledge of the common mental mechanisms, comparatively less satisfactory so that one had to consider how to bring the therapeutic ability into harmony with the newly acquired knowledge, which had progressed so far ahead.

Our own presentation, described from this point of view, represents the beginning of a phase which we should like, in contrast to the previous ones, to call the phase of experience. Whereas formerly, one tried to obtain the therapeutic result as a reaction to the enlightenment of the patient, we now try to place the knowledge obtained by psychoanalysis directly in the service of our therapy, by directly provoking the corresponding personal experience on the basis of our insight, and explaining to the patient only this experience, which is naturally directly evident to him also.

The knowledge on the basis of which we are able to intervene at the right place, and in the requisite degree, consists essentially of the conviction of the universal importance of certain fundamental early experiences—as for example the Oedipus conflict,—the traumatic effect of which in the analysis, like a provocative treatment in medicine, is kindled again and, under the influence of living through the experience consciously for the first time, is brought to a useful ending.

This kind of therapy is related, in a certain sense, to a technique of education because—like education itself—it consists, on account of the affective relation to the teacher, far more in experience than in the factor of enlightenment. Here also, as in medicine, the tremendous progress from purely intuitive—and therefore often mistaken—intervention to the introduction of the conscious analytical experience based on knowledge, repeats itself.

CHAPTER VI.

Although we could scarcely, as we said in the beginning, succeed in giving a complete picture of the history of psycho-analysis, under the heading of the reciprocal effect of theory and practice, we think that we have nevertheless sketched the history of its development, in broad outlines, and consider that we are in a position to foretell its future paths of development.

The evolution, as we have frequently described, starting from Breuer's catharsis, led to the actual Freudian psycho-analysis which, simultaneously with its constantly increasing technical development, became a scientific theoretic system which was the foundation of an entirely new psychology. We showed how the misunderstanding of this double rôle of psycho-analysis, and the unavoidable one-sidedness could result, indeed, had to result, in sometimes this meaning, sometimes that, being overestimated at the expense of the other. The last extreme swing of the pendulum was the excessive interest in theorizing, which showed itself according to the general impression, at the Berlin Congress (September, 1922). In our critical exposition, in view of this, we tried to give the necessary balance, by more strongly emphasizing the practical aspects, in doing which one could hardly avoid, indeed it was perhaps even necessary at times, to fall into the other extreme.

This warning to ourselves must not, however, keep us from thinking out possible further developments in this direction, if only in general terms, so that by consistently following out these thoughts we may come somewhere near the truth, at least in certain points.

In his speech at the Budapest Congress (September, 1918) on "Wege der Psychoanalytischer Therapie" (The Ways of Psycho-analytic Therapy) Freud has already predicted the essentials as he sees them. One is only surprised that such important ideas have, in practice, not been given the attention due them from our point of view.[28] Finally, indeed, it began to look as though psycho-analysis, which preëminently serves a practical purpose, was to be over-flooded by a wave of theoretic speculation. This caused us to take these arguments of Freud as a point of departure in order to emphasize once more the practical point of view also in its therapeutic importance, which Freud himself never lost sight of.

Psycho-therapists before Breuer were extremely active, as is well known, but they were merely active, by which we mean that they lacked the insight into the mental mechanisms of the illness, as well as into their own behavior and its effect. In so far as they instinctively happened upon what was correct for the case in question, they obtained, and certainly do obtain, results. These sprang from the kind of activity (energetic or affectionate) which they for the time being preferred, operating somewhat beneficially upon the patient without any knowledge of the process. The important advance, represented by Freud's psycho-analysis over Breuer's catharsis, for the therapy in general was the insight into the fundamental importance of the transference. All other progress in analytic technique

[28] The attempt to create polyclinic institutions is a commendable exception; their foundation goes back, as is well known, to this suggestion of Freud. See "Bericht uber die Berliner Psychoanalytische Poliklinik" (März, 1920, bis Juni, 1922). (Report on the Berlin Psychoanalytic Polyclinic) by Dr. M. Eitingon (Internat. Zeitschrf. VIII, 1922; also separately published by the International Psycho-Analytic Press).

since then can be regarded essentially as the consistent development, and utilization of this fundamental insight which was Freud's advance over Breuer. But the essential theoretic advances of Freud also resulted from this practical point of view—for example the recognition of the infantile Oedipus kernel in the transference situation. And greatly as psycho-analytic therapy has developed in breadth and depth since its beginnings, Freud has never departed in his technique from the fundamental conception that the affective factor of experience is the essential factor of the cure.

This, of course, required the rare faculty of constantly reapplying the increasing knowledge to advance the actual therapeutic task. Evidently the ability is not given to everyone of purposely keeping the theoretic interest apart from the practical necessities, and at the same time of being able to combine the two to such an extent as is beneficial to each. Thus we can understand the theoretical exaggerations in practice, against which our critical remarks were chiefly directed, whereas our descriptive considerations were intended to show, by way of suggestion, how the entire psychological knowledge won from analysis can, and must be used in practice, that is as a factor of analytic experience.

It would be a mistake to conclude from the above that we underestimate the theory or the knowledge in itself. Such is in no way the case. Only we believe that in this respect a change in the previous attitude is unavoidable. We were always of the opinion that the analyst, like the specialist in every other subject, can never know enough, but we deny the necessity of initiating the patient into our whole knowledge every time, or of discovering afresh in every single case the psychological and theoretical knowledge derived from analysis, and thus trying to acquire a conviction which one should have brought with one.

This standpoint leads to a remark in regard to the possibilities of learning psycho-analysis. There was no such possibility for a long time. Beginning analysts were entirely dependent upon the knowledge they could get out of books. This knowledge was therefore theoretic and they simply tried to apply it to the patient. If they wished to go further than this there remained nothing to do except, as is usual in other branches of medicine, to treat the patient at the same time as a subject of investigation. In consequence of the purely theoretic preparation, this research on the *anima vili* was directed chiefly towards the theory. From such experiences it gradually became clear that the only proper preparation must be the actual experience of an analysis. Therefore the training schools attached to the polyclinics have made the rule that every one who wishes to devote himself to analysis shall first be analyzed by an experienced analyst. But just as in the therapeutic analyses the mere imparting of academic knowledge belongs, as it were, to the pediatrics of this subject, we believe that the correct didactic analysis is one that does not in the least differ from the curative treatment. How, indeed, shall the future analyst learn the technique if he does not experience it just exactly as he is to apply it later? Moreover, it depends upon the results of the analysis whether in a given case it is a question of didactic or a therapeutic analysis, whether the intention and qualification for the profession of psycho-analysis remain firm after the treatment.

In view of certain experiences, one might be tempted to ask oneself, whether our therapeutic analyses have not up to now often been too "didactic", whereas the so-called didactic analyses taught less analysis than the theory, which should only have been acquired separately later on.

We could formulate our standpoint in these questions somewhat thus: *too much knowledge on the part of the patient should be replaced by more knowledge on the part of the analyst.* The analyst should not impart the theoretic knowledge which "occurs" to him in connection with the association material of the patient; that is he should not express, as it were, his own parallel associations, but he should work over the whole material in himself and only impart that which the patient absolutely requires for the analytic experience, and its understanding.

By placing the accent on the knowledge and the action of the analyst the picture of the analytic treatment could, at least outwardly, in time in a certain sense more nearly approximate that of the usual methods of treatment in nonanalytic psycho-therapy, or in general medicine. The enormous difference consists in the fact that the analyst can, on the basis of properly combining his knowledge with the individual material which the patient offers, determine exactly the time, the kind and the degree of his intervention, whereas this is determined in all other kinds of psycho-therapy either by sheer force, or by "artificial" intuition.

In hypnosis, for example, the physician generally obtained merely temporary and not radical results, because its application covered over all the vital psychic motives. This was why Freud gave up hypnosis and used the method of free association which gave us our first insight into the play of mental forces. However, one must admit with Freud that hypnosis owes its undeniable successes to the complete elimination of the intellectual (ethical, esthetic, etc.) resistances. If one could, for example, combine the inestimable advantage of the technique of hypnosis with the advantage of the analytic ability to free the hypnotic affect situation, a tremendous advance in our therapeutic ability would be achieved.

Psycho-analysis has already shed enough light on this problem to enable us to recognize the Oedipus situation as the nucleus of the hypnotic affect relation. But it has not yet been able to give us the deepest understanding of what is really specific to the hypnotic state. When we have fully understood the nature of the hypnotic attachment to the physician, which has not yet been really cleared up by the recognition of the nature of the transference, it is possible that we may come to a point when the analyst can use hynosis as a part of his technique, without being obliged to fear that he may not be able in the end to loosen the affective umbilical cord which attaches the patient to him. This possibility of readmitting hypnosis, or other suggestive methods, into our analytic therapy would perhaps be the culmination of the simplification of the analytic technique, towards which, according to our interpretation, we should be and are actually tending. The final goal of psycho-analysis is to substitute, by means of the technique, affective factors of experience for intellectual processes. It is well known that this is just what is achieved in an extreme way in hypnosis, in which conscious material is called forth or eliminated according to need.

An elimination, particularly of the intellectual resistances, is being increasingly required since psycho-analysis has begun to penetrate more generally into society, and people bring this knowledge as a means of resistance into the cure. This fact was not the least among the motives which obliged us unintentionally to change our technique and must force us to adjust it to the increasing enlightenment of society as to the cause and nature of the neuroses.

According to Freud the spread of psycho-analytic knowledge will, in time, automatically bring about the disappearance of those forms of neuroses which we have known up to now.

We see here again two kinds of knowledge at work, one that helps the therapy, that can even, by prophylaxis, prevent the neuroses (the analytic education of children), the other which takes the form of a hindrance in the cure. This last difficulty is paralyzed by the fact that, for the present, at any rate, the knowledge of the analyst is still always a good deal in advance of and superior to general knowledge.

Thus the whole development of the technique of psycho-analysis tends, according to us, to become essentially simplified in the near future. It is possible that this will increase the appearance of a certain monotony and sticking to formula, but after all the correct practitioner was always a craftsman also and, perhaps, should essentially be so. The application of such formulæ to the individual material which here represent simply the residue of hard won knowledge, still remains the essential in psycho-analysis, thus offering sufficient opportunity to the specially gifted as well as for further research. The reduction of the method to more simple actual facts—which our increasing knowledge should also require—would in any case in time achieve, the not to be underestimated practical result, that on the one hand, it would be much easier for doctors (not only psycho-therapeutists) to acquire psycho-analytic knowledge, but on the other hand to shorten and simplify the treatment.

From this point of view of the practical application the splendid isolation which was indispensable to the creation and development of psycho-analysis need then no longer be strictly adhered to: indeed, we should not wonder, if the point were finally reached when other psycho-therapeutic methods which had proven themselves useful according to analytic understanding (as we tried to show, for example, in hypnosis) were legitimately combined with psycho-analysis. Freud himself had such future possibility of the mass application of psycho-analytic therapy in mind when he expressed the opinion that it was very probable that "the pure gold of analysis might be freely alloyed with the copper of direct suggestion and that the hypnotic means of influence might again find its place." [29]

Of course when psycho-analytic knowledge has penetrated into general medical thinking in the form of a better understanding of human nature, the result will be that all intervention will be based on a more accurate estimate of the mental factors also, and therefore will be more purposeful and effective. Already to-day farsighted general practitioners, gynecologists, and surgeons have attempted the application of psycho-analysis and, in so far as they were successful, were undeniably able to reach results which were surprising to other specialists. For us, of course, these results are not surprising, since we expect an essential advance in all branches of medicine from the definite analytic training of all doctors. One may even expect that psycho-analytic knowledge, that is the knowledge of mankind, may become the nucleus of all medical knowledge and bring about the unification of this science, which has been so dismembered by the extensive growth of the specialties. The old family physician, the friend and counselor of the family, would thus again play his former important rôle with an even deeper meaning. He would watch with understanding and know intimately the whole

[29] Wege der Psychoanalytischen Therapie, 1918.

personality and would be able to exert an intelligent influence upon the development of a human being from his
birth onwards, on his education, to throw some light on the
difficulties of puberty and the choice of a profession, and
on marriage, all more or less trying mental conflicts, as
well as to deal with organic illnesses and mental disorders.
His rôle of counselor would not be restricted to bodily ailments, but he would give competent advice about the almost
more important mental factors, such as the mutual influence
of the mental and the physical.

This doctor of souls would naturally exert through the
family a still unconceived amount of influence upon society,
its morals and its customs, and thus indirectly effect an
improvement in education, and in this way again contribute
to the prophylaxis of the neuroses.   The uniting, in the
person of the physician, of knowledge which has up to now
appeared to be so heterogeneous might possibly contribute
towards the unification of the sciences in general, which up
to now have been much too sharply separated into the
natural and the mental sciences.   We can already say that
the penetration of psycho-analytic knowledge has, for example, greatly furthered the study of biology, by laying
the foundation for an entirely new theory of the instincts
which could then point out the way for a new theory of
development.   The results of reapplying psycho-analysis,
for example, to physiological chemistry (inner secretions,
etc.) in its modern trends can as yet scarcely be estimated;
and the analysis of the neuroses finally strikes upon the
chemistry of sex, the importance of which Freud laid down
in principle in his "Three Contributions to the Theory of
Sex."   And the toxic etiology of the psychoses which had
previously been considered only from the one point of view,

might, in connection with the psycho-analyses of these illnesses, still lead to therapeutic surprises.

In the future, not only will psycho-analytic knowledge be the common property of all physicians, which will be as indispensable as to-day, for example, the knowledge of anatomy and physiology, but there will, of course, be specially trained therapeutists who, as is frequently the case to-day, need not necessarily be doctors since education as well as the care of mental life, are really psycho-therapeutic or prophylactic tasks. This settles the somewhat elaborate questioning of certain specialists as to whether "laymen", that is, nonmedical people, shall analyze at all. As the situation stands to-day physicians limited by their one-sided training in the natural sciences are actually laymen in psychological matters.[30] Indeed, one may truthfully say that their purely physiological way of thinking has, to a certain extent, limited their understanding of the mental side. On the other hand, the fundamental conceptions of psycho-analysis rest on a few general hypotheses common to human nature, so that aside from a thorough analytical training, a good general education suffices for its understanding and mastery and a knowledge of medicine is not necessarily advantageous as follows from what Freud says on this subject.[31] This was why the meaning of psycho-analysis was so much more recognized and appreciated up to now by nonmedical than by medical people, so much so that recently a young representative of modern psychiatry

[30] Only very recently has one thought of giving psychological training in medical schools.

[31] Ueber Psychoanalyse, 1910. ''The physician who through his training has come to know so much which is a closed chapter to the layman, is helpless before hysterical phenomena in spite of his knowledge.'' ''He himself is a layman in the face of hysteria; he cannot understand it.'' Therefore, Freud also says that it is only advantageous to us to go with the physician up to the point of diagnosis, but that we can then separate from him.

could in an open meeting of a congress reproach his colleagues with the fact that they, who really were called upon
to be the leaders in psycho-analysis, had let the subject slip
out of their hands.[32] This state of affairs should, however,
improve in the near future and it looks as though in certain
countries official medicine were beginning to take a different stand, so that the looked-for penetration of psycho-
analysis into the general knowledge of mankind will bring
about the disappearance of disputes about borderline cases
among specialists.

What Freud was already able to foretell in "The Future
Chances of Psycho-analytic Therapy" (in his Congress
speech, 1910), that our therapeutic results will be much
better when we shall have obtained the authority commonly
attributed to other specialists, has since then come to pass
to some extent. However, the full effectiveness of these
social factors, which must in no way be underestimated,
will only be achieved when the resistances—intellectual and
others—will have disintegrated, perhaps with the assistance of changes in the technique which take these points
into account.

If we have attempted in the foregoing pages, venturing
from the present direct facts, to forecast the prospects of
psycho-analysis, this seems to us more than an idle play
of phantasy. Indeed, if we carry these thoughts to their
logical conclusion, we come to a point at which our interpretation appears in so far to be justified as it fits in with
that of a great, if indirect, organic development. The most
important advance in psycho-analysis consists finally in a
great increase of consciousness, or expressed according to
our meta-psychology, in raising the instinctive unconscious
mental content to the level of pre-conscious thinking. This,

[32] See Prinzhorn's Review of (his own work) Inter-n. Zeitschrift f. PsA.
VIII, 1922.

however, from our point of view, means such an important step in the development of mankind, that it may actually be regarded as a biologic advance, and indeed as one which for the first time takes place under a kind of self-control.

Under the influence of this increase in consciousness the physician, who has developed from the medicine man, sorcerer, charlatan, and magic healer, and who at his best often remains somewhat an artist, will develop increasing knowledge of mental mechanisms, and in this sense, prove the saying that medicine is the oldest art and the youngest science.

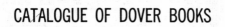
CATALOGUE OF DOVER BOOKS

Psychology

YOGA: A SCIENTIFIC EVALUATION, Kovoor T. Behanan. A complete reprinting of the book that for the first time gave Western readers a sane, scientific explanation and analysis of yoga. The author draws on controlled laboratory experiments and personal records of a year as a disciple of a yoga, to investigate yoga psychology, concepts of knowledge, physiology, "supernatural" phenomena, and the ability to tap the deepest human powers. In this study under the auspices of Yale University Institute of Human Relations, the strictest principles of physiological and psychological inquiry are followed throughout. Foreword by W. A. Miles, Yale University. 17 photographs. Glossary. Index. xx + 270pp. 5⅜ x 8. T505 Paperbound **$2.00**

CONDITIONED REFLEXES: AN INVESTIGATION OF THE PHYSIOLOGICAL ACTIVITIES OF THE CEREBRAL CORTEX, I. P. Pavlov. Full, authorized translation of Pavlov's own survey of his work in experimental psychology reviews entire course of experiments, summarizes conclusions, outlines psychological system based on famous "conditioned reflex" concept. Details of technical means used in experiments, observations on formation of conditioned reflexes, function of cerebral hemispheres, results of damage, nature of sleep, typology of nervous system, significance of experiments for human psychology. Trans. by Dr. G. V. Anrep, Cambridge Univ. 235-item bibliography. 18 figures. 445pp. 5⅜ x 8. S614 Paperbound **$2.35**

EXPLANATION OF HUMAN BEHAVIOUR, F. V. Smith. A major intermediate-level introduction to and criticism of 8 complete systems of the psychology of human behavior, with unusual emphasis on theory of investigation and methodology. Part I is an illuminating analysis of the problems involved in the explanation of observed phenomena, and the differing viewpoints on the nature of causality. Parts II and III are a closely detailed survey of the systems of McDougall, Gordon Allport, Lewin, the Gestalt group, Freud, Watson, Hull, and Tolman. Biographical notes. Bibliography of over 800 items. 2 Indexes. 38 figures. xii + 460pp. 5½ x 8¾. T253 Clothbound **$6.00**

SEX IN PSYCHO-ANALYSIS (formerly CONTRIBUTIONS TO PSYCHO-ANALYSIS), S. Ferenczi. Written by an associate of Freud, this volume presents countless insights on such topics as impotence, transference, analysis and children, dreams, symbols, obscene words, masturbation and male homosexuality, paranoia and psycho-analysis, the sense of reality, hypnotism and therapy, and many others. Also includes full text of THE DEVELOPMENT OF PSYCHO-ANALYSIS by Ferenczi and Otto Rank. Two books bound as one. Total of 406pp. 5⅜ x 8. T324 Paperbound **$1.85**

BEYOND PSYCHOLOGY, Otto Rank. One of Rank's most mature contributions, focussing on the irrational basis of human behavior as a basic fact of our lives. The psychoanalytic techniques of myth analysis trace to their source the ultimates of human existence: fear of death, personality, the social organization, the need for love and creativity, etc. Dr. Rank finds them stemming from a common irrational source, man's fear of final destruction. A seminal work in modern psychology, this work sheds light on areas ranging from the concept of immortal soul to the sources of state power. 291pp. 5⅜ x 8. T485 Paperbound **$2.00**

ILLUSIONS AND DELUSIONS OF THE SUPERNATURAL AND THE OCCULT, D. H. Rawcliffe. Holds up to rational examination hundreds of persistent delusions including crystal gazing, automatic writing, table turning, mediumistic trances, mental healing, stigmata, lycanthropy, live burial, the Indian Rope Trick, spiritualism, dowsing, telepathy, clairvoyance, ghosts, ESP, etc. The author explains and exposes the mental and physical deceptions involved, making this not only an exposé of supernatural phenomena, but a valuable exposition of characteristic types of abnormal psychology. Originally titled "The Psychology of the Occult." 14 illustrations. Index. 551pp. 5⅜ x 8. T503 Paperbound **$2.00**

THE PRINCIPLES OF PSYCHOLOGY, William James. The full long-course, unabridged, of one of the great classics of Western literature and science. Wonderfully lucid descriptions of human mental activity, the stream of thought, consciousness, time perception, memory, imagination, emotions, reason, abnormal phenomena, and similar topics. Original contributions are integrated with the work of such men as Berkeley, Binet, Mills, Darwin, Hume, Kant, Royce, Schopenhauer, Spinoza, Locke, Descartes, Galton, Wundt, Lotze, Herbart, Fechner, and scores of others. All contrasting interpretations of mental phenomena are examined in detail — introspective analysis, philosophical interpretation, and experimental research. "A classic," JOURNAL OF CONSULTING PSYCHOLOGY. "The main lines are as valid as ever," PSYCHO-ANALYTICAL QUARTERLY. "Standard reading . . . a classic of interpretation," PSYCHIATRIC QUARTERLY. 94 illustrations. 1408pp. 2 volumes. 5⅜ x 8.   Vol. 1, T381 Paperbound **$2.50**
Vol. 2, T382 Paperbound **$2.50**

THE DYNAMICS OF THERAPY IN A CONTROLLED RELATIONSHIP, Jessie Taft. One of the most important works in literature of child psychology, out of print for 25 years. Outstanding disciple of Rank describes all aspects of relationship or Rankian therapy through concise, simple elucidation of theory underlying her actual contacts with two seven-year olds. Therapists, social caseworkers, psychologists, counselors, and laymen who work with children will all find this important work an invaluable summation of method, theory of child psychology. xix + 296pp. 5⅜ x 8. T325 Paperbound **$1.75**

Books Explaining Science and Mathematics

WHAT IS SCIENCE?, N. Campbell. The role of experiment and measurement, the function of mathematics, the nature of scientific laws, the difference between laws and theories, the limitations of science, and many similarly provocative topics are treated clearly and without technicalities by an eminent scientist. "Still an excellent introduction to scientific philosophy," H. Margenau in PHYSICS TODAY. "A first-rate primer . . . deserves a wide audience," SCIENTIFIC AMERICAN. 192pp. 5⅜ x 8.   S43 Paperbound **$1.25**

THE NATURE OF PHYSICAL THEORY, P. W. Bridgman. A Nobel Laureate's clear, non-technical lectures on difficulties and paradoxes connected with frontier research on the physical sciences. Concerned with such central concepts as thought, logic, mathematics, relativity, probability, wave mechanics, etc. he analyzes the contributions of such men as Newton, Einstein, Bohr, Heisenberg, and many others. "Lucid and entertaining . . . recommended to anyone who wants to get some insight into current philosophies of science," THE NEW PHILOSOPHY. Index. xi + 138pp. 5⅜ x 8.   S33 Paperbound **$1.25**

EXPERIMENT AND THEORY IN PHYSICS, Max Born. A Nobel Laureate examines the nature of experiment and theory in theoretical physics and analyzes the advances made by the great physicists of our day: Heisenberg, Einstein, Bohr, Planck, Dirac, and others. The actual process of creation is detailed step-by-step by one who participated. A fine examination of the scientific method at work. 44pp. 5⅜ x 8.   S308 Paperbound **75¢**

THE PSYCHOLOGY OF INVENTION IN THE MATHEMATICAL FIELD, J. Hadamard. The reports of such men as Descartes, Pascal, Einstein, Poincaré, and others are considered in this investigation of the method of idea-creation in mathematics and other sciences and the thinking process in general. How do ideas originate? What is the role of the unconscious? What is Poincaré's forgetting hypothesis? are some of the fascinating questions treated. A penetrating analysis of Einstein's thought processes concludes the book. xiii + 145pp. 5⅜ x 8.   T107 Paperbound **$1.25**

THE NATURE OF LIGHT AND COLOUR IN THE OPEN AIR, M. Minnaert. Why are shadows sometimes blue, sometimes green, or other colors depending on the light and surroundings? What causes mirages? Why do multiple suns and moons appear in the sky? Professor Minnaert explains these unusual phenomena and hundreds of others in simple, easy-to-understand terms based on optical laws and the properties of light and color. No mathematics is required but artists, scientists, students, and everyone fascinated by these "tricks" of nature will find thousands of useful and amazing pieces of information. Hundreds of observational experiments are suggested which require no special equipment. 200 illustrations; 42 photos. xvi + 362pp. 5⅜ x 8.   T196 Paperbound **$2.00**

***MATHEMATICS IN ACTION, O. G. Sutton.** Everyone with a command of high school algebra will find this book one of the finest possible introductions to the application of mathematics to physical theory. Ballistics, numerical analysis, waves and wavelike phenomena, Fourier series, group concepts, fluid flow and aerodynamics, statistical measures, and meteorology are discussed with unusual clarity. Some calculus and differential equations theory is developed by the author for the reader's help in the more difficult sections. 88 figures. Index. viii + 236pp. 5⅜ x 8.   T440 Clothbound **$3.50**

SOAP-BUBBLES: THEIR COLOURS AND THE FORCES THAT MOULD THEM, C. V. Boys. For continuing popularity and validity as scientific primer, few books can match this volume of easily-followed experiments, explanations. Lucid exposition of complexities of liquid films, surface tension and related phenomena, bubbles' reaction to heat, motion, music, magnetic fields. Experiments with capillary attraction, soap bubbles on frames, composite bubbles, liquid cylinders and jets, bubbles other than soap, etc. Wonderful introduction to scientific method, natural laws that have many ramifications in areas of modern physics. Only complete edition in print. New Introduction by S. Z. Lewin, New York University. 83 illustrations; 1 full-page color plate. xii + 190pp. 5⅜ x 8½.   T542 Paperbound **95¢**

CATALOGUE OF DOVER BOOKS

THE STORY OF X-RAYS FROM RÖNTGEN TO ISOTOPES, A. R. Bleich, M.D. This book, by a member of the American College of Radiology, gives the scientific explanation of x-rays, their applications in medicine, industry and art, and their danger (and that of atmospheric radiation) to the individual and the species. You learn how radiation therapy is applied against cancer, how x-rays diagnose heart disease and other ailments, how they are used to examine mummies for information on diseases of early societies, and industrial materials for hidden weaknesses. 54 illustrations show x-rays of flowers, bones, stomach, gears with flaws, etc. 1st publication. Index. xix + 186pp. 5⅜ x 8. **T622 Paperbound $1.35**

SPINNING TOPS AND GYROSCOPIC MOTION, John Perry. A classic elementary text of the dynamics of rotation — the behavior and use of rotating bodies such as gyroscopes and tops. In simple, everyday English you are shown how quasi-rigidity is induced in discs of paper, smoke rings, chains, etc., by rapid motions; why a gyrostat falls and why a top rises; precession; how the earth's motion affects climate; and many other phenomena. Appendix on practical use of gyroscopes. 62 figures. 128pp. 5⅜ x 8. **T416 Paperbound $1.00**

SNOW CRYSTALS, W. A. Bentley, M. J. Humphreys. For almost 50 years W. A. Bentley photographed snow flakes in his laboratory in Jericho, Vermont; in 1931 the American Meteorological Society gathered together the best of his work, some 2400 photographs of snow flakes, plus a few ice flowers, windowpane frosts, dew, frozen rain, and other ice formations. Pictures were selected for beauty and scientific value. A very valuable work to anyone in meteorology, cryology; most interesting to layman; extremely useful for artist who wants beautiful, crystalline designs. All copyright free. Unabridged reprint of 1931 edition. 2453 illustrations. 227pp. 8 x 10½. **T287 Paperbound $3.00**

A DOVER SCIENCE SAMPLER, edited by George Barkin. A collection of brief, non-technical passages from 44 Dover Books Explaining Science for the enjoyment of the science-minded browser. Includes work of Bertrand Russell, Poincaré, Laplace, Max Born, Galileo, Newton; material on physics, mathematics, metallurgy, anatomy, astronomy, chemistry, etc. You will be fascinated by Martin Gardner's analysis of the sincere pseudo-scientist, Moritz's account of Newton's absentmindedness, Bernard's examples of human vivisection, etc. Illustrations from the Diderot Pictorial Encyclopedia and De Re Metallica. 64 pages. **FREE**

THE STORY OF ATOMIC THEORY AND ATOMIC ENERGY, J. G. Feinberg. A broader approach to subject of nuclear energy and its cultural implications than any other similar source. Very readable, informal, completely non-technical text. Begins with first atomic theory, 600 B.C. and carries you through the work of Mendelejeff, Röntgen, Madame Curie, to Einstein's equation and the A-bomb. New chapter goes through thermonuclear fission, binding energy, other events up to 1959. Radioactive decay and radiation hazards, future benefits, work of Bohr, moderns, hundreds more topics. "Deserves special mention . . . not only authoritative but thoroughly popular in the best sense of the word," Saturday Review. Formerly, "The Atom Story." Expanded with new chapter. Three appendixes. Index. 34 illustrations. vii + 243pp. 5⅜ x 8. **T625 Paperbound $1.60**

THE STRANGE STORY OF THE QUANTUM, AN ACCOUNT FOR THE GENERAL READER OF THE GROWTH OF IDEAS UNDERLYING OUR PRESENT ATOMIC KNOWLEDGE, B. Hoffmann. Presents lucidly and expertly, with barest amount of mathematics, the problems and theories which led to modern quantum physics. Dr. Hoffmann begins with the closing years of the 19th century, when certain trifling discrepancies were noticed, and with illuminating analogies and examples takes you through the brilliant concepts of Planck, Einstein, Pauli, Broglie, Bohr, Schroedinger, Heisenberg, Dirac, Sommerfeld, Feynman, etc. This edition includes a new, long postscript carrying the story through 1958. "Of the books attempting an account of the history and contents of our modern atomic physics which have come to my attention, this is the best," H. Margenau, Yale University, in "American Journal of Physics." 32 tables and line illustrations. Index. 275pp. 5⅜ x 8. **T518 Paperbound $1.50**

SPACE AND TIME, E. Borel. Written by a versatile mathematician of world renown with his customary lucidity and precision, this introduction to relativity for the layman presents scores of examples, analogies, and illustrations that open up new ways of thinking about space and time. It covers abstract geometry and geographical maps, continuity and topology, the propagation of light, the special theory of relativity, the general theory of relativity, theoretical researches, and much more. Mathematical notes. 2 Indexes. 4 Appendices. 15 figures. xvi + 243pp. 5⅜ x 8. **T592 Paperbound $1.45**

FROM EUCLID TO EDDINGTON: A STUDY OF THE CONCEPTIONS OF THE EXTERNAL WORLD, Sir Edmund Whittaker. A foremost British scientist traces the development of theories of natural philosophy from the western rediscovery of Euclid to Eddington, Einstein, Dirac, etc. The inadequacy of classical physics is contrasted with present day attempts to understand the physical world through relativity, non-Euclidean geometry, space curvature, wave mechanics, etc. 5 major divisions of examination: Space; Time and Movement; the Concepts of Classical Physics; the Concepts of Quantum Mechanics; the Eddington Universe. 212pp. 5⅜ x 8. **T491 Paperbound $1.35**

*THE EVOLUTION OF SCIENTIFIC THOUGHT FROM NEWTON TO EINSTEIN, A. d'Abro. A detailed account of the evolution of classical physics into modern relativistic theory and the concommitant changes in scientific methodology. The breakdown of classical physics in the face of non-Euclidean geometry and the electromagnetic equations is carefully discussed and then an exhaustive analysis of Einstein's special and general theories of relativity and their implications is given. Newton, Riemann, Weyl, Lorentz, Planck, Maxwell, and many others are considered. A non-technical explanation of space, time, electromagnetic waves, etc. as understood today. "Model of semi-popular exposition," NEW REPUBLIC. 21 diagrams. 482pp. 5⅜ x 8.
T2 Paperbound **$2.25**

EINSTEIN'S THEORY OF RELATIVITY, Max Born. Nobel Laureate explains Einstein's special and general theories of relativity, beginning with a thorough review of classical physics in simple, non-technical language. Exposition of Einstein's work discusses concept of simultaneity, kinematics, relativity of arbitrary motions, the space-time continuum, geometry of curved surfaces, etc., steering middle course between vague popularizations and complex scientific presentations. 1962 edition revised by author takes into account latest findings, predictions of theory and implications for cosmology, indicates what is being sought in unified field theory. Mathematics very elementary, illustrative diagrams and experiments informative but simple. Revised 1962 edition. Revised by Max Born, assisted by Gunther Leibfried and Walter Biem. Index. 143 illustrations. vii + 376pp. 5⅜ x 8.
S769 Paperbound **$2.00**

PHILOSOPHY AND THE PHYSICISTS, L. Susan Stebbing. A philosopher examines the philosophical aspects of modern science, in terms of a lively critical attack on the ideas of Jeans and Eddington. Such basic questions are treated as the task of science, causality, determinism, probability, consciousness, the relation of the world of physics to the world of everyday experience. The author probes the concepts of man's smallness before an inscrutable universe, the tendency to idealize mathematical construction, unpredictability theorems and human freedom, the supposed opposition between 19th century determinism and modern science, and many others. Introduces many thought-stimulating ideas about the implications of modern physical concepts. xvi + 295pp. 5⅜ x 8. T480 Paperbound **$1.65**

THE RESTLESS UNIVERSE, Max Born. A remarkably lucid account by a Nobel Laureate of recent theories of wave mechanics, behavior of gases, electrons and ions, waves and particles, electronic structure of the atom, nuclear physics, and similar topics. "Much more thorough and deeper than most attempts . . . easy and delightful," CHEMICAL AND ENGINEERING NEWS. Special feature: 7 animated sequences of 60 figures each showing such phenomena as gas molecules in motion, the scattering of alpha particles, etc. 11 full-page plates of photographs. Total of nearly 600 illustrations. 351pp. 6⅛ x 9¼. T412 Paperbound **$2.00**

THE COMMON SENSE OF THE EXACT SCIENCES, W. K. Clifford. For 70 years a guide to the basic concepts of scientific and mathematical thought. Acclaimed by scientists and laymen alike, it offers a wonderful insight into concepts such as the extension of meaning of symbols, characteristics of surface boundaries, properties of plane figures, measurement of quantities, vectors, the nature of position, bending of space, motion, mass and force, and many others. Prefaces by Bertrand Russell and Karl Pearson. Critical introduction by James Newman. 130 figures. 249pp. 5⅜ x 8. T61 Paperbound **$1.60**

MATTER AND LIGHT, THE NEW PHYSICS, Louis de Broglie. Non-technical explanations by a Nobel Laureate of electro-magnetic theory, relativity, matter, light and radiation, wave mechanics, quantum physics, philosophy of science, and similar topics. This is one of the simplest yet most accurate introductions to the work of men like Planck, Einstein, Bohr, and others. Only 2 of the 21 chapters require a knowledge of mathematics. 300pp. 5⅜ x 8.
T35 Paperbound **$1.85**

SCIENCE, THEORY AND MAN, Erwin Schrödinger. This is a complete and unabridged reissue of SCIENCE AND THE HUMAN TEMPERAMENT plus an additional essay: "What Is an Elementary Particle?" Nobel Laureate Schrödinger discusses such topics as nature of scientific method, tne nature of science, chance and determinism, science and society, conceptual models for physical entities, elementary particles and wave mechanics. Presentation is popular and may be followed by most people with little or no scientific training. "Fine practical preparation for a time when laws of nature, human institutions . . . are undergoing a critical examination without parallel," Waldemar Kaempffert, N. Y. TIMES. 192pp. 5⅜ x 8.
T428 Paperbound **$1.35**

CONCERNING THE NATURE OF THINGS, Sir William Bragg. The Nobel Laureate physicist in his Royal Institute Christmas Lectures explains such diverse phenomena as the formation of crystals, how uranium is transmuted to lead, the way X-rays work, why a spinning ball travels in a curved path, the reason why bubbles bounce from each other, and many other scientific topics that are seldom explained in simple terms. No scientific background needed—book is easy enough that any intelligent adult or youngster can understand it. Unabridged. 32pp. of photos; 57 figures. xii + 232pp. 5⅜ x 8. T31 Paperbound **$1.35**

*THE RISE OF THE NEW PHYSICS (formerly THE DECLINE OF MECHANISM), A. d'Abro. This authoritative and comprehensive 2 volume exposition is unique in scientific publishing. Written for intelligent readers not familiar with higher mathematics, it is the only thorough explanation in non-technical language of modern mathematical-physical theory. Combining both history and exposition, it ranges from classical Newtonian concepts up through the electronic theories of Dirac and Heisenberg, the statistical mechanics of Fermi, and Einstein's relativity theories. "A must for anyone doing serious study in the physical sciences," J. OF FRANKLIN INST. 97 illustrations. 991pp. 2 volumes. T3 Vol. 1, Paperbound **$2.25**
T4 Vol. 2, Paperbound **$2.25**

SCIENCE AND HYPOTHESIS, Henri Poincaré. Creative psychology in science. How such concepts as number, magnitude, space, force, classical mechanics were developed and how the modern scientist uses them in his thought. Hypothesis in physics, theories of modern physics. Introduction by Sir James Larmor. "Few mathematicians have had the breadth of vision of Poincaré, and none is his superior in the gift of clear exposition," E. T. Bell. Index. 272pp. 5⅜ x 8.
S221 Paperbound **$1.35**

THE VALUE OF SCIENCE, Henri Poincaré. Many of the most mature ideas of the "last scientific universalist" conveyed with charm and vigor for both the beginning student and the advanced worker. Discusses the nature of scientific truth, whether order is innate in the universe or imposed upon it by man, logical thought versus intuition (relating to mathematics through the works of Weierstrass, Lie, Klein, Riemann), time and space (relativity, psychological time, simultaneity), Hertz's concept of force, interrelationship of mathematical physics to pure math, values within disciplines of Maxwell, Carnot, Mayer, Newton, Lorentz, etc. Index. iii + 147pp. 5⅜ x 8.
S469 Paperbound **$1.35**

THE SKY AND ITS MYSTERIES, E. A. Beet. One of the most lucid books on the mysteries of the universe; covers history of astronomy from earliest observations to modern theories of expanding universe, source of stellar energy, birth of planets, origin of moon craters, possibilities of life on other planets. Discusses effects of sunspots on weather; distance, age of stars; methods and tools of astronomers; much more. Expert and fascinating. "Eminently readable book," London Times. Bibliography. Over 50 diagrams, 12 full-page plates. Fold-out star map. Introduction. Index. 238pp. 5¼ x 7½.
T627 Clothbound **$3.50**

OUT OF THE SKY: AN INTRODUCTION TO METEORITICS, H. H. Nininger. A non-technical yet comprehensive introduction to the young science of meteoritics: all aspects of the arrival of cosmic matter on our planet from outer space and the reaction and alteration of this matter in the terrestrial environment. Essential facts and major theories presented by one of the world's leading experts. Covers ancient reports of meteors; modern systematic investigations; fireball clusters; meteorite showers; tektites; planetoidal encounters; etc. 52 full-page plates with over 175 photographs. 22 figures. Bibliography and references. Index. viii + 336pp. 5⅜ x 8.
T519 Paperbound **$1.85**

THE REALM OF THE NEBULAE, E. Hubble. One of great astronomers of our day records his formulation of concept of "island universes." Covers velocity-distance relationship; classification, nature, distances, general types of nebulae; cosmological theories. A fine introduction to modern theories for layman. No math needed. New introduction by A. Sandage. 55 illustrations, photos. Index. iv + 201pp. 5⅜ x 8.
S455 Paperbound **$1.50**

AN ELEMENTARY SURVEY OF CELESTIAL MECHANICS, Y. Ryabov. Elementary exposition of gravitational theory and celestial mechanics. Historical introduction and coverage of basic principles, including: the ecliptic, the orbital plane, the 2- and 3-body problems, the discovery of Neptune, planetary rotation, the length of the day, the shapes of galaxies, satellites (detailed treatment of Sputnik I), etc. First American reprinting of successful Russian popular exposition. Follow actual methods of astrophysicists with only high school math! Appendix. 58 figures. 165pp. 5⅜ x 8.
T756 Paperbound **$1.25**

GREAT IDEAS AND THEORIES OF MODERN COSMOLOGY, Jagjit Singh. Companion volume to author's popular "Great Ideas of Modern Mathematics" (Dover, $1.55). The best non-technical survey of post-Einstein attempts to answer perhaps unanswerable questions of origin, age of Universe, possibility of life on other worlds, etc. Fundamental theories of cosmology and cosmogony recounted, explained, evaluated in light of most recent data: Einstein's concepts of relativity, space-time; Milne's a priori world-system; astrophysical theories of Jeans, Eddington; Hoyle's "continuous creation;" contributions of dozens more scientists. A faithful, comprehensive critical summary of complex material presented in an extremely well-written text intended for laymen. Original publication. Index. xii + 276pp. 5⅜ x 8½.
T925 Paperbound **$1.85**

BASIC ELECTRICITY, Bureau of Naval Personnel. Very thorough, easily followed course in basic electricity for beginner, layman, or intermediate student. Begins with simplest definitions, presents coordinated, systematic coverage of basic theory and application: conductors, insulators, static electricity, magnetism, production of voltage, Ohm's law, direct current series and parallel circuits, wiring techniques, electromagnetism, alternating current, capacitance and inductance, measuring instruments, etc.; application to electrical machines such as alternating and direct current generators, motors, transformers, magnetic magnifiers, etc. Each chapter contains problems to test progress; answers at rear. No math needed beyond algebra. Appendices on signs, formulas, etc. 345 illustrations. 448pp. 7½ x 10.
S973 Paperbound **$3.00**

ELEMENTARY METALLURGY AND METALLOGRAPHY, A. M. Shrager. An introduction to common metals and alloys; stress is upon steel and iron, but other metals and alloys also covered. All aspects of production, processing, working of metals. Designed for student who wishes to enter metallurgy, for bright high school or college beginner, layman who wants background on extremely important industry. Questions, at ends of chapters, many microphotographs, glossary. Greatly revised 1961 edition. 195 illustrations, tables. ix + 389pp. 5⅜ x 8.
S138 Paperbound **$2.25**

BRIDGES AND THEIR BUILDERS, D. B. Steinman & S. R. Watson. Engineers, historians, and every person who has ever been fascinated by great spans will find this book an endless source of information and interest. Greek and Roman structures, Medieval bridges, modern classics such as the Brooklyn Bridge, and the latest developments in the science are retold by one of the world's leading authorities on bridge design and construction. BRIDGES AND THEIR BUILDERS is the only comprehensive and accurate semi-popular history of these important measures of progress in print. New, greatly revised, enlarged edition. 23 photos; 26 line-drawings. Index. xvii + 401pp. 5⅜ x 8.   T431 Paperbound **$2.00**

FAMOUS BRIDGES OF THE WORLD, D. B. Steinman. An up-to-the-minute new edition of a book that explains the fascinating drama of how the world's great bridges came to be built. The author, designer of the famed Mackinac bridge, discusses bridges from all periods and all parts of the world, explaining their various types of construction, and describing the problems their builders faced. Although primarily for youngsters, this cannot fail to interest readers of all ages. 48 illustrations in the text. 23 photographs. 99pp. 6⅛ x 9¼.   T161 Paperbound **$1.00**

HOW DO YOU USE A SLIDE RULE? by A. A. Merrill. A step-by-step explanation of the slide rule that presents the fundamental rules clearly enough for the non-mathematician to understand. Unlike most instruction manuals, this work concentrates on the two most important operations: multiplication and division. 10 easy lessons, each with a clear drawing, for the reader who has difficulty following other expositions. 1st publication. Index. 2 Appendices. 10 illustrations. 78 problems, all with answers. vi + 36 pp. 6⅛ x 9¼.   T62 Paperbound **60¢**

HOW TO CALCULATE QUICKLY, H. Sticker. A tried and true method for increasing your "number sense" — the ability to see relationships between numbers and groups of numbers. Addition, subtraction, multiplication, division, fractions, and other topics are treated through techniques not generally taught in schools: left to right multiplication, division by inspection, etc. This is not a collection of tricks which work only on special numbers, but a detailed well-planned course, consisting of over 9,000 problems that you can work in spare moments. It is excellent for anyone who is inconvenienced by slow computational skills. 5 or 10 minutes of this book daily will double or triple your calculation speed. 9,000 problems, answers. 256pp. 5⅜ x 8.   T295 Paperbound **$1.00**

MATHEMATICAL FUN, GAMES AND PUZZLES, Jack Frohlichstein. A valuable service for parents of children who have trouble with math, for teachers in need of a supplement to regular upper elementary and junior high math texts (each section is graded—easy, average, difficult —for ready adaptation to different levels of ability), and for just anyone who would like to develop basic skills in an informal and entertaining manner. The author combines ten years of experience as a junior high school math teacher with a method that uses puzzles and games to introduce the basic ideas and operations of arithmetic. Stress on everyday uses of math: banking, stock market, personal budgets, insurance, taxes. Intellectually stimulating and practical, too. 418 problems and diversions with answers. Bibliography. 120 illustrations. xix + 306pp. 5⅝ x 8½.   T789 Paperbound **$1.75**

GREAT IDEAS OF MODERN MATHEMATICS: THEIR NATURE AND USE, Jagjit Singh. Reader with only high school math will understand main mathematical ideas of modern physics, astronomy, genetics, psychology, evolution, etc. better than many who use them as tools, but comprehend little of their basic structure. Author uses his wide knowledge of non-mathematical fields in brilliant exposition of differential equations, matrices, group theory, logic, statistics, problems of mathematical foundations, imaginary numbers, vectors, etc. Original publication. 2 appendixes. 2 indexes. 65 illustr. 322pp. 5⅜ x 8.   S587 Paperbound **$1.75**

THE UNIVERSE OF LIGHT, W. Bragg. Sir William Bragg, Nobel Laureate and great modern physicist, is also well known for his powers of clear exposition. Here he analyzes all aspects of light for the layman: lenses, reflection, refraction, the optics of vision, x-rays, the photoelectric effect, etc. He tells you what causes the color of spectra, rainbows, and soap bubbles, how magic mirrors work, and much more. Dozens of simple experiments are described. Preface. Index. 199 line drawings and photographs, including 2 full-page color plates. x + 283pp. 5⅜ x 8.   T538 Paperbound **$1.85**

*INTRODUCTION TO SYMBOLIC LOGIC AND ITS APPLICATIONS, Rudolph Carnap. One of the clearest, most comprehensive, and rigorous introductions to modern symbolic logic, by perhaps its greatest living master. Not merely elementary theory, but demonstrated applications in mathematics, physics, and biology. Symbolic languages of various degrees of complexity are analyzed, and one constructed. "A creation of the rank of a masterpiece," Zentralblatt für Mathematik und Ihre Grenzgebiete. Over 300 exercises. 5 figures. Bibliography. Index. xvi + 241pp. 5⅜ x 8.   S453 Paperbound **$1.85**

*HIGHER MATHEMATICS FOR STUDENTS OF CHEMISTRY AND PHYSICS, J. W. Mellor. Not abstract, but practical, drawing its problems from familiar laboratory material, this book covers theory and application of differential calculus, analytic geometry, functions with singularities, integral calculus, infinite series, solution of numerical equations, differential equations, Fourier's theorem and extensions, probability and the theory of errors, calculus of variations, determinants, etc. "If the reader is not familiar with this book, it will repay him to examine it," CHEM. & ENGINEERING NEWS. 800 problems. 189 figures. 2 appendices; 30 tables of integrals, probability functions, etc. Bibliography. xxi + 641pp. 5⅜ x 8.
S193 Paperbound **$2.50**

CATALOGUE OF DOVER BOOKS

THE FOURTH DIMENSION SIMPLY EXPLAINED, edited by Henry P. Manning. Originally written as entries in contest sponsored by "Scientific American," then published in book form, these 22 essays present easily understood explanations of how the fourth dimension may be studied, the relationship of non-Euclidean geometry to the fourth dimension, analogies to three-dimensional space, some fourth-dimensional absurdities and curiosities, possible measurements and forms in the fourth dimension. In general, a thorough coverage of many of the simpler properties of fourth-dimensional space. Multi-points of view on many of the most important aspects are valuable aid to comprehension. Introduction by Dr. Henry P. Manning gives proper emphasis to points in essays, more advanced account of fourth-dimensional geometry. 82 figures. 251pp. 5⅜ x 8. T711 Paperbound **$1.35**

TRIGONOMETRY REFRESHER FOR TECHNICAL MEN, A. A. Klaf. A modern question and answer text on plane and spherical trigonometry. Part I covers plane trigonometry: angles, quadrants, trigonometrical functions, graphical representation, interpolation, equations, logarithms, solution of triangles, slide rules, etc. Part II discusses applications to navigation, surveying, elasticity, architecture, and engineering. Small angles, periodic functions, vectors, polar coordinates, De Moivre's theorem, fully covered. Part III is devoted to spherical trigonometry and the solution of spherical triangles, with applications to terrestrial and astronomical problems. Special time-savers for numerical calculation. 913 questions answered for you! 1738 problems; answers to odd numbers. 494 figures. 14 pages of functions, formulae. Index. x + 629pp. 5⅜ x 8. T371 Paperbound **$2.00**

CALCULUS REFRESHER FOR TECHNICAL MEN. A. A. Klaf. Not an ordinary textbook but a unique refresher for engineers, technicians, and students. An examination of the most important aspects of differential and integral calculus by means of 756 key questions. Part I covers simple differential calculus: constants, variables, functions, increments, derivatives, logarithms, curvature, etc. Part II treats fundamental concepts of integration: inspection, substitution, transformation, reduction, areas and volumes, mean value, successive and partial integration, double and triple integration. Stresses practical aspects! A 50 page section gives applications to civil and nautical engineering, electricity, stress and strain, elasticity, industrial engineering, and similar fields. 756 questions answered. 556 problems; solutions to odd numbers. 36 pages of constants, formulae. Index. v + 431pp. 5⅜ x 8. T370 Paperbound **$2.00**

PROBABILITIES AND LIFE, Emile Borel. One of the leading French mathematicians of the last 100 years makes use of certain results of mathematics of probabilities and explains a number of problems that for the most part, are related to everyday living or to illness and death: computation of life expectancy tables, chances of recovery from various diseases, probabilities of job accidents, weather predictions, games of chance, and so on. Emphasis on results not processes, though some indication is made of mathematical proofs. Simple in style, free of technical terminology, limited in scope to everyday situations, it is comprehensible to laymen, fine reading for beginning students of probability. New English translation. Index. Appendix. vi + 87pp. 5⅜ x 8½. T121 Paperbound **$1.00**

POPULAR SCIENTIFIC LECTURES, Hermann von Helmholtz. 7 lucid expositions by a pre-eminent scientific mind: "The Physiological Causes of Harmony in Music," "On the Relation of Optics to Painting," "On the Conservation of Force," "On the Interaction of Natural Forces," "On Goethe's Scientific Researches" into theory of color, "On the Origin and Significance of Geometric Axioms," "On Recent Progress in the Theory of Vision." Written with simplicity of expression, stripped of technicalities, these are easy to understand and delightful reading for anyone interested in science or looking for an introduction to serious study of acoustics or optics. Introduction by Professor Morris Kline, Director, Division of Electromagnetic Research, New York University, contains astute, impartial evaluations. Selected from "Popular Lectures on Scientific Subjects," 1st and 2nd series. xii + 286pp. 5⅜ x 8½. T799 Paperbound **$1.45**

SCIENCE AND METHOD, Henri Poincaré. Procedure of scientific discovery, methodology, experiment, idea-germination—the intellectual processes by which discoveries come into being. Most significant and most interesting aspects of development, application of ideas. Chapters cover selection of facts, chance, mathematical reasoning, mathematics, and logic; Whitehead, Russell, Cantor; the new mechanics, etc. 288pp. 5⅜ x 8. S222 Paperbound **$1.50**

HEAT AND ITS WORKINGS, Morton Mott-Smith, Ph.D. An unusual book; to our knowledge the only middle-level survey of this important area of science. Explains clearly such important concepts as physiological sensation of heat and Weber's law, measurement of heat, evolution of thermometer, nature of heat, expansion and contraction of solids, Boyle's law, specific heat. BTU's and calories, evaporation, Andrews's isothermals, radiation, the relation of heat to light, many more topics inseparable from other aspects of physics. A wide, non-mathematical yet thorough explanation of basic ideas, theories, phenomena for laymen and beginning scientists illustrated by experiences of daily life. Bibliography. 50 illustrations. x + 165pp. 5⅜ x 8½. T978 Paperbound **$1.00**

Classics of Science

THE DIDEROT PICTORIAL ENCYCLOPEDIA OF TRADES AND INDUSTRY, MANUFACTURING AND THE TECHNICAL ARTS IN PLATES SELECTED FROM "L'ENCYCLOPEDIE OU DICTIONNAIRE RAISONNE DES SCIENCES, DES ARTS, ET DES METIERS" OF DENIS DIDEROT, edited with text by C. Gillispie. The first modern selection of plates from the high point of 18th century French engraving, Diderot's famous Encyclopedia. Over 2000 illustrations on 485 full page plates, most of them original size, illustrating the trades and industries of one of the most fascinating periods of modern history, 18th century France. These magnificent engravings provide an invaluable glimpse into the past for the student of early technology, a lively and accurate social document to students of cultures, an outstanding find to the lover of fine engravings. The plates teem with life, with men, women, and children performing all of the thousands of operations necessary to the trades before and during the early stages of the industrial revolution. Plates are in sequence, and show general operations, closeups of difficult operations, and details of complex machinery. Such important and interesting trades and industries are illustrated as sowing, harvesting, beekeeping, cheesemaking, operating windmills, milling flour, charcoal burning, tobacco processing, indigo, fishing, arts of war, salt extraction, mining, smelting iron, casting iron, steel, extracting mercury, zinc, sulphur, copper, etc., slating, tinning, silverplating, gilding, making gunpowder, cannons, bells, shoeing horses, tanning, papermaking, printing, dying, and more than 40 other categories. 920pp. 9 x 12. Heavy library cloth.   T421 Two volume set **$18.50**

THE PRINCIPLES OF SCIENCE, A TREATISE ON LOGIC AND THE SCIENTIFIC METHOD, W. Stanley Jevons. Treating such topics as Inductive and Deductive Logic, the Theory of Number, Probability, and the Limits of Scientific Method, this milestone in the development of symbolic logic remains a stimulating contribution to the investigation of inferential validity in the natural and social sciences. It significantly advances Boole's logic, and describes a machine which is a foundation of modern electronic calculators. In his introduction, Ernest Nagel of Columbia University says, "(Jevons) . . . continues to be of interest as an attempt to articulate the logic of scientific inquiry." Index. liii + 786pp. 5⅜ x 8.
S446 Paperbound **$2.98**

*DIALOGUES CONCERNING TWO NEW SCIENCES, Galileo Galilei. A classic of experimental science which has had a profound and enduring influence on the entire history of mechanics and engineering. Galileo based this, his finest work, on 30 years of experimentation. It offers a fascinating and vivid exposition of dynamics, elasticity, sound, ballistics, strength of materials, and the scientific method. Translated by H. Crew and A. de Salvio. 126 diagrams. Index. xxi + 288pp. 5⅜ x 8.   S99 Paperbound **$1.75**

DE MAGNETE, William Gilbert. This classic work on magnetism founded a new science. Gilbert was the first to use the word "electricity," to recognize mass as distinct from weight, to discover the effect of heat on magnetic bodies; invented an electroscope, differentiated between static electricity and magnetism, conceived of the earth as a magnet. Written by the first great experimental scientist, this lively work is valuable not only as an historical landmark, but as the delightfully easy-to-follow record of a perpetually searching, ingenious mind. Translated by P. F. Mottelay. 25 page biographical memoir. 90 fix. lix + 368pp. 5⅜ x 8.   S470 Paperbound **$2.00**

*OPTICKS, Sir Isaac Newton. An enormous storehouse of insights and discoveries on light, reflection, color, refraction, theories of wave and corpuscular propagation of light, optical apparatus, and mathematical devices which have recently been reevaluated in terms of modern physics and placed in the top-most ranks of Newton's work! Foreword by Albert Einstein. Preface by I. B. Cohen of Harvard U. 7 pages of portraits, facsimile pages, letters, etc. cxvi + 412pp. 5⅜ x 8.   S205 Paperbound **$2.25**

A SURVEY OF PHYSICAL THEORY, M. Planck. Lucid essays on modern physics for the general reader by the Nobel Laureate and creator of the quantum revolution. Planck explains how the new concepts came into being; explores the clash between theories of mechanics, electro-dynamics, and thermodynamics; and traces the evolution of the concept of light through Newton, Huygens, Maxwell, and his own quantum theory, providing unparalleled insights into his development of this momentous modern concept. Bibliography. Index. vii + 121pp. 5⅜ x 8.
S650 Paperbound **$1.15**

A SOURCE BOOK IN MATHEMATICS, D. E. Smith. English translations of the original papers that announced the great discoveries in mathematics from the Renaissance to the end of the 19th century: succinct selections from 125 different treatises and articles, most of them unavailable elsewhere in English—Newton, Leibniz, Pascal, Riemann, Bernoulli, etc. 24 articles trace developments in the field of number, 18 cover algebra, 36 are on geometry, and 13 on calculus. Biographical-historical introductions to each article. Two volume set. Index in each. Total of 115 illustrations. Total of xxviii + 742pp. 5⅜ x 8.   S552 Vol I Paperbound **$2.00**
S553 Vol II Paperbound **$2.00**
The set, boxed **$4.00**

CATALOGUE OF DOVER BOOKS

*THE THIRTEEN BOOKS OF EUCLID'S ELEMENTS, edited by T. L. Heath. This is the complete EUCLID — the definitive edition of one of the greatest classics of the western world. Complete English translation of the Heiberg text with spurious Book XIV. Detailed 150-page introduction discusses aspects of Greek and medieval mathematics: Euclid, texts, commentators, etc. Paralleling the text is an elaborate critical exposition analyzing each definition, proposition, postulate, etc., and covering textual matters, mathematical analyses, refutations, extensions, etc. Unabridged reproduction of the Cambridge 2nd edition. 3 volumes. Total of 995 figures, 1426pp. 5⅜ x 8.   S88, 89, 90 — 3 vol. set, Paperbound **$6.75**

*THE GEOMETRY OF RENE DESCARTES. The great work which founded analytic geometry. The renowned Smith-Latham translation faced with the original French text containing all of Descartes' own diagrams! Contains: Problems the Construction of Which Requires Only Straight Lines and Circles; On the Nature of Curved Lines; On the Construction of Solid or Supersolid Problems. Notes. Diagrams. 258pp.   S68 Paperbound **$1.60**

*A PHILOSOPHICAL ESSAY ON PROBABILITIES, P. Laplace. Without recourse to any mathematics above grammar school, Laplace develops a philosophically, mathematically and historically classical exposition of the nature of probability: its functions and limitations, operations in practical affairs, calculations in games of chance, insurance, government, astronomy, and countless other fields. New introduction by E. T. Bell. viii + 196pp. S166 Paperbound **$1.35**

DE RE METALLICA, Georgius Agricola. Written over 400 years ago, for 200 years the most authoritative first-hand account of the production of metals, translated in 1912 by former President Herbert Hoover and his wife, and today still one of the most beautiful and fascinating volumes ever produced in the history of science! 12 books, exhaustively annotated, give a wonderfully lucid and vivid picture of the history of mining, selection of sites, types of deposits, excavating pits, sinking shafts, ventilating, pumps, crushing machinery, assaying, smelting, refining metals, making salt, alum, nitre, glass, and many other topics. This definitive edition contains all 289 of the 16th century woodcuts which made the original an artistic masterpiece. It makes a superb gift for geologists, engineers, libraries, artists, historians, and everyone interested in science and early illustrative art. Biographical, historical introductions. Bibliography, survey of ancient authors. Indices. 289 illustrations. 672pp. 6¾ x 10¾. Deluxe library edition.   S6 Clothbound **$10.00**

GEOGRAPHICAL ESSAYS, W. M. Davis. Modern geography and geomorphology rest on the fundamental work of this scientist. His new concepts of earth-processes revolutionized science and his broad interpretation of the scope of geography created a deeper understanding of the interrelation of the landscape and the forces that mold it. This first inexpensive unabridged edition covers theory of geography, methods of advanced geographic teaching, descriptions of geographic areas, analyses of land-shaping processes, and much besides. Not only a factual and historical classic, it is still widely read for its reflections of modern scientific thought. Introduction. 130 figures. Index. vi + 777pp. 5⅜ x 8.
                 S383 Paperbound **$3.50**

CHARLES BABBAGE AND HIS CALCULATING ENGINES, edited by P. Morrison and E. Morrison. Friend of Darwin, Humboldt, and Laplace, Babbage was a leading pioneer in large-scale mathematical machines and a prophetic herald of modern operational research—true father of Harvard's relay computer Mark I. His Difference Engine and Analytical Engine were the first successful machines in the field. This volume contains a valuable introduction on his life and work; major excerpts from his fascinating autobiography, revealing his eccentric and unusual personality; and extensive selections from "Babbage's Calculating Engines," a compilation of hard-to-find journal articles, both by Babbage and by such eminent contributors as the Countess of Lovelace, L. F. Menabrea, and Dionysius Lardner. 11 illustrations. Appendix of miscellaneous papers. Index. Bibliography. xxxviii + 400pp. 5⅜ x 8.   T12 Paperbound **$2.00**

*THE WORKS OF ARCHIMEDES WITH THE METHOD OF ARCHIMEDES, edited by T. L. Heath. All the known works of the greatest mathematician of antiquity including the recently discovered METHOD OF ARCHIMEDES. This last is the only work we have which shows exactly how early mathematicians discovered their proofs before setting them down in their final perfection. A 186 page study by the eminent scholar Heath discusses Archimedes and the history of Greek mathematics. Bibliography. 563pp. 5⅜ x 8.   S9 Paperbound **$2.45**

Puzzles, Mathematical Recreations

SYMBOLIC LOGIC and THE GAME OF LOGIC, Lewis Carroll. "Symbolic Logic" is not concerned with modern symbolic logic, but is instead a collection of over 380 problems posed with charm and imagination, using the syllogism, and a fascinating diagrammatic method of drawing conclusions. In "The Game of Logic" Carroll's whimsical imagination devises a logical game played with 2 diagrams and counters (included) to manipulate hundreds of tricky syllogisms. The final section, "Hit or Miss" is a lagniappe of 101 additional puzzles in the delightful Carroll manner. Until this reprint edition, both of these books were rarities costing up to $15 each. Symbolic Logic: Index. xxxi + 199pp. The Game of Logic: 96pp. 2 vols. bound as one. 5⅜ x 8.　　　　　　　　　　　　　　　　　T492 Paperbound **$1.50**

PILLOW PROBLEMS and A TANGLED TALE, Lewis Carroll. One of the rarest of all Carroll's works, "Pillow Problems" contains 72 original math puzzles, all typically ingenious. Particularly fascinating are Carroll's answers which remain exactly as he thought them out, reflecting his actual mental process. The problems in "A Tangled Tale" are in story form, originally appearing as a monthly magazine serial. Carroll not only gives the solutions, but uses answers sent in by readers to discuss wrong approaches and misleading paths, and grades them for insight. Both of these books were rarities until this edition, "Pillow Problems" costing up to $25, and "A Tangled Tale" $15. Pillow Problems: Preface and Introduction by Lewis Carroll. xx + 109pp. A Tangled Tale: 6 illustrations. 152pp. Two vols. bound as one. 5⅜ x 8.　　　　　　　　　　　　　　　　T493 Paperbound **$1.50**

AMUSEMENTS IN MATHEMATICS, Henry Ernest Dudeney. The foremost British originator of mathematical puzzles is always intriguing, witty, and paradoxical in this classic, one of the largest collections of mathematical amusements. More than 430 puzzles, problems, and paradoxes. Mazes and games, problems on number manipulation, unicursal and other route problems, puzzles on measuring, weighing, packing, age, kinship, chessboards, joiners', crossing river, plane figure dissection, and many others. Solutions. More than 450 illustrations. vii + 258pp. 5⅜ x 8.　　　　　　　　　　　　　　　　　T473 Paperbound **$1.25**

THE CANTERBURY PUZZLES, Henry Dudeney. Chaucer's pilgrims set one another problems in story form. Also Adventures of the Puzzle Club, the Strange Escape of the King's Jester, the Monks of Riddlewell, the Squire's Christmas Puzzle Party, and others. All puzzles are original, based on dissecting plane figures, arithmetic, algebra, elementary calculus and other branches of mathematics, and purely logical ingenuity. "The limit of ingenuity and intricacy," The Observer. Over 110 puzzles. Full Solutions. 150 illustrations. vii + 225pp. 5⅜ x 8.
　　　　　　　　　　　　　　　　　T474 Paperbound **$1.25**

MATHEMATICAL EXCURSIONS, H. A. Merrill. Even if you hardly remember your high school math, you'll enjoy the 90 stimulating problems contained in this book and you will come to understand a great many mathematical principles with surprisingly little effort. Many useful shortcuts and diversions not generally known are included: division by inspection, Russian peasant multiplication, memory systems for pi, building odd and even magic squares, square roots by geometry, dyadic systems, and many more. Solutions to difficult problems. 50 illustrations. 145pp. 5⅜ x 8.　　　　　　　　　　　　　　T350 Paperbound **$1.00**

MAGIC SQUARES AND CUBES, W. S. Andrews. Only book-length treatment in English, a thorough non-technical description and analysis. Here are nasik, overlapping, pandiagonal, serrated squares; magic circles, cubes, spheres, rhombuses. Try your hand at 4-dimensional magical figures! Much unusual folklore and tradition included. High school algebra is sufficient. 754 diagrams and illustrations. viii + 419pp. 5⅜ x 8.　　　　　　　T658 Paperbound **$1.85**

CALIBAN'S PROBLEM BOOK: MATHEMATICAL, INFERENTIAL AND CRYPTOGRAPHIC PUZZLES, H. Phillips (Caliban), S. T. Shovelton, G. S. Marshall. 105 ingenious problems by the greatest living creator of puzzles based on logic and inference. Rigorous, modern, piquant; reflecting their author's unusual personality, these intermediate and advanced puzzles all involve the ability to reason clearly through complex situations; some call for mathematical knowledge, ranging from algebra to number theory. Solutions. xi + 180pp. 5⅜ x 8.
　　　　　　　　　　　　　　　　　T736 Paperbound **$1.25**

MATHEMATICAL PUZZLES FOR BEGINNERS AND ENTHUSIASTS, G. Mott-Smith. 188 mathematical puzzles based on algebra, dissection of plane figures, permutations, and probability, that will test and improve your powers of inference and interpretation. The Odic Force, The Spider's Cousin, Ellipse Drawing, theory and strategy of card and board games like tit-tat-toe, go moku, salvo, and many others. 100 pages of detailed mathematical explanations. Appendix of primes, square roots, etc. 135 illustrations. 2nd revised edition. 248pp. 5⅜ x 8.
　　　　　　　　　　　　　　　　　T198 Paperbound **$1.00**

MATHEMAGIC, MAGIC PUZZLES, AND GAMES WITH NUMBERS, R. V. Heath. More than 60 new puzzles and stunts based on the properties of numbers. Easy techniques for multiplying large numbers mentally, revealing hidden numbers magically, finding the date of any day in any year, and dozens more. Over 30 pages devoted to magic squares, triangles, cubes, circles, etc. Edited by J. S. Meyer. 76 illustrations. 128pp. 5⅜ x 8.　　　　T110 Paperbound **$1.00**

MATHEMATICAL RECREATIONS, M. Kraitchik. One of the most thorough compilations of unusual mathematical problems for beginners and advanced mathematicians. Historical problems from Greek, Medieval, Arabic, Hindu sources. 50 pages devoted to pastimes derived from figurate numbers, Mersenne numbers, Fermat numbers, primes and probability. 40 pages of magic, Euler, Latin, panmagic squares. 25 new positional and permutational games of permanent value: fairy chess, latruncles, reversi, jinx, ruma, lasca, tricolor, tetrachrome, etc. Complete rigorous solutions. Revised second edition. 181 illustrations. 333pp. 5⅜ x 8.
T163 Paperbound **$1.75**

MATHEMATICAL PUZZLES OF SAM LOYD, selected and edited by M. Gardner. Choice puzzles by the greatest American puzzle creator and innovator. Selected from his famous collection, "Cyclopedia of Puzzles," they retain the unique style and historical flavor of the originals. There are posers based on arithmetic, algebra, probability, game theory, route tracing, topology, counter, sliding block, operations research, geometrical dissection. Includes the famous "14-15" puzzle which was a national craze, and his "Horse of a Different Color" which sold millions of copies. 117 of his most ingenious puzzles in all, 120 line drawings and diagrams. Solutions. Selected references. xx + 167pp. 5⅜ x 8. T498 Paperbound **$1.00**

MATHEMATICAL PUZZLES OF SAM LOYD, Vol. II, selected and edited by Martin Gardner. The outstanding 2nd selection from the great American innovator's "Cyclopedia of Puzzles": speed and distance problems, clock problems, plane and solid geometry, calculus problems, etc. Analytical table of contents that groups the puzzles according to the type of mathematics necessary to solve them. 166 puzzles, 150 original line drawings and diagrams. Selected references. xiv + 177pp. 5⅜ x 8. T709 Paperbound **$1.00**

ARITHMETICAL EXCURSIONS: AN ENRICHMENT OF ELEMENTARY MATHEMATICS, H. Bowers and J. Bowers. A lively and lighthearted collection of facts and entertainments for anyone who enjoys manipulating numbers or solving arithmetical puzzles: methods of arithmetic never taught in school, little-known facts about the most simple numbers, and clear explanations of more sophisticated topics; mysteries and folklore of numbers, the "Hin-dog-abic" number system, etc. First publication. Index. 529 numbered problems and diversions, all with answers. Bibliography. 60 figures. xiv + 320pp. 5⅜ x 8. T770 Paperbound **$1.65**

CRYPTANALYSIS, H. F. Gaines. Formerly entitled ELEMENTARY CRYPTANALYSIS, this introductory-intermediate level text is the best book in print on cryptograms and their solution. It covers all major techniques of the past, and contains much that is not generally known except to experts. Full details about concealment, substitution, and transposition ciphers; periodic mixed alphabets, multafid, Kasiski and Vigenere methods, Ohaver patterns, Playfair, and scores of other topics. 6 language letter and word frequency appendix. 167 problems, now furnished with solutions. Index. 173 figures. vi + 230pp. 5⅜ x 8.
T97 Paperbound **$2.00**

CRYPTOGRAPHY, L. D. Smith. An excellent introductory work on ciphers and their solution, the history of secret writing, and actual methods and problems in such techniques as transposition and substitution. Appendices describe the enciphering of Japanese, the Baconian biliteral cipher, and contain frequency tables and a bibliography for further study. Over 150 problems with solutions. 160pp. 5⅜ x 8. T247 Paperbound **$1.00**

PUZZLE QUIZ AND STUNT FUN, J. Meyer. The solution to party doldrums. 238 challenging puzzles, stunts and tricks. Mathematical puzzles like The Clever Carpenter, Atom Bomb; mysteries and deductions like The Bridge of Sighs, The Nine Pearls, Dog Logic; observation puzzles like Cigarette Smokers, Telephone Dial; over 200 others including magic squares, tongue twisters, puns, anagrams, and many others. All problems solved fully. 250pp. 5⅜ x 8.
T337 Paperbound **$1.00**

101 PUZZLES IN THOUGHT AND LOGIC, C. R. Wylie, Jr. Brand new problems you need no special knowledge to solve! Take the kinks out of your mental "muscles" and enjoy solving murder problems, the detection of lying fishermen, the logical identification of color by a blindman, and dozens more. Introduction with simplified explanation of general scientific method and puzzle solving. 128pp. 5⅜ x 8. T367 Paperbound **$1.00**

MY BEST PROBLEMS IN MATHEMATICS, Hubert Phillips ("Caliban"). Only elementary mathematics needed to solve these 100 witty, catchy problems by a master problem creator. Problems on the odds in cards and dice, problems in geometry, algebra, permutations, even problems that require no math at all—just a logical mind, clear thinking. Solutions completely worked out. If you enjoy mysteries, alerting your perceptive powers and exercising your detective's eye, you'll find these cryptic puzzles a challenging delight. Original 1961 publication. 100 puzzles, solutions. x + 107pp. 5⅝ x 8. T91 Paperbound **$1.00**

MY BEST PUZZLES IN LOGIC AND REASONING, Hubert Phillips ("Caliban"). A new collection of 100 inferential and logical puzzles chosen from the best that have appeared in England, available for first time in U.S. By the most endlessly resourceful puzzle creator now living. All data presented are both necessary and sufficient to allow a single unambiguous answer. No special knowledge is required for problems ranging from relatively simple to completely original one-of-a-kinds. Guaranteed to please beginners and experts of all ages. Original publication. 100 puzzles, full solutions. x + 107pp. 5⅜ x 8. T119 Paperbound **$1.00**

CATALOGUE OF DOVER BOOKS

THE BOOK OF MODERN PUZZLES, G. L. Kaufman. A completely new series of puzzles as fascinating as crossword and deduction puzzles but based upon different principles and techniques. Simple 2-minute teasers, word labyrinths, design and pattern puzzles, logic and observation puzzles — over 150 braincrackers. Answers to all problems. 116 illustrations. 192pp. 5⅜ x 8.
.T143 Paperbound **$1.00**

NEW WORD PUZZLES, G. L. Kaufman. 100 ENTIRELY NEW puzzles based on words and their combinations that will delight crossword puzzle, Scrabble and Jotto fans. Chess words, based on the moves of the chess king; design-onyms, symmetrical designs made of synonyms; rhymed double-crostics; syllable sentences; addle letter anagrams; alphagrams; linkograms; and many others all brand new. Full solutions. Space to work problems. 196 figures. vi + 122pp. 5⅜ x 8.
T344 Paperbound **$1.00**

MAZES AND LABYRINTHS: A BOOK OF PUZZLES, W. Shepherd. Mazes, formerly associated with mystery and ritual, are still among the most intriguing of intellectual puzzles. This is a novel and different collection of 50 amusements that embody the principle of the maze: mazes in the classical tradition; 3-dimensional, ribbon, and Möbius-strip mazes; hidden messages; spatial arrangements; etc.—almost all built on amusing story situations. 84 illustrations. Essay on maze psychology. Solutions. xv + 122pp. 5⅜ x 8.
T731 Paperbound **$1.00**

MAGIC TRICKS & CARD TRICKS, W. Jonson. Two books bound as one. 52 tricks with cards, 37 tricks with coins, bills, eggs, smoke, ribbons, slates, etc. Details on presentation, misdirection, and routining will help you master such famous tricks as the Changing Card, Card in the Pocket, Four Aces, Coin Through the Hand, Bill in the Egg, Afghan Bands, and over 75 others. If you follow the lucid exposition and key diagrams carefully, you will finish these two books with an astonishing mastery of magic. 106 figures. 224pp. 5⅜ x 8. T909 Paperbound **$1.00**

PANORAMA OF MAGIC, Milbourne Christopher. A profusely illustrated history of stage magic, a unique selection of prints and engravings from the author's private collection of magic memorabilia, the largest of its kind. Apparatus, stage settings and costumes; ingenious ads distributed by the performers and satiric broadsides passed around in the streets ridiculing pompous showmen; programs; decorative souvenirs. The lively text, by one of America's foremost professional magicians, is full of anecdotes about almost legendary wizards: Dede, the Egyptian; Philadelphia, the wonder-worker; Robert-Houdin, "the father of modern magic;" Harry Houdini; scores more. Altogether a pleasure package for anyone interested in magic, stage setting and design, ethnology, psychology, or simply in unusual people. A Dover original. 295 illustrations; 8 in full color. Index. viii + 216pp. 8⅜ x 11¼.
T774 Paperbound **$2.25**

HOUDINI ON MAGIC, Harry Houdini. One of the greatest magicians of modern times explains his most prized secrets. How locks are picked, with illustrated picks and skeleton keys; how a girl is sawed into twins; how to walk through a brick wall — Houdini's explanations of 44 stage tricks with many diagrams. Also included is a fascinating discussion of great magicians of the past and the story of his fight against fraudulent mediums and spiritualists. Edited by W.B. Gibson and M.N. Young. Bibliography. 155 figures, photos. xv + 280pp. 5⅜ x 8.
T384 Paperbound **$1.35**

MATHEMATICS, MAGIC AND MYSTERY, Martin Gardner. Why do card tricks work? How do magicians perform astonishing mathematical feats? How is stage mind-reading possible? This is the first book length study explaining the application of probability, set theory, theory of numbers, topology, etc., to achieve many startling tricks. Non-technical, accurate, detailed! 115 sections discuss tricks with cards, dice, coins, knots, geometrical vanishing illusions, how a Curry square "demonstrates" that the sum of the parts may be greater than the whole, and dozens of others. No sleight of hand necessary! 135 illustrations. xii + 174pp. 5⅜ x 8.
T335 Paperbound **$1.00**

EASY-TO-DO ENTERTAINMENTS AND DIVERSIONS WITH COINS, CARDS, STRING, PAPER AND MATCHES, R. M. Abraham. Over 300 tricks, games and puzzles will provide young readers with absorbing fun. Sections on card games; paper-folding; tricks with coins, matches and pieces of string; games for the agile; toy-making from common household objects; mathematical recreations; and 50 miscellaneous pastimes. Anyone in charge of groups of youngsters, including hard-pressed parents, and in need of suggestions on how to keep children sensibly amused and quietly content will find this book indispensable. Clear, simple text, copious number of delightful line drawings and illustrative diagrams. Originally titled "Winter Nights Entertainments." Introduction by Lord Baden Powell. 329 illustrations. v + 186pp. 5⅜ x 8½.
T921 Paperbound **$1.00**

STRING FIGURES AND HOW TO MAKE THEM, Caroline Furness Jayne. 107 string figures plus variations selected from the best primitive and modern examples developed by Navajo, Apache, pygmies of Africa, Eskimo, in Europe, Australia, China, etc. The most readily understandable, easy-to-follow book in English on perennially popular recreation. Crystal-clear exposition; step-by-step diagrams. Everyone from kindergarten children to adults looking for unusual diversion will be endlessly amused. Index. Bibliography. Introduction by A. C. Haddon. 17 full-page plates. 960 illustrations. xxiii + 401pp. 5⅜ x 8½.
T152 Paperbound **$2.00**

Language Books and Records

GERMAN: HOW TO SPEAK AND WRITE IT. AN INFORMAL CONVERSATIONAL METHOD FOR SELF STUDY, Joseph Rosenberg. Eminently useful for self study because of concentration on elementary stages of learning. Also provides teachers with remarkable variety of aids: 28 full- and double-page sketches with pertinent items numbered and identified in German and English; German proverbs, jokes; grammar, idiom studies; extensive practice exercises. The most interesting introduction to German available, full of amusing illustrations, photographs of cities and landmarks in German-speaking cities, cultural information subtly woven into conversational material. Includes summary of grammar, guide to letter writing, study guide to German literature by Dr. Richard Friedenthal. Index. 400 illustrations. 384pp. 5⅜ x 8½.
T271 Paperbound **$2.00**

FRENCH: HOW TO SPEAK AND WRITE IT. AN INFORMAL CONVERSATIONAL METHOD FOR SELF STUDY, Joseph Lemaitre. Even the absolute beginner can acquire a solid foundation for further study from this delightful elementary course. Photographs, sketches and drawings, sparkling colloquial conversations on a wide variety of topics (including French culture and custom), French sayings and quips, are some of aids used to demonstrate rather than merely describe the language. Thorough yet surprisingly entertaining approach, excellent for teaching and for self study. Comprehensive analysis of pronunciation, practice exercises and appendices of verb tables, additional vocabulary, other useful material. Index. Appendix. 400 illustrations. 416pp. 5⅜ x 8½.
T268 Paperbound **$2.00**

DICTIONARY OF SPOKEN SPANISH, Spanish-English, English-Spanish. Compiled from spoken Spanish, emphasizing idiom and colloquial usage in both Castilian and Latin-American. More than 16,000 entries containing over 25,000 idioms—the largest list of idiomatic constructions ever published. Complete sentences given, indexed under single words—language in immediately useable form, for travellers, businessmen, students, etc. 25 page introduction provides rapid survey of sounds, grammar, syntax, with full consideration of irregular verbs. Especially apt in modern treatment of phrases and structure. 17 page glossary gives translations of geographical names, money values, numbers, national holidays, important street signs, useful expressions of high frequency, plus unique 7 page glossary of Spanish and Spanish-American foods and dishes. Originally published as War Department Technical Manual TM 30-900. iv + 513pp. 5⅜ x 8.
T495 Paperbound **$1.75**

SPEAK MY LANGUAGE: SPANISH FOR YOUNG BEGINNERS, M. Ahlman, Z. Gilbert. Records provide one of the best, and most entertaining, methods of introducing a foreign language to children. Within the framework of a train trip from Portugal to Spain, an English-speaking child is introduced to Spanish by a native companion. (Adapted from a successful radio program of the N. Y. State Educational Department.) Though a continuous story, there are a dozen specific categories of expressions, including greetings, numbers, time, weather, food, clothes, family members, etc. Drill is combined with poetry and contextual use. Authentic background music is heard. An accompanying book enables a reader to follow the records, and includes a vocabulary of over 350 recorded expressions. Two 10" 33⅓ records, total of 40 minutes. Book. 40 illustrations. 69pp. 5¼ x 10½.
T890 The set **$4.95**

AN ENGLISH-FRENCH-GERMAN-SPANISH WORD FREQUENCY DICTIONARY, H. S. Eaton. An indispensable language study aid, this is a semantic frequency list of the 6000 most frequently used words in 4 languages—24,000 words in all. The lists, based on concepts rather than words alone, and containing all modern, exact, and idiomatic vocabulary, are arranged side by side to form a unique 4-language dictionary. A simple key indicates the importance of the individual words within each language. Over 200 pages of separate indexes for each language enable you to locate individual words at a glance. Will help language teachers and students, authors of textbooks, grammars, and language tests to compare concepts in the various languages and to concentrate on basic vocabulary, avoiding uncommon and obsolete words. 2 Appendixes. xxi + 441pp. 6½ x 9¼.
T738 Paperbound **$2.45**

NEW RUSSIAN-ENGLISH AND ENGLISH-RUSSIAN DICTIONARY, M. A. O'Brien. Over 70,000 entries in the new orthography! Many idiomatic uses and colloquialisms which form the basis of actual speech. Irregular verbs, perfective and imperfective aspects, regular and irregular sound changes, and other features. One of the few dictionaries where accent changes within the conjugation of verbs and the declension of nouns are fully indicated. "One of the best," Prof. E. J. Simmons, Cornell. First names, geographical terms, bibliography, etc. 738pp. 4½ x 6¼.
T208 Paperbound **$2.00**

96 MOST USEFUL PHRASES FOR TOURISTS AND STUDENTS in English, French, Spanish, German, Italian. A handy folder you'll want to carry with you. How to say "Excuse me," "How much is it?", "Write it down, please," etc., in four foreign languages. Copies limited, no more than 1 to a customer.
FREE

Say It language phrase books

These handy phrase books (128 to 196 pages each) make grammatical drills unnecessary for an elementary knowledge of a spoken foreign language. Covering most matters of travel and everyday life each volume contains:

Over 1000 phrases and sentences in immediately useful forms — foreign language plus English.

Modern usage designed for Americans. Specific phrases like, "Give me small change," and "Please call a taxi."

Simplified phonetic transcription you will be able to read at sight.

The only completely indexed phrase books on the market.

Covers scores of important situations: — Greetings, restaurants, sightseeing, useful expressions, etc.

These books are prepared by native linguists who are professors at Columbia, N.Y.U., Fordham and other great universities. Use them independently or with any other book or record course. They provide a supplementary living element that most other courses lack. Individual volumes in:

Russian 75¢	Italian 75¢	Spanish 75¢	German 75¢
Hebrew 75¢	Danish 75¢	Japanese 75¢	Swedish 75¢
Dutch 75¢	Esperanto 75¢	Modern Greek 75¢	Portuguese 75¢
Norwegian 75¢	Polish 75¢	French 75¢	Yiddish 75¢
Turkish 75¢		English for German-speaking people 75¢	
English for Italian-speaking people 75¢		English for Spanish-speaking people 75¢	

Large clear type. 128-196 pages each. 3½ x 5¼. Sturdy paper binding.

Listen and Learn language records

LISTEN & LEARN is the only language record course designed especially to meet your travel and everyday needs. It is available in separate sets for FRENCH, SPANISH, GERMAN, JAPANESE, RUSSIAN, MODERN GREEK, PORTUGUESE, ITALIAN and HEBREW, and each set contains three 33⅓ rpm long-playing records—1½ hours of recorded speech by eminent native speakers who are professors at Columbia, New York University, Queens College.

Check the following special features found only in LISTEN & LEARN:

- **Dual-language recording.** 812 selected phrases and sentences, over 3200 words, spoken first in English, then in their foreign language equivalents. A suitable pause follows each foreign phrase, allowing you time to repeat the expression. You learn by unconscious assimilation.
- **128 to 206-page manual** contains everything on the records, plus a simple phonetic pronunciation guide.
- **Indexed for convenience.** The only set on the market that is completely indexed. No more puzzling over where to find the phrase you need. Just look in the rear of the manual.
- **Practical.** No time wasted on material you can find in any grammar. LISTEN & LEARN covers central core material with phrase approach. Ideal for the person with limited learning time.
- **Living, modern expressions,** not found in other courses. Hygienic products, modern equipment, shopping—expressions used every day, like "nylon" and "air-conditioned."
- **Limited objective.** Everything you learn, no matter where you stop, is immediately useful. You have to finish other courses, wade through grammar and vocabulary drill, before they help you.
- **High-fidelity recording.** LISTEN & LEARN records equal in clarity and surface-silence any record on the market costing up to $6.

"Excellent . . . the spoken records . . . impress me as being among the very best on the market," **Prof. Mario Pei,** Dept. of Romance Languages, Columbia University. "Inexpensive and well-done . . . it would make an ideal present," CHICAGO SUNDAY TRIBUNE. "More genuinely helpful than anything of its kind which I have previously encountered," **Sidney Clark,** well-known author of "ALL THE BEST" travel books.

UNCONDITIONAL GUARANTEE. Try LISTEN & LEARN, then return it within 10 days for full refund if you are not satisfied.

Each set contains three twelve-inch 33⅓ records, manual, and album.

SPANISH	the set $5.95	GERMAN	the set $5.95
FRENCH	the set $5.95	ITALIAN	the set $5.95
RUSSIAN	the set $5.95	JAPANESE	the set $5.95
PORTUGUESE	the set $5.95	MODERN GREEK	the set $5.95
MODERN HEBREW	the set $5.95		

Orientalia

ORIENTAL RELIGIONS IN ROMAN PAGANISM, F. Cumont. A study of the cultural meeting of east and west in the Early Roman Empire. It covers the most important eastern religions of the time from their first appearance in Rome, 204 B.C., when the Great Mother of the Gods was first brought over from Syria. The ecstatic cults of Syria and Phrygia — Cybele, Attis, Adonis, their orgies and mutilatory rites; the mysteries of Egypt — Serapis, Isis, Osiris, the dualism of Persia, the elevation of cosmic evil to equal stature with the deity, Mithra; worship of Hermes Trismegistus; Ishtar, Astarte; the magic of the ancient Near East, etc. Introduction. 55pp. of notes; extensive bibliography. Index. xxiv + 298pp. 5⅜ x 8.
T321 Paperbound **$2.00**

THE MYSTERIES OF MITHRA, F. Cumont. The definitive coverage of a great ideological struggle between the west and the orient in the first centuries of the Christian era. The origin of Mithraism, a Persian mystery religion, and its association with the Roman army is discussed in detail. Then utilizing fragmentary monuments and texts, in one of the greatest feats of scholarly detection, Dr. Cumont reconstructs the mystery teachings and secret doctrines, the hidden organization and cult of Mithra. Mithraic art is discussed, analyzed, and depicted in 70 illustrations. 239pp. 5⅜ x 8.
T323 Paperbound **$1.85**

CHRISTIAN AND ORIENTAL PHILOSOPHY OF ART, A. K. Coomaraswamy. A unique fusion of philosopher, orientalist, art historian, and linguist, the author discusses such matters as: the true function of aesthetics in art, the importance of symbolism, intellectual and philosophic backgrounds, the role of traditional culture in enriching art, common factors in all great art, the nature of medieval art, the nature of folklore, the beauty of mathematics, and similar topics. 2 illustrations. Bibliography. 148pp. 5⅜ x 8.
T378 Paperbound **$1.35**

TRANSFORMATION OF NATURE IN ART, A. K. Coomaraswamy. Unabridged reissue of a basic work upon Asiatic religious art and philosophy of religion. The theory of religious art in Asia and Medieval Europe (exemplified by Meister Eckhart) is analyzed and developed. Detailed consideration is given to Indian medieval aesthetic manuals, symbolic language in philosophy, the origin and use of images in India, and many other fascinating and little known topics. Glossaries of Sanskrit and Chinese terms. Bibliography. 41pp. of notes. 245pp. 5⅜ x 8.
T368 Paperbound **$1.75**

BUDDHIST LOGIC, F.Th. Stcherbatsky. A study of an important part of Buddhism usually ignored by other books on the subject: the Mahayana buddhistic logic of the school of Dignaga and his followers. First vol. devoted to history of Indian logic with Central Asian continuations, detailed exposition of Dignaga system, including theory of knowledge, the sensible world (causation, perception, ultimate reality) and mental world (judgment, inference, logical fallacies, the syllogism), reality of external world, and negation (law of contradiction, universals, dialectic). Vol. II contains translation of Dharmakirti's Nyayabindu with Dharmamottara's commentary. Appendices cover translations of Tibetan treatises on logic, Hindu attacks on Buddhist logic, etc. The basic work, one of the products of the great St. Petersburg school of Indian studies. Written clearly and with an awareness of Western philosophy and logic; meant for the Asian specialist and for the general reader with only a minimum of background. Vol. I, xii + 559pp. Vol. II, viii + 468pp. 5⅜ x 8½.
T955 Vol. I Paperbound **$2.50**
T956 Vol. II Paperbound **$2.50**
The set **$5.00**

THE TEXTS OF TAOISM. The first inexpensive edition of the complete James Legge translations of the Tao Te King and the writings of Chinese mystic Chuang Tse. Also contains several shorter treatises: the T'ai Shang Tractate of Actions and Their Retributions; the King Kang King, or Classic of Purity; the Yin Fu King, or Classic of the Harmony of the Seen and Unseen; the Yu Shu King, or Classic of the Pivot of Jade; and the Hsia Yung King, or Classic of the Directory for a Day. While there are other translations of the Tao Te King, this is the only translation of Chuang Tse and much of other material. Extensive introduction discusses differences between Taoism, Buddhism, Confucianism; authenticity and arrangement of Tao Te King and writings of Chuang Tse; the meaning of the Tao and basic tenets of Taoism; historical accounts of Lao-tse and followers; other pertinent matters. Clarifying notes incorporated into text. Originally published as Volumes 39, 40 of SACRED BOOKS OF THE EAST series, this has long been recognized as an indispensible collection. Sinologists, philosophers, historians of religion will of course be interested and anyone with an elementary course in Oriental religion or philosophy will understand and profit from these writings. Index. Appendix analyzing thought of Chuang Tse. Vol. I, xxiii + 396pp. Vol. II, viii + 340pp. 5⅜ x 8½.
T990 Vol. I Paperbound **$2.25**
T991 Vol. II Paperbound **$2.25**

EPOCHS OF CHINESE AND JAPANESE ART, Ernest T. Fenollosa. Although this classic of art history was written before the archeological discovery of Shang and Chou civilizations, it is still in many respects the finest detailed study of Chinese and Japanese art available in English. It is very wide in range, covering sculpture, carving, painting, metal work, ceramics, textiles, graphic arts and other areas, and it considers both religious and secular art, including the Japanese woodcut. Its greatest strength, however, lies in its extremely full, detailed, insight-laden discussion of historical and cultural background, and in its analysis of the religious and philosophical implications of art works. It is also a brilliant stylistic achievement, written with enthusiasm and verve, which can be enjoyed and read with profit by both the Orientalist and the general reader who is interested in art. Index. Glossary of proper names. 242 illustrations. Total of 704 pages. 5⅜ x 8½.
T364-5 Two vol. set, paperbound **$5.00**

THE VEDANTA SUTRAS OF BADARAYANA WITH COMMENTARY BY SANKARACHARYA. The definitive translation of the consummation, foremost interpretation of Upanishads. Originally part of SACRED BOOKS OF THE EAST, this two-volume translation includes exhaustive commentary and exegesis by Sankara; 128-page introduction by translator, Prof. Thibaut, that discusses background, scope and purpose of the sutras, value and importance of Sankara's interpretation; copious footnotes providing further explanations. Every serious student of Indian religion or thought, philosophers, historians of religion should read these clear, accurate translations of documents central to development of important thought systems in the East. Unabridged republication of Volumes 34, 38 of the Sacred Books of the East. Translated by George Thibaut. General index, index of quotations and of Sanskrit. Vol. I, cxxv + 448pp. Vol. II, iv + 506pp. 5⅜ x 8½.
T994 Vol. I Paperbound **$2.00**
T995 Vol. II Paperbound **$2.00**

THE UPANISHADS. The Max Müller translation of the twelve classical Upanishads available for the first time in an inexpensive format: Chandogya, Kena, Aitareya aranyaka and upanishad, Kaushitaki, Isa, Katha, Mundaka, Taittiriyaka Brhadaranyaka, Svetarasvatara. Prasna — all of the classical Upanishads of the Vedanta school—and the Maitriyana Upanishad. Originally volumes 1, 15 of SACRED BOOKS OF THE EAST series, this is still the most scholarly translation. Prof. Müller, probably most important Sanskritologist of nineteenth century, provided invaluable introduction that acquaints readers with history of Upanishad translations, age and chronology of texts, etc. and a preface that discusses their value to Western readers. Heavily annotated. Stimulating reading for anyone with even only a basic course background in Oriental philosophy, religion, necessary to all Indologists, philosophers, religious historians. Transliteration and pronunciation guide. Vol. I, ciii + 320pp. Vol. II, liii + 350pp.
T992 Vol. I Paperbound **$2.25**
T993 Vol. II Paperbound **$2.25**
The set **$4.50**

Prices subject to change without notice.

Dover publishes books on art, music, philosophy, literature, languages, history, social sciences, psychology, handcrafts, orientalia, puzzles and entertainments, chess, pets and gardens, books explaining science, intermediate and higher mathematics, mathematical physics, engineering, biological sciences, earth sciences, classics of science, etc. Write to:

Dept. catrr.
Dover Publications, Inc.
180 Varick Street, N.Y. 14, N.Y.